Sexual Subversions

Current books in Women's Studies

ELIZABETH GROSZ

Sexual Subversions

Three French Feminists

Sydney
ALLEN & UNWIN
Wellington   London   Boston

© Elizabeth Grosz 1989
This book is copyright under the Berne Convention. No reproduction
without permission. All rights reserved.

First published in 1989
Allen & Unwin Australia Pty Ltd
An Unwin Hyman company
8 Napier Street, North Sydney NSW 2059 Australia

Allen & Unwin New Zealand Limited
60 Cambridge Terrace, Wellington, New Zealand

Unwin Hyman Limited
15–17 Broadwick Street, London W1V 1FP England

Unwin Hyman Inc.
8 Winchester Place, Winchester, Mass 01890 USA

National Library of Australia
Cataloguing-in-Publication entry:
Grosz, E.A. (Elizabeth A.).
    Sexual subversions: three French feminists.

    Bibliography.
    Includes index:
    ISBN 0 04 351072 8.
    ISBN 0 04 301292 2 (Hardback).

    1. Kristeva, Julia, 1941–   . 2. Irigaray, Luce.
    3. Le Doeuff, Michèle. 4. Feminism—France. 5. Sex
    (Philosophy). I. Title.

305.4

Set in 10.5/11.5 pt Bodoni and produced by
SRM Production Service Sdn Bhd, Malaysia

Contents

Preface

THIS book was conceived as a response to problems that emerged in teaching feminist theory to undergraduate students. While it is difficult at the best of times to 'teach' feminism, this difficulty is magnified when the material is unavailable in English, and when secondary sources (with some notable exceptions) tend to border on the obscure or are based on misunderstandings of primary sources. This is especially striking when attempting to teach French feminisms to a non-French-reading audience, anxious to receive these texts but unable to understand them with any rigour. This book is meant to rectify some of the obscurities surrounding the works of three French feminists, and to provide a teaching resource in an area where there are few sustained or detailed discussions of the work of these difficult yet immensely rewarding writers. At the same time this book hopefully reaches beyond the confines of pedagogy to raise theoretical and political issues of more general relevance to those engaged in feminist research. It actively participates in a number of debates and controversies surrounding the nature of feminist theory, the relations feminist intellectuals have to male-dominated knowledges and the strategies they are able to utilise in developing non-patriarchal, autonomous or woman-centered knowledges.

This book, then, is an introduction to and overview of the writings of three of the more well-known, even if not well-read, French feminists—Julia Kristeva, Luce Irigaray and Michèle Le Doeuff. No book on French feminisms would be complete without including the work of Kristeva and Irigaray: their influence on the production of feminist theory both inside and beyond France is inestimable. Le Doeuff's work is perhaps less well known outside of France. A number of her shorter papers have been translated into English; her longer writings are as yet unavailable in translation. She seems to have had less impact on Anglophone feminisms, generating less discussion in feminist journals although her work is no less worthy of critical attention. This neglect may be the result of her work being more narrowly discipline-based — it is located firmly within the history of philosophy — although her work may have implications well beyond traditional philosophy. Rather than include other, more familiar names (Hélène Cixous and Marguerite Duras spring to mind), I felt that Le Doeuff would bring a different perspective to bear on the question of sexual difference. In any case Cixous and Duras have been the subjects of considerable feminist research and their work has a number of similarities, especially with Irigaray's. Moreover, had either been included, this book would have been too heavily oriented to a literary field, and would consequently have been unrepresentative of the range and scope of feminist scholarship in France. While clearly interested in and reliant on literary modes of analysis, Le Doeuff's more philosophical and historical project provides a balance to the more directly literary frameworks from which Kristeva and Irigaray tend to be read. The inclusion of Le Doeuff's work enables that of the others to be read in a more philosophical context; she makes it difficult to *reduce* Irigaray's writings to mere poetry, without real philosophical content; or to ignore Kristeva's contributions to theories of subjectivity and critiques of knowledge. Her inclusion may provide something of a counterbalance to literary appropriations of French feminisms by Anglo-American audiences.

Kristeva, Irigaray and Le Doeuff are the focal points of this study precisely because each challenges the works of the others. Each highlights the *differences* of the others, putting into stark contrast the underlying frameworks to which the others are committed. Each counterpoints weaknesses and problems in the others' projects; and each, in some sense, supplements the insights of the others. While there is agreement on a number of basic issues — a fundamental antihumanism and materialism, a recognition of the powers of prevailing (patriarchal) modes of representation and knowledge, a recognition of the cultural debt owed to women and to maternity, a concern with the social, institutional and discursive construction of sexual identity — what seems most striking in comparing their positions are the serious disagreements and differences in method, goals and the privileged texts on which each relies. These differences imply that, while they may be labelled 'feminists of difference', the heterogeneity of their works must be recognised. They do not present a coherent political or theoretical position, form a 'school' or share a common doctrine.

Yet there is a sense in which each is appropriately labelled a 'feminist of difference', insofar as each addresses the question of women's autonomy from male definition. Each remains interested in affirming the sexual specificity of women, rather than seeing women only in their relations to men. Each seeks out a femininity that women can use to question the patriarchal norms and ideals of femininity. Each refuses to accept the preordained positions patriarchy has relegated to women.

The problematic of *difference* within which each is positioned dates from Nietzsche's scathing condemnations of the postulate of logical identity. Identity, in which A=A, is the most basic axiom in Aristotelian logic; it underlies our received notions of personal identity, as well as the foundations of Western ontology and epistemology. In opposing a logic of identity, a logic of Being, and in advocating a 'logic' of difference or becoming, Nietzsche initiated a major critical trajectory in contemporary theory. Ferdinand de Saussure demonstrated that such a 'logic' of difference is necessary to explain the complexity and functioning of language, and representation more generally. He claimed that the apparent unities or identities presumed in linguistics — the identity of signs or texts — is made possible only through the play of signifying differences: the play of differences between signifiers, between signifieds, and between one sign and others. This 'logic' of difference explains not only how we are able, for the purposes of analysis and reflection, to delimit linguistic identities or entities, but also how language itself undermines and problematises the very identities it establishes. A sign is self-identical (A=A), but it is also always something else, something more, another sign, dependent on a whole network of signs.

The logic of identity received a further blow with Freud's postulate of the unconscious. No longer could the self-identity presumed by the Cartesian *cogito* go unquestioned. If there is an unconscious radically heteromorphic to consciousness, if there is a part of the subject opaque to itself, then the presumed identity of psychical existence has no adequate justification. The subject is different from itself, radically split and incapable of self-knowledge. It is a 'field' in which forces play out their differences rather than a fixed identity. Freud's interrogation of the unconscious wishes and impulses fragmenting and interrupting consciousness demonstrated that the presumption of a philosophical subject — the knowing subject — is based on a wishful perfection unattainable by a being who is unaware of its own internal rifts. Freud also raised for the first time the question of *sexual* difference, the question of the (social) meaning of sexual specificity. Indeed, given the link between the oedipus complex and the formation of the unconscious through the constitution of the superego, Freud linked the question of the subject's incapacity to know itself to the repression of the idea of sexual difference: the only way the child can resolve the question of its sexual identity is through the repression of ideas incompatible with its socially designated sexual position, through, that is, the creation of a repository of all it must 'forget'.

Jacques Derrida's assault on the 'logic of identity'—which he labels 'logocentrism'—relies on a number of Saussure's and Freud's insights. Yet his interest is not directed to the sign (as Saussure's was) nor to the subject (as Freud's was): instead he focuses on the logic of difference as it functions within philosophical/literary/theoretical *texts*. Derrida demonstrates that there is a logic at work within texts that outstrips the text's intentions and avowed aims. Texts always say more than they are able to control. The identity of the *Book* is possible only with the suppression of the play of differences which constitute it and which continually threaten to undermine it. Where the identity of the sign, the subject and the text are put into question, there still remains a residual identity presumed for the body, particularly the body as it is represented in purely biological terms. Michel Foucault's genealogical writings are largely responsible for questioning the presumed unity, cohesion and ahistorical identity attributed to the human body. He demonstrates that the body, as much as other cultural objects, is the product and effect of various systems of training, discipline and construction. Bodies are not the brute effects of a pregiven nature, but are historically specific effects of forms of social and institutional production and inscription. Just as a history of the production of knowledges is possible, so, too, is a history of the production of bodies. Whatever (historical) identity the body has, this is the result of a play of forces unifying and codifying the different organs, processes and functions which comprise it. These forces are never capable of completely subduing the bodies and bodily energies they thereby produce, for there is a resistance to the imposition of discipline, and a potential for revolt in the functioning of any regime of power.

These philosophers or theorists of difference provide the context and framework within which the work of the French feminists is to be located. Chapter 1 is devoted to a more detailed discussion of the intellectual background of contemporary French theory, a background I believe is necessary to explain the particular revisions and subversion of male theory effected by French feminisms. Yet, as I argue, none of these male theorists adequately addresses the question of sexual difference. They do, however, provide many of the raw materials through which this question may be addressed. Relying in different ways on these raw materials, Kristeva, Irigaray and Le Doeuff raise the question of women's difference from, rather than opposition to, men, and thus also the question of the differences posed by feminist theory in its attempts to move beyond a position of opposition to or negation of male theory.

The contemporary French obsession with antihumanism, anti-essentialism and difference explains many apparent differences between the concerns of French feminists and their English-speaking counterparts. Anglo-American and Australian feminists seem more concerned with the ways in which feminism can be integrated with other theories and political positions, particularly marxism and liberalism. While it is common to differentiate feminist positions into three categories — liberal, marxist and 'radical' feminism — in overviews of Anglophone feminism, it is not clear that these hard-and-fast categories are readily applicable to the three French feminists discussed here (nor indeed to the range of English-speaking feminisms). Liberal feminism is generally defined as a feminism which seeks to attain women's equality with men; marxist feminism could rather crudely be described as a position which seeks to integrate an understanding of the oppressed position of women within patriarchy into an understanding of other forms of domination — both class and race — in capitalism and imperialism. So-called 'radical' feminism, it is claimed, seeks to understand women's oppression as women within patriarchy, without, however, relying on patriarchal or masculinist concepts. At its extreme this amounts to a kind of 'theoretical separatism' in which the pre-patriarchal or non-patriarchal nature of woman is sought as a basis for providing methods and criteria for the production and assessment of feminist knowledge.

While clearly sharing some interests with Anglo-American feminists, Kristeva, Irigaray and Le Doeuff are not interested simply in the question of equality (which implies the presumption of an underlying sameness or identity with men); nor are they interested in discovering or recovering some untinged female essence or feminine attributes. And while they are cognisant of marxist theory, exhibiting greater or lesser adherence to its principles, Kristeva, Irigaray and Le Doeuff write against a background within which marxism is readily presumed. They do not write as feminists committed to and obliged by a marxist framework. This does not imply, however, that they are *anti*marxist; it simply means that marxism is one among a number of sources of influence, one among many possible frameworks, no more privileged than psychoanalysis or Derridean deconstruction or Foucauldian genealogy.

Because their writings are not homogenous with the ready-made categories of Anglophone feminisms, they are often treated as exotic imports, fascinating because of their foreignness and unfamiliarity, and difficult to assimilate — the latest 'fashions' from the Parisian intellectual market. This attitude combines an excessive reverence with strong scepticism; it is a common response to the theoreticism of French writing when contrasted with the apparently pragmatic orientation of English-speaking feminists. Yet the writings of French feminists are neither insuperably difficult nor unassimilable to the interests and projects of Anglo-American feminists. It is not simply a matter of amalgamating or welding together bits of indigenous theory with components of imported theories; nor is it a matter of seeing them as irreconcilably opposed. Some sort of interaction between English- and French-language texts is necessary. This, however, means that the contribution French theorists have to offer English-speaking feminists needs to be recognised in its context and its concreteness. A number of feminists have already addressed the question of the importation of theory (for example, Jardine [1981]; Felman [1981]; Spivak [1981]; Marks and Courtivron [1981]; Morris [1979]), each indicating the continuing need for ongoing exchange between feminists from different nations and continents. This book is an attempt to provide some form of access to the writings of three French feminists whom I believe are extremely useful for and relevant to feminist researches in Australia, North America and Britain.

Chapters 2 and 3 provide an overview of Kristeva's understanding of the production and functioning of the speaking subject, its discursive possibilities and its capacity for social subversion. These two chapters are based on analyses of her earlier and more recent writings respectively, divided by the years 1979–80, which mark a transition in and reorientation of her views. Chapters 4 and 5 introduce and survey Irigaray's understanding of sexual difference and her critique of phallocentrism. These two chapters are also chronologically divided, Chapter 4 concentrating on her earlier writings, before about 1979; Chapter 5 being devoted to more recent researches, especially those directed towards the concept of the divine, ethics and the possibilities of exchange between sexually different beings. Chapter 6 analyses Le Doeuff's notion of the philosophical imaginary, and the role of women and femininity in the history of philosophy.

Many have directly or indirectly assisted in the publication of this book. My thanks go to the Humanities Research Centre at the Australian National University, which enabled me to spend four months researching material in 1986 during their 'Feminism and the Humanities' year. Special thanks must go to Professors Ian Donaldson and Graeme Clarke, and to the convenor, Dr Susan Sheridan. Because much of the material I have used is not available in English translation, I have had to rely on a number of private or unpublished translations. Professor Max Deutscher has been extremely generous in giving me access to a number of translations of Le Doeuff's work. I must heartily thank Dr Caroline Sheaffer-Jones for her patience and willingness to cheerfully check my rough translations of Irigaray, and for those she has undertaken herself; and to Carolyn Burke for sending me some of her unpublished papers and for providing encouragement in this project. I remain grateful to the suggestions, discussions and occasional disagreements with Dr Moira Gatens: these provided real insights and inspiration. Meaghan Morris deserves thanks for her support and advice; as does Dr Judith Allen for our many conversations on Australian feminism and the relevance of French feminisms to an Australian context; and members of the Department of General Philosophy at Sydney University are thanked for their support during difficult times. My students, who have been guinea pigs for some of the material in the book, have always provided great stimulation for research, and well-needed feedback whenever I have been less than clear. Cecily Williams has my gratitude for her patience, support and understanding. I would like also to thank my parents who have, in ways they may not recognise, provided stability and an anchor when the going was tough. Finally, I would like to thank John Iremonger and Allen & Unwin for the suggestion that I publish this book and for their continuing support for the publication of feminist texts in Australia.

Elizabeth Grosz,
Sydney, 1988

Glossary

Alterity A form of otherness irreducible to and unable to be modelled on any form of projection of or identification with the subject. The term refers to a notion of the other outside the binary opposition between self and other, an independent and autonomous other with its own qualities and attributes. The other is outside of, unpredictable by and ontologically prior to the subject (*see also* **Ethics** and **Dichotomy**).

Avant garde The term refers specifically to the transgressive and code-breaking symbolic and representational systems (within the visual, plastic, performative and verbal arts) developing from the end of the nineteenth century until the outbreak of the second World War. Kristeva uses the term to refer to the work of a select number of transgressive writers and artists— Mallarmè, Artaud, Lautréamont, Joyce, Beckett in literature; and Cage and Stockhausen in music. In the second case, the term refers more generally to experimental, innovative, subversive, representational practices, those which refuse the historically relative norms or conventional forms of representation to embark on various experiments and procedures to break down these conventions. The term refers to those historically located 'texts' which transgress or subvert the social codes providing their context, even if these transgressive experiments are later recodified into new norms, which may themselves require transgression (*see also* **Representation**, **Semiotic** and **Symbolic**).

Corporeality (also **Bodies**) Conventionally conceived within the history of philosophy as the polar opposite of mind, corporeality, or the body, is associated with a series of negative terms within pairs of binary opposites. Where the mind is traditionally correlated with reason, subject, consciousness, interiority, activity and masculinity, the body is implicitly associated with the opposites of these terms, passion, object, non-conscious, exteriority, passivity and femininity. Where mind is the provenance of philosophy and psychology, the body is regarded as the object of biological and medical investigation. Mind is understood as distinctively human, the motor of progress and the cause and measure of human achievement. By contrast, the body is assumed to be brute, animalistic, inert, outside of history, culture and socio-political life. While it may be the bearer or medium of mind or subjectivity, it is also an obstacle to or intervention into the pure operations of the mind. French feminists, among them Kristeva, Irigaray and Cixous, however, wish to reclaim a notion of the body which refuses traditional binary oppositions and places it firmly within a socio-historical context. Following psychoanalytic precepts, they see the structure of subjectivity as an effect of the ways in which the subject represents and understands its own body. One implication of this view which is undeveloped by Freud himself is the claim that the specificities of the body (its sex in particular) make a difference to the subjectivity of the subject. Masculinity is the effect of representing the body as phallic; and femininity is an effect of the representation of the body as castrated. For Irigaray, not only is subjectivity structured with reference to the (symbolic) meaning of the body, but the body itself is the product and effect of symbolic inscriptions which produce it as a particular, socially appropriate type of body. Dominant systems of discourse and representation are active ingredients of this social inscription of the sexed body, producing it as phallic (in the case of men) and as castrated (in the case of women). The body is thus the site of the intersection of psychical projections; and of social inscriptions. Understood in this way, it can no longer be considered pre- or acultural. Common feminist objections to theories utilising notions of the body — the charges of essentialism, naturalism and biologism — are not appropriate in this case (*see also* **Morphology**).

Deconstruction Along with the terms 'grammatology', 'différance', 'the double science', 'supplementary reading', Derrida uses this term to describe his procedures for the active interrogation of logocentric texts. Deconstruction is neither a destruction of prevailing intellectual norms and theoretical ideals, nor their replacement or reconstruction by new, more acceptable forms. Deconstruction in its technical sense refers to a series of tactics and devices rather than a method: strategies to reveal the unarticulated presuppositions on which metaphysical and logocentric texts are based. Derrida uses the term to designate a three-fold intervention into the metaphysical structures of binary oppositions: 1 the strategic reversal of binary terms, so that the term occupying the negative position in a binary pair is placed in the positive position, and the positive term, in the negative position; 2 the movement of displacement, in which the negative term is displaced from its dependent position and located as the very condition of the positive term; and 3 the creation or discovery of a term which is undecidable within a binary logic, insofar as it includes both binary terms, and yet exceeds their scope. It is a term which is simultaneously *both* and *neither* of the binary terms. By means of these procedures, Derrida not only contests the underlying presumptions of metaphysics, but also explains their historical tenacity and dominance within our received intellectual history. It is a series of strategies to make explicit what must remain unsaid for this domination to continue; and an attempt to replace this structure of domination with a more fluid and less coercive conceptual organisation of terms (*see also* **Dichotomy** and **Logocentrism**).

Desire A pivotal term within two quite different intellectual traditions. In the first tradition, within which Plato, Hegel and Lacan can be located, desire is conceived as a fundamental lack in being, an incompletion or absence within the subject which the subject experiences as a disquieting loss, and which prompts it into the activity of seeking an appropriate object to fill the lack and thus to satisfy itself. In Hegel, and following him, Lacan, desire seeks an 'object' which will both satisfy it, yet sustain it as desire, that is, an object, which, while yielding satisfaction, does not obliterate desire by filling it: thus desire always desires another('s) desire, desire seeks to be desired by another. For Lacan, desire is always marked by the desire of the Other. It is an ontological lack which ensures the separation of the subject from the immediacy of its natural and social environment, and the impulse of that subject to fill in this space through, in the first instance, the desire of the (m)other; and in the second, through its access to language and systems of meaning. Desire is the excess or residue left unsatisfied through the gratifi- cation of need or instinct, and left unspoken by the articulation of demand. This first tradition sees desire as negative, a hole, an unfillable absence. In a second tradition, within which Spinoza, Nietzsche, Foucault and Deleuze are placed, desire is not a lack but a positive force of production. It is no longer identified with a purely psychical and signifying relation, but is a force or energy which creates links between objects, which makes things, forges alliances, produces connections. In this sense, desire may function at a sub- human level, on the level of organs or biological impulses; it may also function at the level of the subject, insofar as the subject desires the expansion or maximisation of its power; and at the supra-human level, where the human subject is merely one small part of a larger assemblage or collectivity. In this second sense, desire is not a particularly psychical structure but permeates all modes of production, and all linkages, psychical, social, mechanical. Here desire is not an unactualised or latent potential; it is always active and real. Feminists have usually used the Hegelian and psychoanalytic notion of desire as a lack to explain women's positions within patriarchy as the objects of men's desire; however more recently, a number have turned to the Nietzschean notion, which links desire directly and without mediation to power and resistance (*see also* **Imaginary** and **Symbolic**).

Dichotomy (also **Distinction, Opposition**)   When a continuous spectrum is divided into discrete self-contained elements, these elements exist in opposition to each other. When the system of boundaries or divisions operates by means of the construction of binaries or pairs of opposed terms, these terms are not only mutually exclusive, but also mutually exhaustive. They divide the spectrum into one term and its opposite, with no possibility of a term which is neither one nor the other, or which is both. Dichotomous structures take the form of A and not-A relations, in which one term is positively defined and the other is defined only as the negative of the first. The relation between the binary terms is regulated by the law of contradiction, which can be formulated as 'either A or not-A', or alternatively as 'Not (A and not-A)'. Within this structure, one term (A) has a positive status and an existence independent of the other; the other term is purely negatively defined, and has no contours of its own; its limiting boundaries are those which define the positive term. Dichotomies are inherently non-reversible, non-reciprocal hierarchies, and thus describe systems of domination (*see also* **Difference** and **Logocentrism**).

Différance Along with deconstruction, this is one of the names Derrida uses to describe his own techniques of reading philosophical and logocentric texts. In his work, the term refers to three related concepts: first, to the movement or energy preconditioning the creation of binary oppositions. It is the un-acknowledged ground of the opposition between identity (or sameness) and difference. In this sense, différance precedes oppositions. Second, it refers to an excess or an unincorporated remainder which resists the imperative of binary organisation. Différance is *both* as well as *neither* identity and difference. In this sense, différance exceeds binary oppositions. And third, it is the name of Derrida's own procedures for reading and locating this différance. The term thus refers to a difference within difference itself, a difference which distinguishes difference from distinction, a different difference from that which opposes identity (*see also* **Deconstruction**, **Difference** and **Logo-centrism**).

Difference This term needs to be differentiated from distinction or dichotomy above. Where dichotomy defines a pair of terms by a relation of presence and absence, or affirmation and denial, difference implies that each of the two (or more) terms has an existence autonomous from the other. Each term exists in its own right. Where there are two terms marked by difference, they are mutually exclusive but not mutually exhaustive. They are regulated by the law of contrariety: if one is true, the other must be false. Both cannot be true, but it is possible that both are false. The concept of difference in the context of Saussurian linguistics refers to the fact that no sign has any positive characteristics in and of itself. Each sign can only be defined in terms of what it is not. This concept of linguistic difference has served as a useful metaphor for defining the relations between the sexes without privileging one sex and defining the other as its opposite. Moreover, unlike binary oppositions, terms related by difference can admit a third, fourth etc term. Where dichotomies take on the A/not-A form, differences take the form of A/B relations.

Ethics A term commonly used as a synonym for morality, is often opposed to the notion of politics. However, this is possible only on the assumption that politics is social and collective, while ethics only pertains to the behaviour of individuals. Morality is a code of norms which regulate the behaviour of individuals (and groups). In the work of French feminists, ethics is not opposed to politics but is a continuation of it within the domain of relations between self and other. Ethics need not imply a moral or normative code, or a series of abstract regulative principles. Rather, it is the working out or negotiation between an other (or others) seen as prior to and pre-given for the subject, and a subject. Ethics is a response to the recognition of the primacy of alterity over identity. Ethics, particularly in the work of Emmanuel Levinas, is that field defined by the other's needs, the other's calling on the subject for a response. In this case, the paradigm of an ethical relation is that of a mother's response to the needs or requirements of a child. Ethics means being called by and responding to the other's otherness. It thus defines a long-term goal for feminists seeking autonomy for both sexes. Only when each sex is recognised as an independent otherness by the other is an ethical relation between them possible. It is thus the culmination and a response to political struggles by feminists to grant women sexual, economic and representational autonomy from men and from systems of male definition (*see also* **Alterity** and **Difference**).

Genealogy The term refers to the construction of a non-continuous history and lineage of descent. Derived from Nietzsche, for whom the term has etymological and hereditary resonances, it is a retrospective reconstruction of the past from the vantage point of present institutions and practices. Foucault uses the term to refer to his (and Nietzsche's) methods of historical analysis, in which history is not conceived in linear or progressivist terms or according to causal connections (which imply a one-way relation between cause and effect). For Foucault, history is an irregular, discontinuous, unpredictable interaction of events, in which lateral connections between events are as significant as causal or developmental connections. For Foucault, a genealogy maps the interconnections between the production of knowledges, bodies and powers. It is thus a motivated history, a history of the 'birth' and transformations of contemporary institutions, practices and procedures. For Irigaray, however, the term is closely associated with heraldry and naming. Family genealogies are lines of descent which can only be traced through the inheritance of the proper name, the name of the father. Consequently, genealogies are precisely those histories in which women have no place and no mark, being represented only provisionally, by virtue of a name that is not their own. Women's names change with the transformation of their status from daughters to wives. They form part of this genealogy only insofar as they can take on the name of another, only insofar as they are defined relative to (men's) proper names.

Imaginary This term has two distinct contexts and meanings. First, and generally, it refers to Lacan's understanding of the formation of the ego and the vital role played by the child's identification with its own image in the mirror-stage. The ego operates within an imaginary order, an order in which it strives to see itself reflected in its relations to others. Lacan's English translator, Alan Sheridan, presents the following explanation: 'The imaginary is ... the world, the register, the dimension of images, conscious and unconscious, perceived or imagined. In this respect, "imaginary" is not simply the opposite of "real": the image certainly belongs to reality ...' (Sheridan, in Lacan, 1977a, ix). The imaginary is thus the narcissistic structure of investments which transforms the image of otherness into a representation of the self. In Lacan's work, this order roughly corresponds to what Freud defines as the pre-oedipal. Like the pre-oedipal, it returns in adult life in certain privileged moments (particularly love relations). Together with the symbolic, and the real, the imaginary is one of the three orders regulating human biological, interpersonal and social life.

However, when Michèle Le Doeuff uses the term, she distinguishes her notion sharply from Lacan's. It is not a psychological term describing the narcissistic and identificatory structure of two-person relations; rather, it is a rhetorical term which refers to the use of figures or imagery in philosophical and other texts. She sees it as a kind of 'thinking-in-images', the use of narrative, pictorial or analogical structures within knowledges. In this sense, the imaginary is symptomatic of an (intellectual and political) elision: it marks those places within philosophical texts where the discourse is unable to admit its founding assumptions and must cover them over. It signals thus a point of critical vulnerability within texts and arguments, a site for what remains otherwise unspeakable and yet necessary for a text to function (*see also* **Semiotic**, **Specular** and **Symbolic**).

Jouissance This term tends to remain untranslated in English texts because of its ambiguity in French. The term refers undecidably to pleasure understood in orgasmic terms, and a more generally corporeal, non-genital pleasure. Sometimes translated by 'bliss', the term does not, however, carry the religious associations of the English term. Sheridan provides the following description: ' "Enjoyment" conveys the sense, contained in *jouissance*, of enjoyment of rights, of property etc. Unfortunately, in modern English, the word has lost the sexual connotations it still retains in French. "Pleasure", on the other hand, is pre-empted by "plaisir" ... "Pleasure" obeys the law of homeostasis that Freud evokes in "Beyond the Pleasure Principle", whereby, through discharge, the psyche seeks the lowest possible level of tension. "*Jouissance*" transgresses this law and, in that respect, it is *beyond* the pleasure principle.' (Sheridan, in Lacan, 1977a, x).

Logos, Logocentrism These terms designate the dominant form of metaphysics in Western thought. The *logos*, logic, reason, knowledge, represents a singular and unified conceptual order, one which seems to grasp the presence or immediacy of things. Logocentrism is a system of thought centred around the dominance of this singular logic of presence. It is a system which seeks, beyond signs and representation, the real and the true, the presence of being, of knowing and reality, to the mind—an access to concepts and things in their pure, unmediated form. Logocentric systems rely heavily on a logic of identity which is founded on the exclusion and binary polarisation of difference (*see also* **Deconstruction**, **Dichotomy**, **Difference** and **Phallocentrism**).

Morphology This is a term used by Irigaray to refer to the ways in which the body and anatomy of each sex is lived by the subject and represented in culture. A psycho-social and significatory concept, it replaces the biologism and essentialism of notions of 'anatomical destiny' pervasive in psychoanalysis. For Irigaray, it is not women's anatomies but the psychical and social meanings of women's bodies within patriarchy that is seen as castrated. Morphologies are the effects of the psychological meanings of the developing child's sexual zones and pleasures, meanings communicated through the hierarchical structures of the nuclear family; they are also the effect of a socio-symbolic inscription of the body, producing bodies as discursive effects. In this sense, patriarchal discourses and phallic/castrated bodies are *isomorphic*, sharing the same shape. If discourses and representations give the body its form and meaning, then feminist struggles must direct themselves to the representational or symbolic order which shapes women's bodies only in the (inverted) image of men's. Women's oppression is not caused by their anatomies or physiologies; but through the transmission and internalisation of the social meaning and value accorded to women's bodies by a misogynist culture (*see also* **Corporeality** and **Phallus**).

Ontology A technical term within philosophy which refers to what exists, to concepts of Being. No theory can avoid making ontological commitments about what (things) exist, and the status of what it posits. For example, we perceive that beings other than ourselves exist. But what status is to be attributed to these other beings? Are they material existents? Figments of our imagination? Existents with a status different from our own? Ontology refers to the ways in which theories conceptualise their universe of relevance, to the mode or status of this universe.

Phallocentrism This is a form of logocentrism in which the phallus takes on the function of the *logos*. The term refers to the ways in which patriarchal systems of representation always submit women to models and images defined by and for men. It is the submission of women to representations in which they are reduced to a relation of dependence on men. There are three forms phallocentrism generally takes: whenever women are represented as the opposites or negatives of men; whenever they are represented in terms the same as or similar to men; and whenever they are represented as men's complements. In all three cases, women are seen as variations or versions of masculinity — either through negation, identity or unification into a greater whole. When this occurs, two sexual symmetries (each representing the point of view of one sex regarding itself and the other) are reduced to one (the male), which takes it upon itself to adequately represent the other (*see also* **Logocentrism**).

Phallus Although the term is derived from Freud's understanding of the phallic stage, in which he claims that only one sexual organ — the penis — is relevant for both sexes, in Lacan's reading, the term has two meanings. In the first place (chronologically and logically) the phallus does not refer to a biological organ but to an imaginary organ, the detachable penis, the penis that the child believes the mother to possess. The phallus is thus the effect of an imaginary fantasy of bodily completion, represented by the mother, against which the child compares itself. In the second place, as a result of the castration complex and the child's acknowledgement of the mother's castration, the phallus is no longer a detachable organ, but a signifier which makes an absence present. As the key signifier of the law of the father, and as the threshold term for the child's access to the symbolic order, it can be conceived in three closely related ways. It is the 'signifier of desire', the 'object' to which the other's desire is directed: it is insofar as he *has* the phallus that man is the object of woman's desire; and it is insofar as she *is* the phallus that a woman is a man's object of desire. In this sense, the phallus is the heir to the primordial lost object (the mother). Second, as a signifier it is the pivotal term in the child's acceptance of the law and name of the father, the term with reference to which the child positions itself as male or not-male (i.e. female); third, it represents the exchange of immediate pleasures for a place as a speaking being. It is thus the 'signifier of signifiers', the emblem of the law of language itself, the term which guides the child to its place as an 'I' within the symbolic (*see also* **Desire, Imaginary** and **Symbolic**).

Representations (also **Signs, Representational Systems**) All systems of representations, whether linguistic (as in texts, discourses and utterances), visual (painting, cinema, photography, images), or kinaesthetic (performance, dance, music), are composed of signs. In Saussurian linguistics, signs are composed of the combination of a signifier and a signified, that is, a material and a conceptual component. Although Saussure himself is largely interested in linguistic signs, and takes language as the model or ideal of all other representational systems, nevertheless, his semiotic understanding implies that any material object is, under certain conditions, capable of signifying or meaning something. For this, two conditions must be satisfied: it must be coupled with one (or more) concepts (this process is what Saussure described as 'signification'); and it must form part of a larger system of signs, where it is necessarily related to and contrasted with other signs (Saussure described this as the relation of value). Signs which compose representational systems have, for Saussure, no positive or substantive identity — they are not autonomous things. The identity of each sign comes only from its differential relation to all other signs. The sign is thus not the name of a thing, but a relation of 'pure difference'. Signs thus need not refer to a reality that exists outside of or before representation. Signs, in other words, need not be referential (and thus either true or false) in order to have meaning (*see also* **Semiotic** and **Symbolic**).

Semiotic The term is derived initially from Ferdinand de Saussure who uses it to refer to the scientific study of signs and sign-systems. However, in Julia Kristeva's usage, it refers to one of the two modalities comprising all psychical and signifying relations. She refers to the psychoanalytic notion of pre-oedipal or imaginary relations, in which the child's sexual drives are not yet organised or hierarchised under the domination of the phallus. The semiotic thus refers to both a decentered libidinal organisation in the child's psycho-sexual life, one which requires repression if the child is to become a social and speaking subject; and to the unrepresented conditions of representations, the drives, energies, impulses and materiality signification must harness as its unformed raw materials, before and beyond the imposition of unity, logic, coherence and stability provided by the symbolic and the oedipal. The semiotic is understood by Kristeva as a pre-oedipal, maternal space and energy subordinated to the law-like functioning of the symbolic, but, at times, breaching the boundaries of the symbolic in privileged moments of social transgression, when, like the repressed, it seeks to intervene into the symbolic to subvert its operations. This is the distinctive contribution of the avant garde: they rupture the symbolic, thereby giving the semiotic a space in representation (*see also* **Avant garde, Imaginary, Jouissance** and **Symbolic**).

Specular (also **Speculate, Speculum**) The specular relation is the imaginary relation the mirror-stage child develops with its own image in the mirror. In identifying with its specular image, the child develops the rudimentary outlines of its ego or sense of self. However, in her critique of Lacan and psychoanalysis, Irigaray argues that the only subject analytic theory recognises is the masculine subject. The reflected image is therefore simply the inversion of masculinity. Irigaray will use this specular model as a shorthand representation of the relations between masculinity and femininity within phallocentric theory: the only representations of women made possible within such systems are those in which women are the duplicates, the opposites or inversions of men. The flat mirror, she claims, is only capable of reflecting the (one) subject who is able to look at itself, reflect itself. She links the masculinity of the specular relation, a relation between man and his double, with the masculine domination of the realm of intellectual or philosophical speculation. Within phallocentric discourses, masculinity has taken upon itself the right to speculate about the world, about women and about itself: above all, it eschews the right to self-reflection, the right to self-speculation, self-critique and self-justification. This speculative mode, in which male reason claims to be able to know itself and its limits, Irigaray claims, leaves no space for self-determined representations of women, for women's self-reflections. Her critique of psychoanalysis and phallocentrism more generally involves an attempt to turn the mirror back on itself, to demonstrate the sexual specificity (the masculinity) of the self-reflecting subject. In other words, she conceives of her project as a shattering of the order of self-representation, traversing the mirror surface so that women may move beyond their positions as men's others. Through the looking glass, she posits a land of wonder in which women may be able to represent themselves and the world from their perspectives. One of her metaphors for this critical and constructive movement to the 'other side' is the conversion of the flat (or Platonic) mirror into the curved and convoluted speculum. The speculum is not only a gynecological instrument by which male medicine can observe the (lack that is the) form of female sexuality; more importantly, the speculum enables women to see themselves, to examine themselves, to see and understand their sexual specificity. The mirror comes to the aid of the speculum without subordinating it. Instead of acting as a symmetrical tool of female self-representation to the male mirror, the speculum does not reflect the other as the image or double of the subject: the speculum has no other: the subject reflects only herself in her specificity. This metaphor renders explicit the male fantasy of self-mastery embedded within those discourses aspiring to self-completion and self-critique: thus only through the obliteration of its particularity and its concomitant elevation to the position of the universal can phallocentrism evade its sexual origins. The speculum is not an instrument of self-mastery, but an exploratory tool, one relevant to women only in their specificity as women (*see also* **Difference**, **Imaginary**, **Phallocentrism**).

Symbolic Lacan opposes this term to the imaginary, as Kristeva does to her notion of the semiotic. For Lacan, it refers to the social and signifying order governing culture, to the post-oedipal position the subject must occupy in order to be a subject. The term is used in three senses in Lacan's writings, and Kristeva's notion is closely based on his usage. First, it refers to the organisation of the social order according to the imperatives of paternal authority. If the imaginary is dominated by the figure of the mother, the symbolic is regulated by the law of the father. In place of the dyadic structure of identifications supporting the imaginary, the symbolic initiates triadic social relations, relations which are founded on exchange (with the phallus functioning as the object of exchange). Second, it refers to the order of language, and particularly to language considered as a rule-governed system of signification, organised with reference to the 'I', the speaking subject. The symbolic is the order of representation. And third, insofar as the father's law not only regulates social exchange, but also requires the child's repression of its incestual, pre-oedipal love relations, the symbolic structures the unconscious. This may explain why Lacan claims that 'the unconscious is structured like a language'. The symbolic is the order of law, language and exchange, and is founded on the repression of the imaginary (*see also* **Desire**, **Imaginary**, **Phallus** and **Semiotic**).

1 Modern French philosophy

FRENCH philosophy has exerted a powerful, even dispro-portionate influence on the way contemporary politics is conceived. Kristeva, Irigaray and Le Doeuff form part of this current of influence. In considering the contributions of French feminists, it is not enough simply to position women's writing as a revision or augmentation of male political theory. These feminists do not simply repeat the work of their intellectual predecessors; in each case their projects entail a particular rewriting and rereading of masculine positions and a thoroughgoing displacement and reorientation of their theoretical categories, presumptions and methods.

French theory is considered appealingly or irritatingly — depending on one's taste — intellectualised and abstract; it seems peripheral to those committed to transforming women's lives in more concrete or direct ways. While their various projects may not directly address many of the pragmatic issues facing women's movements, nevertheless they may prove crucial in contesting the ways in which the world, everyday life and knowledges are under-stood. Kristeva, Le Doeuff and Irigaray provide neither handbooks for action, directions for political programs nor information directly applicable to day-to-day struggles. They say little of direct rel-evance to setting up women's refuges or rape crisis centres. But they may indirectly provide a way of understanding women, women's place in culture and women's future possibilities in terms different from prevailing patriarchal depictions.

In this chapter I explore some of the intellectual background and theoretical context of contemporary French feminisms. This may help make their work more accessible to English-speaking feminists. Clearly this chapter can only provide the most general outlines of the numerous positions and issues raised in French political and intellectual life. Nevertheless, such a sketch may provide an outline of the space that feminists today contest and/or (re)claim in their attempts to develop non-patriarchal and non-oppressive knowledges.

Although we should begin an overview of contemporary French thought in the seventeenth century with Descartes and explore its development through Spinoza, Kant, Hegel and Nietzsche, I will only signal the relevance of these figures indirectly through outlining the controversies and different positions emerging in French politics and philosophy since the 1930s. Although earlier philosophical movements — from Cartesianism to Bergsonianism, associationism and utopian socialism — may illuminate the kinds of issues developed in the 1930s and after, these will not be elaborated here.

Following Vincent Descombes (1980), I divide modern French thought into two broad categories or generations, the first located in the traditions of humanism and structuralism (which begin with Descartes and Kant respectively, and, more recently are associated with Hegel, Heidegger and Husserl); the second dates from the 1960s, its major sources being the great antihumanists of the nineteenth century, Marx, Freud and Nietzsche. The second, 1960s generation (amongst whom Lacan, Althusser, Levi-Strauss, Foucault, Deleuze and Derrida are major figures) provides the immediate context within and against which the three feminists at the centre of this book, Kristeva, Irigaray and Le Doeuff, need to be positioned.

Kojève, Hippolyte and Hegel

Linking together the disparate fields of phenomenology and marxism is the figure of Alexandre Kojève, whose 1933–39 lectures on Hegel are preserved in his posthumously published text *Introduction to the Reading of Hegel* (1969). His lectures had an enormous impact on an entire generation of French intellectuals who would later come to prominence as phenomenologists (Sartre, de Beauvoir, Merleau-Ponty), structuralists (Lacan, Levi-Strauss, Althusser) and cultural and literary theorists (Barthes, Bataille, Klossowski). His position regarding textual interpretation (or 'reading'), the constitutive social conditions of human existence, the dialectical dynamic of history, the role of relations of oppression in the progress of history, and the relations between the rational and the Real, provided germinal ideas that blossomed in the work of others, often with a delayed impact and emerging sometimes only a decade or more later.

Kojève's reading of Hegel focuses almost exclusively on Hegel's 1807 text *The Phenomenology of Spirit*, which Kojève reads as an account of the dialectical unfolding of a history that is the consequence of the slave's supercession of his (physical, conceptual and social) slavery. For Hegel, the precondition for historical development or dialectical change is provided by the postulate of a self-consciousness, a self-identical being, a being confronting another self-consciousness fundamentally similar to itself, distinguished from everything other than itself by a radical *negativity*. Self-consciousness sees its object only in terms of negativity, as a thing to be used, transformed, obliterated: 'what is other for it exists as an object without essential-reality, as an object marked with the character of a negative-entity' (Kojève, 1969:10). It is only when the object of this self-consciousness turns out to be another self-consciousness that history (as dialectical overcoming) can be said to begin: it is only from the 'moment' there is contradiction and dialectical antagonism that history and thus development and change become possible.

Each self-consciousness may have 'subjective certainty' of itself, but this certainty has no objective confirmation without the complicity of the other. Each self-consciousness requires the recognition of the other in order to attain its self-certainty.[1] For self-consciousness to be certain of itself, it must be recognised by another self-consciousness fundamentally the same as itself. This other also requires self-consciousness to recognise it as a subject in turn. Indeed, each must be prepared to risk its animal life, its mere physical existence, in order to attain the self-certainty or identity it craves. As the dialectic between these two similar beings unfolds, their relation becomes a *life and death struggle*, where each strives to assert its superiority over the other. If this struggle leads to the death of one or both protagonists, the certainty and confirmation from the other for which each struggles would be impossible. This struggle can have only one possible outcome if history as we know it is to develop. If one or both parties perish, self-consciousness does not gain the recognition of an other like itself, and thus reverts to its (mythical) proto-historical isolation and brute existence. It is only when one of the antagonists values autonomy and freedom, prestige and recognition more highly than animal life, when the subject is prepared to risk life itself; and when the other in turn values life above freedom — that is, when one vanquishes the other in the struggle for pure prestige — history 'begins'.[2]

The first becomes the master, the second, the bondsman or slave.

The first now exists for himself; while the second now exists for another, for the master. The master is autonomous; the slave dependent. We have in Hegel the primordial genesis of authority and relations of domination and subordination in the encounter of two subjects, the meeting of mirror-doubles. This model of abstract struggle has proved crucial in the development of contemporary accounts of the structure of oppression directly informing French feminisms.

The master thus gains the recognition he needs to have his self-certainty objectively confirmed. The slave by contrast 'binds himself completely to the things on which he depends' (Kojève, 1969:17), thus becoming like a thing himself. Ironically, while the master is recognised as subject-for-himself by the slave, the master is not recognised by a subject that *he* himself recognises or values as an equal self-consciousness. The slave's recognition, in other words, has no value for the master, for it is a recognition bestowed by an *object* not by an *Other*.

Kojève's point seems to be that history belongs to and is made by the slave, not the master. The master's position is ultimately a dead end, fixed, an 'existential impasse' (Kojève, 1969:19):

> *The master, therefore, was on the wrong track. After the fight that made him Master, he is not what he wanted to be in starting the fight: a man recognized by another man. Therefore: if man can be satisfied only by recognition, the man who behaves as a Master will never be satisfied. And since — in the beginning — man is either Master or Slave, the satisfied man will necessarily be a Slave; or more exactly, the man has been a Slave, who has passed Slavery, who has 'dialectically overcome' his slavery. (Kojève, 1969:19–20)*

In other words history is the consequence of the slave's attempt to transcend the ensnarements of that slavery by which he is bound. History is his supercession of himself *qua* slave. History is self-exceeding, self-transforming labour: the overcoming of the inertia of brute existence, the terror of subjection by the other or master, and the refusal of any idea of freedom and autonomy that is isolated from material self-sustaining and transforming labour, and self-productive social, political and intellectual life. For Kojève, history is the movement of transcendence, the acquisition of a *lived truth of the subject* in an intersubjective and socio-political world.

Kojève was largely responsible for kindling interest in radical readings of Hegel in France. Together with Jean Hyppolite, who translated *The Phenomenology of Spirit* into French in 1941, he provided a political vindication of Hegel, reading him retrospectively in the light of Marx's account of class struggle. In Hegel, Kojève saw the earliest detailed anticipation of Marx's materialist dialectic. Through his reading of Hegel he forged a direct link between individual, psychical or self-conscious subjectivity, and socio-political, cultural and historical development—the 'private' and the 'public', the 'psychical' and the 'social'—as we will see, a major contribution to the character of French philosophy today.

Where Kojève's reading stresses the master-slave dynamic as the motor or force of history, Hyppolite reads *The Phenomenology* largely in the light of Hegel's understanding of the 'unhappy consciousness' *(faute de mieux)*—the striving of the creative mind for stability within a chaotic world, the 'alienated soul' (Hegel, 1967:251–67). Hyppolite's reading functions in terms of the psychology of the subject in the face of the world. It is a reading that emphasises the partiality of the subject's claims to truth and knowledge in comparison with the totality or wholeness of Absolute Knowledge. Hyppolite compared *The Phenomenology* to a 'terrestial repetition of Dante's *Divine Comedy*' (Hyppolite, 1969:vi). It can be read as the analysis of the alienation and the overcoming of alienation in and by subjectivity. Where Kojève reads Hegel through the retrospective validation of Marx, Hyppolite reads Hegel through his deferred effect in Kierkegaard, phenomenology and psychoanalysis.

To summarise some of the implications of the 'discovery' of Hegel for French feminisms, the following points may be relevant:

1 Kojève demonstrated through his reading of Hegel that the logic of history is inseparable from the question of oppression and struggle. Power, domination and freedom are the essential ingredients of history.
2 He makes the question of subjectivity, self-consciousness and identity not just a relevant issue to the arena of politics, but places it at its very centre. The subject's relations to other subjects, to culture and to knowledge is the field on which history is played out.
3 Instead of a narrowly deterministic understanding of history as a reflection of the powerful—the masters—Kojève stresses the *productivity* of the position of the slave. Progress and development come from struggle and resistance, not domination, control or even enlightenment of masters. The history produced by

struggle is the history of the slave's struggle for genuine self-determination.

4 While Kojève stresses the crucial role of subjectivity in history, he also emphasises the lack at the centre of subjectivity — a lack defined as desire, negation — in opposition to the fullness Descartes attributed to the pregiven *cogito*.

5 Self-knowledge is not given to the subject in isolation from others or the world, as Descartes asserts. Rather, where it occurs, it is the result of a congruence between the self-conscious subject, a political community, social institutions and knowledges. Absolute knowledge as a self-reflective activity is possible only at the 'end of history'.

6 Perhaps most significantly for feminist theory, he establishes the intimate link between identity and alterity: the fate of the subject is necessarily bound up with the existence of the other. The other is the essential condition of self-consciousness.

Kojève and Hyppolite link Hegel and Hegelianism to a series of other philosophical texts and positions — Marx's, Freud's, Kierkegaard's, Husserl's — thereby ensuring that Hegel is no longer read as an anachronistic nineteenth-century romantic metaphysician, but as a dynamic theorist of subjectivity and struggle, whose dialectical methods are still highly relevant to contemporary politics.

Phenomenology, marxism and structuralism

Since Kojève's reading of Hegel, French intellectual and political life has been polarised around two competing positions. The first is humanist, phenomenological or existential; the second is anti-humanist, scientific and marxist. Jean-Paul Sartre and Maurice Merleau-Ponty are perhaps the best known of the first position; while Georges Politzer, Paul Nizan, Henri Lefebvre, Georges Friedmann and Edgar Morin (Hirsch, 1981:20–21), lesser-known figures outside of France, could be included in the second. There are of course anomalous figures who are not easily classified according to this schema — such as Emmanuel Levinas, Maurice Blanchot, Pierre Klossowski and Georges Bataille — whose works are of special relevance to the post-1968 generation.

Sartre published *Being and Nothingness* in 1943. In it he humanises and individualises Husserlian phenomenology. Humanism is the belief that all values, meanings, history and culture are the products of human consciousness and individual activity. It conflates the subject and consciousness, granting primary value to consciousness in making choices, and judging, creating and transforming social relations. Sartre's own version of phenomenology — existentialism — espouses the primacy of the subject's experiences in ontological, political, social and interpersonal relations.

For Sartre, the human being has at least one immutable, fixed characteristic: its essence is determined by its existence. It is paradoxically forced to be free, to give meaning and value to its existence by its own choices. Sartre divides the subject into three modes-of-being: being-in-itself (the subject's brute, given or fixed nature, including its physiology, its past and what is unchangeable); being-for-itself (consciousness, self-reflective awareness); and being-for-others (the subject considered as another by another subject, social and interpersonal identity). Being-for-itself or consciousness is privileged insofar as choice, freedom, is located here. Being-in-itself is given, and being-for-others is beyond one's control. The subject is a consciousness constrained to be free. The conscious subject is surrounded by a gap or lack, a 'nothingness', which separates it from itself (it can never simply *be* what it *is* or coincide with itself, it must become what it might be), from its projects (nothingness as the gap between intention and action that may engender *bad faith*) and from others (insofar as the other, while separated from me, can invade me by means of *the look*). The subject is intrinsically given identity, integrity and cohesion by its choices and acts. It is a self-contained entity positioned in but not a part of the material world, a being capable of transcendence.

The subject's awareness of its lack of being or essence may lead to anguish and nausea because it can never simply be what it is: it must continually make and remake itself through choice. The subject is alone responsible for its freedom. Its attempts to evade this responsibility, with its attendant anguish, Sartre calls 'bad faith'. Bad faith occurs whenever the subject reduces its being-for-itself to a being-in-itself or a being-for-others, that is, whenever it substitutes one mode of its being for another. In the subject's relations to the other, the other is both a guarantee of being-for-itself through an act of Hegelian recognition, and a threat to the subject's freedom, for it can rob the subject of its self-certainty. By means of the look, the other can steal away the subject's freedom to define itself and reduce it to an object. The other is the frustrating (because free) object of desire, and limit on the subject's freedom.

While sharing many similarities with Sartre, Merleau-Ponty's version of phenomenology strikingly departs from Sartre on several crucial issues: he rejects Sartre's distinction between the in-itself and the for-itself, between immanence and transcendence and between self and other. He brings together terms usually regarded as dichotomous, defined in either/or terms, creating instead a both/and relation. As V. Descombes suggests:

> *Merleau-Ponty's entire philosophy [consists in] 1. the alternatives of classical philosophy are rejected: man as he exists is neither pure 'in itself'. (A thing, a material body in the scientific sense) nor a pure 'for itself' (a res cogitans, a sovereign freedom) ... But in its turn the solution of antitheses is found neither in a synthesis which might reconcile the two points of view, nor in a rejection of the assumption which gives rise to the antithesis. The solution is sought 'between the two' in a 'finite' synthesis, that is, an unfinished and precarious one. (Descombes, 1980:56)*

Merleau-Ponty sees the subject as neither mind nor body, neither immanent nor transcendent, but through the filter of 'lived experience', which attests to its simultaneous and irreducible corporeal *and* conceptual existence. For Merleau-Ponty, the subject is a point of orientation for a meaningful, historical and social world. It is the being which gives significance to the world insofar as language and culture are internal conditions of subjectivity. He brings together Husserlian notions of the phenomenological, lived subject with empirical researches in physiology, neurology, anatomy, psychoanalysis and psychiatry, demonstrating the fundamental interconnectedness of the psychical and the physical.

The official doctrine of the French Communist Party — the PCF — denounced existentialism as bourgeois, idealist and individualist. In the 1940s and 1950s the PCF was narrowly Stalinist in policy and attitude. While proclaiming, in accordance with Marx, that class struggle is the motor of history, it conceives of class in narrowly economistic terms. It claims that history progresses inevitably towards the dissolution of class relations, revolution and a new socialist, egalitarian social order. Marxism itself was conceived as a science; its method, dialectical materialism, is the only valid one in analysing history, culture and class relations. Marxism is seen as a truthful, predictive *science*. Classes and class relations are positivistically reduced to narrowly economic positions; the economy is considered the infrastructure which directly determines the ideological and cultural superstructure.

The PCF considered its role to be that of guide, organiser and representative of the proletariat; it saw itself as the vanguard leading the working classes in a takeover of the forces and relations of production or the State and its various instrumentalities. It supported the Soviet Union as the first living model of socialism, and defended its methods in the face of opposition, particularly after the Soviet invasion of Hungary in 1956. Its adherence to dialectical and historical materialism was based on its commitment to the notion of determinism in understanding history, and to a mechanistic understanding of materialism, which reduces it to brute physicalism.

By the Cold War period of the 1950s and 1960s phenomenology/ existentialism and mechanistic marxism were the two extremes of French leftist politics and theory. Even though there were a number of individuals who attempted to reconcile the two, or who held both positions without attempting to integrate them (for example, Merleau-Ponty, Henri Wallon and others), they still seemed to be opposed. Both humanism and mechanistic marxism were strongly influenced by Kojève's reading of Hegel, though in different directions: Sartre by Hegelian concepts of negativity and otherness, alienation and self-consciousness; marxism by the 'materialisation' of Hegel's idealist dialectic. Existentialism is a psychologically or subjectively oriented account of ontology; marxism is a scientific account of social, political and economic relations. Where existentialism lacks a broad understanding of social and economic relations, or indeed any account of oppression and exploitation, marxism lacks a detailed understanding of the specifically ideological, cultural and interpersonal dynamics of capitalism, and, above all, an explanation of the lived experiences of bourgeois subjects.

From the early 1960s Sartre attempted to integrate these apparently opposed positions (see Sartre, 1968 and 1976). He developed the concept of *praxis*, the humanised practices of individuals and groups, including classes, in an attempt to bridge the gulf between human freedom conceived in existentialist terms, and class powers and structures understood in marxist terms. It represented his attempt to displace the determinism and inevitability of economistic marxism. Individuals and groups *could*, through their concerted, conscious efforts, change oppressive social structures. As a consequence of this 'amalgamation', existentialism was transformed into a political theory through its admission that class oppression may mitigate human freedom. Freedom could no longer be conceived as purely conceptual, a freedom of *attitude* to a given situation, but must also be material, the freedom to change the situation.[3] In both its scientistic/deterministic and its humanist

9

forms, marxism dominated leftist political thought. Praxis and the inevitable unfolding of the materialist dialectic fought each other for supremacy over the terrain of radical politics. These political shifts and realignments, coupled with the rediscovery of the 'holy texts' of Marx, Freud and Nietzsche, provided at least some of the impetus for the emergence of an antihumanist and anti-reductionist marxism, represented in the 1960s by the work of Louis Althusser.

In opposition to phenomenology/existentialism and deterministic marxism, and inspired by the work of linguists like Ferdinand de Saussure and by Freudian psychoanalysis, structuralism emerged as the third major intellectual movement in twentieth-century France. It challenged the existential primacy of the experiences and consciousness of the subject and its reduction of social relations to the meaning they offer to consciousness — the phenomenological vision of the subject as the master of meaning and source of knowledge. Through Saussurian semiology, structuralists such as Claude Lévi-Strauss, Roland Barthes and Jacques Lacan criticise the notion of the pregiven subject and the sign as the bearer of a self-constituted meaning.

The sign is understood as an arbitrary coupling of concept and matter, fundamentally dependent for its meaning and value on the entire system of signs. Saussure argues that the sign is produced by and relies on its 'pure difference' from other signs. Its differential relations with other signs, not the animation by the subject's intentions, gives the sign its meaning. In opposition to the pre-eminence of consciousness, structuralists stress the Freudian postulate of an unconscious which functions independently of conscious awareness to betray the subject's conscious intentions. There is more than consciousness in the subject, an excess which refuses to conform to its logic and requirements, continually undermining and betraying them.

Structuralism developed a common method in a number of disciplines, from linguistics to anthropology (Lévi-Strauss), psychology (Jean Piaget), psychoanalysis (Lacan) and other social sciences. Reduced to its simplest form, structuralism contends that the object of social sciences is not empirically given — the word (in linguistics), the text (in literary criticism), the social practice (in anthropology and sociology), the event (in history), the symptom (in psychology) — but is a latent system within which the empirical object finds its context. Structuralism seeks out the underlying structures or relations between empirical elements, seeing the empirically given object merely as a manifestation of this broader system. The system is analysed not materially but formally, in terms of the relations and positions of units and the precise rules and conventions ordering these relations. These rules regulate the ways in which particular elements are able to function and have meaning; they also serve to integrate and accommodate new elements. These rules need not be conceived as historically inflexible, for they are susceptible to diachronic transformations. Lévi-Strauss, for example, does not compare rituals from one culture with apparently similar rituals in another culture without placing one culture's rituals within the context of its entire mythical and religious system. Similarly, in linguistics one does not compare one word in a language to its equivalent in another without understanding the ways in which each language functions as an entire system. Within structuralism the sign is dethroned from the centre of meaning and consciousness is displaced from the centre of subjectivity, much as Copernicus displaced the earth from the centre of the cosmos.

In summary, structuralists claim that:

1 The system, rather than its individual elements, needs analysis; individual persons, actions or objects are not self-sustaining and cannot be understood without examining the context of their underlying systems, of which they are merely symptoms.
2 The individual element, given to observation, is not a reliable index of reality. What is given is the effect of other, latent relations. It cannot be taken as truthful or real, but is symptomatic of a deeper, non-observable system.
3 Structuralism is thus antihumanist, seeing consciousness and experience as the unrecognised effects of complex, unconscious relations of which they are unaware. Knowledge is gained thus only when the given, the conscious, is positioned in its broader context.
4 As an interdisciplinary method, structuralism shows the interconnections of all social phenomena and, above all, the inestimable contribution of language to the advent of social and cultural life. Social, religious, cultural and economic relations are amenable to a scientific analysis, not on the model provided by the natural sciences, but because all are, in some sense, 'structured like a language'. Linguistics thus provides a paradigm of what an appropriate social science might productively emulate.

Althusser's work synthesised the tensions between scientistic marxism, phenomenology and structuralism through his particular reading of the key texts of Marx.

Althusser's theory of ideology

Althusser's conception of subjectivity and ideology needs to be positioned within the context of the debate between humanist and determinist versions of marxism. His position is developed in rigorous opposition to both. In relation to humanism, he denounces the equation of subjectivity with consciousness (consciousness provides a partial and distorted ideological awareness). On the other hand he also rejects the reductionism of mechanistic marxism by claiming that while social and cultural relations depend on economic relations, they are not explicable solely in economic terms. Ideological and cultural relations exhibit a 'relative autonomy' from the economic sphere.

His account of ideology sees consciousness as a distorted reflection of real relations (the critique of humanism); as well as an account of an autonomous, non-economic, social relation (the critique of determinism). His concept of ideology is located somewhere in between the economic 'instance' and the lived experiences of subjects.

In order to transform subjective or ideological experience into scientific knowledge, a scientific method, such as Marx developed in *Capital*, is necessary. This explains what one's 'real' conditions of existence are, and how they generate a distorted or ideological consciousness of class relations. If science analyses the real conditions of existence, and ideology is the distorted lived representation of these relations, ideology is an effect of the subject's unrecognised class position. It is the means by which a match between individual experience and socio-economic imperatives is achieved.

For Althusser, consciousness no longer provides a reliable picture of social reality. In this sense he follows the Hegelian constriction of consciousness to *partial* knowledge which always falls short of the Absolute. Yet his position is distinct from Hegel's insofar as Althusser's is thoroughly materialist. The subject's experiences are neither given in unmediated form (empiricism) nor are they simply the effects of individual choice (existentialism). They are the results of a *systematically* analysable distortion-effect. The norm against which they are measured is not the unfurling of Hegelian 'Spirit', but class relations, conceived in materialist terms.

In order to counter reductive economism, Althusser revives the traditional marxist metaphor of society as a building or structure: the building requires a strong base (the economic forces and relations of production) onto which two floors (the superstructure of State functions and ideological apparatuses, respectively) are placed. The structure rests 'in the last instance' on the economic base, yet the ideological and cultural agencies (including the moral, religious and educational institutions) retain a 'relative autonomy' from any direct determination by it. The realm of ideology exerts a dialectical relation on the economy, providing terms and concepts by which to rationalise and justify it.

Ideology is the precondition of the production of individuals as social subjects; and a defining characteristic of the socio-cultural superstructure. Althusser elaborates his position mainly in one key paper, 'Ideology and Ideological State Apparatuses (Notes Towards an Investigation)' (Althusser, 1971). In it he asks how a social formation produces and reproduces itself over time. He suggests that every social formation must be able not only to reproduce the technical and material means of productions (replacing worn-out tools, technology, raw materials, etc.) but also the labour power needed to work them. Every society must ensure that there is a relative continuity between one generation and the next in values, attitudes, skills and beliefs:

> *[I]t is not enough to ensure for labour power the material conditions of its reproduction if it is to be reproduced as labour power ... the available labour power must be 'competent', that is suitable to be set to work in the complex system of the process of production ... [T]he labour power has to be (diversely) skilled and therefore reproduced as such. Diversely: according to the requirements of the socio-technical division of labour, its different 'jobs' and 'posts'. (Althusser, 1971:126–7)*

Constructing socially appropriate subjects implies the acquisition of various technical, social and interpersonal skills; and a certain mode of ignorance of the procedures constituting it as a subject. Ideology functions to produce the requisite skills, attitudes, a general submission to dominant values — not just, in his words, 'know-how' but also 'subjection to the ruling ideology'.

The subject's subjection to the dominant ideology cannot be adequately explained in terms of coercion or force. Such a model implies a massive social investment of resources in maintaining and guarding the socialisation of subjects. Clearly, however, coercion does occasionally occur (Althusser describes the institutions governing coercive institutions and structures, such as the military, police and penal systems, as 'Repressive State Apparatuses' [RSAs]). In his understanding they function more as a last resort of social control, to be brought into operation only when other means fail. Where the RSAs regulate subjects through terror and external threat, there are more 'efficient' procedures on which all cultures can rely to produce social subjects. Althusser claims that the 'Ideological State Apparatuses' (ISAs) use more insidious, less prohibitive techniques. He includes all socio-cultural institutions, claiming that they function to ensure a cohesive system of representations and rationalisations of the values of the ruling class. He singles out the family-school nexus for a privileged role in the production of social subjectivity. The ISAs and the RSAs between them ensure a harmony or match between the requirements of a social system for suitable labour power and ideological beliefs and the particular kinds of subjectivity thus produced (Althusser, 1971:137–8).

Althusser distinguishes between *ideology in general* and particular ideolog*ies*. For him, the latter are always expressions of concrete, determinate class positions and historical periods. Ideolog*ies* can only be characterised by their position as representations of specific historico-political values, values which serve dominant interests. They vary widely over different cultures and periods, and cannot be given any general features except that they serve class interests — and are presumed by those subjected to them to be natural and unchangeable. If ideologies are always historically specific, by contrast, ideology 'has no history': '...I think it is possible to hold that ideolog*ies* have a history (although determined in the last instance by class struggle); and ... that ideology *in general* has no history' (Althusser, 1971:151).

For Althusser there must always be, 'omnipresent' and 'transhistorically', systems of representation and practices to ensure that each culture socialises subjects according to its specific needs. Thus while particular ideolog*ies*, representing historically determinate interests, may perish or be transformed, *ideology in general* will continue even after the demolition of the capitalist State and its replacement by socialism. Although all cultures must enculturate their subjects, they always do so in concrete, determinate ways. He advances two propositions about ideology in general: first, 'Ideology represents the imaginary relations of individuals to their real conditions of existence' (1971:153); and second, 'Ideology has a material existence' (1971:155).

Ideology necessarily distorts or inverts 'men's' real social conditions, obscuring the effects of class relations and the social positions and interests of ideological subjects. While distorting and hiding real social relations, it does so in a systematic and thus decipherable fashion.

14

... while admitting that they do not correspond to reality, that is, that they constitute an illusion, we admit that they do make allusion to reality and that they need only to be 'interpreted' to discover the reality of the world behind their imaginary representation of that world (ideology = illusion/allusion). (1971:153)

Ideology is a representational system, a system of ideas and values, an 'imaginary representation of real relations'. It cannot be explained by the two major theories of social dominance, which see ideology as either a conspiracy or a form of alienation. For Althusser, ideology is not the result of conspiracy between a ruling clique or dominant, powerful individuals (multinationals, media barons, cartels, etc.) who are somehow in touch with 'the truth' but disseminate falsehood; it is not a lie, a product of collusion among powerful knowers. Nor is it a form of alienation which implies some kind of non-ideological essence from which the subject is severed, and which, moreover, is doomed to disappear 'after the revolution' when the subject will be restored to wholeness and self-knowledge. Because ideology is 'transhistorical' it cannot be overthrown. It is the necessary condition of *all* cultural relations.

The values and interests ideology reflects are not disembodied, immaterial or merely conceptual. On the contrary, these ideas are produced as a consequence of concrete material practices, which are themselves usually embedded within and contextualised by various social institutions or ISAs. The ISAs do not *cause* subjects to be formed with particular characteristics; instead they precondition them, structuring and confirming their attitudes, beliefs and practices.

In short, for Althusser, ideology serves one overall function — to constitute subjects as subjects of a particular type, to produce out of biological 'raw materials' a socially useful and specific subject. Ideology thus functions to 'interpellate', to hail, and thus to constitute biological individuals as social subjects.

To summarise Althusser's theory of ideology:

1 Ideology is the distorted representation of 'men's' real social relations.
2 Ideology is the expression of the unspoken values of the dominant class.
3 Ideology is located in systems of ideas, beliefs, values and practices, which are internalised and lived as true by the subject.

4 Ideology comprises the institutional and cultural framework of any society.
5 Ideology functions to produce social subjects out of biological 'raw materials'.
6 Ideology functions both as a form of recognition (the subject recognises itself in being interpellated) and miscognition (the subject misunderstands its position as ideological effect, instead regarding itself as self-created).
7 Although a scientific analysis of ideology (such as historical materialism provides) is possible, it is not able to undo the lived experiences or effects on the subject.

Althusser's notion of ideology has had a powerful effect on a number of French feminists, particularly those committed to a marxist- or socialist-feminist framework. To again indicate in the briefest terms the force of this effect:

1 Althusser demonstrated that Marx did not simply present an account of the economic structure of society. His work is also capable of explaining non-economic, cultural phenomena.
2 He claims that while Marx provided the methodology necessary for a scientific account of history and class relations, it also needs to harness the insights of a theory like Freud's or Lacan's in order to account adequately for the largely unconscious effects of ideology on individuals.
3 His critique of individualistic humanism and his espousal of a structural and scientific model of individual, social and economic relations have helped provide a model and a series of methods feminists have found useful in analysing patriarchal (and class) ideology.

Partly as a result of his own self-criticisms, partly as a consequence of his position in May 1968, and partly as a result of 'personal' events[4], his work has to a large extent fallen into disrepute. However, he remains a powerful, if today a reluctantly acknowledged, source in the development of contemporary theories of power that have implicitly been at the centre of political analyses developed both within and outside of France.

Lacan and psychoanalysis

If phenomenology, structuralism and marxism occupy one side of the intellectual divide marked by the events of May 1968[5], a different series of names and texts emerge on the other. The political and social upheavals of 1968 consisted in, among other things, large-scale radical disenchantment with the kinds of political practices, theoretical commitments and guidelines of established leftist political orthodoxies. The PCF and the socialists responded to the upheavals by claiming that it was not the right time for revolution, that students, workers and radicals should hold off. Althusser's work was by this time regarded with strong suspicion and he was seen merely as an apologist for the party line. He was accused of conservativism in upholding the primacy of the party in political struggles, and the authority of science in the production and assessment of theory—of dogmatically clinging to established norms.

A less centralised, more diffuse and marginalised notion of political struggle began to emerge. Instead of preset goals (the socialist revolution, 'scientific/historical truth'), prevailing methods (the organisation of workers into hierarchical unions and political parties) and the adoption of ready-made evaluative criteria (judgments in terms of class relations), a politics of spontaneity and specificity, of localised autonomous, non-hierarchical groups —the antithesis of the hierarchised form of the party structure with its delegates, representatives and leaders—emerged as the major hopes for social transformation (Guattari, 1984). A wave of localised, small-scale revolutionary fervour spread through Europe, the United States and Australia in the late 1960s. Its targets were not simply the 'ruling classes' in their classical sense (capitalists, bureaucrats, officials) but also those who propose to speak for or on behalf of others, including leftists, teachers, psychologists, 'experts', etc. Often trained in phenomenology or marxism, this generation was as strongly influenced by the work of Freud and Nietzsche as it was by Hegel and Marx. This was a remarkably rich and tumultuous period, a time of unbounded exuberance and optimism in experimental practices, new forms of social organis-ation, new kinds of theory and new political practices. Second-wave feminism also found its *raison d'être* through the inspiration of or rebellion against this newly emerging political consciousness (see Duchin, 1986:Ch.1). Like their counterparts in Anglo-American contexts, many women developed a feminist conscious-ness as a consequence of disillusionment with the male domination of radical politics.

While Lacan's intervention into psychoanalysis began many years before 1968[6], he was one of the few structuralists or major intellectual figures (along with Sartre and Barthes) to remain

17

generally unscathed by the criticisms developed in 1968. Indeed, his position was even more popular afterwards than it was before this time. There are many anecdotes — some true, others fabricated — about Lacan's position during the riots, his connections with Althusser[7], and with student politics and the educational authorities. For example, Lacan was accused by university authorities of inciting students to subversive activities, of being directly responsible for student unrest!:

> *The director of that august institution [the École Normale Supérieure] decided that the students' uprising in May 68 had been spawned by Lacan's seminar and that he would no longer be permitted to give it on the campus ... Lacan responded by saying that the director reminded him of one of those chains you pull when you flush a toilet; this mobilised student outrage and the director found his office occupied by the Lacanians, in confirmation of his suspicions about the subversiveness of Lacan. (Schneiderman, 1982:29)*

Whatever his position *really* was, his seminars became immensely popular, attracting not only would-be analysts but also students, intellectuals and radicals of all kinds, including a number of women who were to become the best-known names in French feminisms. These seminars were entertaining, sometimes obscure and often highly controversial. Lacan's rereading of Freud was a particularly powerful counterbalance to the disdain and silence greeting Freud's work in France. Although Freud did have a few disciples in Paris (most notably Princess Marie Bonaparte), psychoanalysis had always been greeted with suspicion by French intellectuals, who preferred the lucidity attributed to consciousness by other psychological, therapeutic and philosophical positions. It is largely because of Lacan's invigoration and radicalisation of Freudian analysis that France avoided a problematic *ego psychology* so dominant in the US and Britain. Lacan linked psychoanalysis to *literature* and its associated questions of textuality, reading and interpretation, rather than to science or medicine. This was not dissimilar to Althusser's emphasis on the question of *reading* and the active interpretation of texts in his re-examination of Marx's texts. This may not be surprising, given that Lacan is, besides Marx himself, arguably the single most influential source for Althusser's concept of ideology as the production or constitution of subjectivity.

In opposition to Anglo-American ego psychology, which Lacan scathingly condemned as a form of manipulative consumerism

(Lacan, 1953:12–13), he reads Freud's project *not* as strengthening the ego nor *adapting* the individual through conformity to his or her cultural role. It is nothing more, nor less, than an interrogation of the unconscious. Ego psychologists, he maintains, are in constant danger of repressing the unconscious insofar as they direct themselves only to the assertions and the adequacy of the ego and consciousness without rigorous attention to how consciousness expresses itself, and, more particularly, the incoherences, gaps and flaws in conscious expression which consciousness itself cannot explain. Refusing to position Freud's work in the contexts of medicine, morality or biology, Lacan also refused it the status of normalisation, adjustment or cure. Instead, he insisted on seeing it as a form of listening or reading, placing it in the context of semiotics, linguistics and literature, as Freud himself suggests.

Placed in this context, psychoanalysis challenges many of the central presuppositions of post-Cartesian philosophy and literary analysis. Post-Cartesian philosophy tends to presume a rational, unified self-certain consciousness. It is undermined more effectively by Freud's postulate of the unconscious than it is by the Hegelian assumption of otherness; otherness is the *duplication* of consciousness. The unconscious is the *displacement* of consciousness from the centre or core of subjectivity. The unconscious is 'another scene', another place, where thinking, wishing and desiring take place. It is a locus about which consciousness can have no knowledge, for where there is the unconscious, there is no 'I', no knowing subject.[8] Lacan uses psychoanalysis to disturb many of the key assumptions in linguistics and literary theory as well, particularly those relying on notions of language as a transparent medium or vehicle of expression for concepts, linking one subject's ideas with another's through communication.[9]

In opposition to both, Lacan stresses that the concept of the unconscious subverts the primacy of consciousness, the immediacy of truth and the transparency of communication. The subject is irremediably split, a being located in a conscious agency (which takes itself as master and knower) *and* in an unconscious agency (which is in fact the 'true' locus of [the absence of] identity). Freud, Lacan claims, demonstrated the subject's radical *inability* to know itself.[10] Its self-certainty is a defensive ruse. The subject's identity is not given in consciousness nor in the form of an ego, but comes from being positioned by language as an 'I'. The subject is not the master of language, its controlling speaker, but its result or product.[11]

Freud's work can be roughly divided into two central themes, one an account of the unconscious and the other an account of sexuality. Lacan reworks both through his understanding of the *symbolic order*. The symbolic is the domain of language, which is coincident with the social. For Lacan, subjectivity and sexuality are functions of the material play of a language regulated by the symbolic order. It is governed by the Other. The law described by Lacan as the 'Law of the Father' is the law of patriarchy. Sexuality is produced and restrained by means of the symbolic; and the unconscious operates according to its privileged forms, which is why Lacan claims that 'the unconscious is structured like a language'.

Sexuality and the unconscious can only be understood in terms of the peculiar 'logic' of language. They are structured, organised and made meaningful only in terms of a key or threshold signifier, which represents language and embodies the Father's Law: the phallus. For Lacan, the phallus is not an organ nor a symbol, but a *signifier*.[12] The phallus is emblematic of language itself, a term which circulates and has value only within a system of other terms. The phallus is the term that divides the sexes into two oppositional categories; it is also the term governing relations between them. As a signifier, the phallus cannot be owned or possessed by anyone. No-one can appropriate a linguistic term, which functions only by virtue of the entire structure of language.

The psychical differences between the sexes are not a function of anatomical differences, but of the *meaning* of anatomical differences, of male and female sex organs, when, for example, they are construed on the model of presence and absence (or castration). Likewise, the unconscious cannot be equated with the instinctually governed *id* or with instincts, but is, even in Freud's terminology, bound up with the *ideational representatives* or signs. The unconscious is a repository of repressed images, perceptions, wishes and beliefs. It is not innate, inevitable or preordained, but is created as a result of the act of *primal repression* which occurs at the resolution of the oedipus complex (for the boy at least). Lacan's intervention into and reading of psychoanalysis is thus a *denaturalisation* of psychical processes which repositions them in a signifying or representational framework.

Lacan's concept of the phallus explains how men and women rationalise their identities as masculine or feminine with reference to biology, and how biology has been confused by them with signification. Each sex is constructed as such through his or her relations to the phallus. The masculine is positioned as *having* the phallus by virtue of his illusory conflation of the organ (the penis) with the signifier (the phallus). The feminine is positioned as *being* the phallus by virtue of her anatomical sex being regarded as the absence or loss of the (male) organ. The male is constructed as the active possessor of the phallus, and the woman as its passive receiver. She becomes the (passive) object of male desire. She becomes the phallus, the object of his desire, by becoming desirable for him, confirming that he has what she lacks (and thus wants).

The mirror phase is Lacan's first major contribution to psychoanalytic theory and its antihumanist critique of subjectivity. It explains the child's earliest differentiation from the mother, the genesis of the child's gradually emerging sense of self. The mirror stage is the period, beginning at around six months of age, in which the child's sense of self or ego is formed. The processes by which it is produced are quite complex, and are not the consequence of natural, organic development or learning. The child does not *learn* that it is a subject, distinct from other subjects and from the world. For it to learn this it must have acquired the capacity to imitate, which, however, already entails a distinction between self and other. Lacan begins with Freud's suggestion in 'On Narcissism: An Introduction' (1914) that the ego is the result of a 'new psychical action', distinct from auto-eroticism. In narcissism the ego is able to take itself or a part of its own body as a love object. The ego is that psychical agency providing the conditions under which the child can become a subject and an object, for itself and for others. It is the product of a process of recognition on the part of the child — the recognition of its own image in a mirror.

This striking phenomenon is readily observed in the young child. At a time when it is physiologically incapable of voluntary, controlled behaviour, when it feels fragmented, uncoordinated and its senses are developing at different rates of maturation (see Merleau-Ponty, Schilder, Guillaume), the child has an utter fascination with its own image and the image of others. Its glee and pleasure in the recognition of images is indicative of a complex movement in which the child *identifies* with and internalises images, founding its sense of self. The child internalises as its own image an externalised representation of itself, a view of itself from the outside. This helps to locate it spatially in relation to other objects which are recognised as distinct from it, and are necessary for it to position and integrate its various sensations and corporeal experiences into a singular, unified and bounded body. It locates itself as a subject, separate from the (m)other (a dynamic not unlike the Hegelian dialectic of mutual recognition of self-conscious subjects).

It sees itself reflected in the (m)other, even though the (m)other is different from it (the mirror is, in a sense, only an extremely striking form of a recognition and identificatory process whose major object could also be the mother or nurturer).

Although the mirror stage thus provides the child with the grounds of its identity as a being separate from other beings, it also is the basis of an alienation, a rift which it will forever unsuccessfully attempt to cover over. It is necessarily split between what it feels (fragmentation, 'the body-in-bits-and-pieces') and what it sees (the image of itself as a *gestalt*, as a visual whole), between a sense of its own identity and the identity provided for it by the other/mother/mirror. The mirror image provides it with an illusory or anticipatory identity, an identity it one day hopes to attain, which will form the basis of its ego-ideal. It results in an image of the self modelled on another, a *necessarily social* subject. For this reason Lacan also claims that the ego is an alienated and paranoid construct—always defined by/as the other.

The imaginary order thus originates in the pre-oedipal, two-person self-other relation, whose paradigm is the relation between mother and child. Each strives to see itself reflected in the other; each defines the other's identity, a kind of primordial master-slave dialectic. It is a relation of reciprocity without exchange. It needs to be mediated by a third term, a term outside the dual imaginary structure, usually represented by the (symbolic) father. This third term is the phallus, which represents the Father's Law, the law prohibiting incest. Through the castration threat the Law demands the sacrifice of the boy's corporeal closeness to and pleasure with the mother. In exchange the boy is offered the Name-of-the-Father, a position *like* his father's, a place in the symbolic order as a phallic speaking subject.

While the imaginary provides the preconditions of social and sexual identity, the subject acquires them only as the result of the oedipal or symbolic reorganisation of the imaginary dyad. The imaginary coincides with and establishes the pre-oedipal, 'polymorphous perverse' sexual impulses, which are later repressed or sublimated by the oedipalised subject. It provides the phonemic material, the binary oppositions of signifying matter which the symbolic will form into ordered, articulated speech. It provides the ingredients for adult, heterosexual copulative sexuality (desire is derived from the symbolic organisation of imaginary demands) and the psycho-libidinal body images that provide the basis for sexual identities as masculine or feminine subjects.

The overcoding of the imaginary by the symbolic entails the

advent of repression and the construction of the unconscious. Lacan derives his understanding from Freud's account of dreams (standard edition, vols 4 and 5) and his metapsychological account (standard edition, vol. 14). Defined as an impermeable barrier preventing the entry to forbidden ideas, wishes and impulses into consciousness, the unconscious does not exist in the pre-oedipal child. It is a direct result of the child's primal repression of its sexual impulses directed towards the mother.

For Lacan, the unconscious is a discourse quite different from those ascribed to consciousness. Conscious discourse obeys the imperatives of grammar, syntax, logic and coherence; by contrast, the unconscious articulates itself only through the gaps, silences, moments of indecision and error that intervene in consciousness. On his understanding, the unconscious consists in signs unable to be expressed in consciousness, signs which are literally robbed of their meaning (technically, of their signifieds) to be reduced to signifiers, the material component of the sign. Repression, then, is the robbery of meaning, the severing of the sign's significance. Using Saussurian and structural linguistics, Lacan will claim that what occurs is a 'failure of translation', the splitting of the signifier from the signified. This may explain why the unconscious has no voice of its own, and can thus have no form of expression independent of consciousness: it can only speak *through* or *as* consciousness, as that which intervenes into consciousness as eruption and interruption.

Freud argues that the repressed unconscious material continually strives for conscious expression and access to action. It gains a partial satisfaction when it is able to disguise itself adequately by means of the primary processes. These are two techniques the unconscious has at its disposal for linking unconscious terms to preconscious ones, enabling the latter to act as their delegates or representatives, and thus gaining a compromise pleasure. Freud describes these two techniques as 'condensation' and 'displacement' (standard edition, vol. 5). Condensation occurs when several terms are compressed together on the basis of certain express similarities, while other similarities remain implicit. Displacement occurs when one term transfers its meaning or significance to another which is somehow associated with it and which can then represent it. For Freud, these are the two major procedures, which, coupled with some minor techniques (secondary revision and what he calls 'consideration of the means of representation') enable the unconscious to be expressed and deciphered.

In these psychical procedures Lacan discerns the operation of a language-like system. Using the work of Roman Jakobson, he claims that condensation can be seen as the linguistic or signifying figure of *metaphor*, while displacement can be regarded as the figure of *metonymy*. Metaphor relies on a relation of similarity between two terms, one of which represents while covering over or silencing the other. This process of rendering the signifier latent by covering over it with another signifier similar to it is, Lacan claims, a diagram of the process of *repression*, the burial of one term under another. Displacement is a metonymy, a relation between two terms, both of which remain present but which are related by means of contiguity. It is the movement from one signifier to another, which Lacan claims is the very movement of *desire*, the endless substitution of one object of desire for another, none of which is adequate to fill the original lack propelling desire — the lost or renounced mother.

Through the very precise operations of metaphor and metonymy, the movements of the unconscious can now be understood in detail, using nothing but the speech of the analysand. Psychoanalysis is, indeed, as its most articulate hysteric, Anna O., described it, 'the talking cure'. Its contents are nothing but signs reduced to signifiers, its techniques consist purely in the verbal, playful techniques of language which make poetry possible; and the analyst's function is that of interlocutor. Its objects, methods, processes and aims are shown by Lacan to be structurally identical with language itself.

To sum up Lacan's general relevance to French feminisms and the French intellectual milieu in the late 1960s and 1970s, we can say:

1 Lacan 'decentered' the dominant Cartesian/existential/pheno-menological concepts of the subject which presume a ready-made autonomous subject. The subject is socially, linguistically and libidinally *constructed*. It is the endresult of processes of production which constitute it as an ego, a unified self (in the imaginary order); and a being obedient to the law (through the Name of the Father in the symbolic order), on one side or the other of a sexual division that is marked by the phallus. The subject is not the product of biology or nature, but of its relations to the other and the Other, to other persons in its social world, and the law regulating the social.

2 Lacan's understanding of subjectivity makes it clear that sexuality plays a crucial role in the constitution of identity. Whether male or female, the subject is produced as masculine and/or

feminine through submission to the phallic norm. This is an effect of language's capacity to inscribe the bodies of males and females with specific values and meanings. Masculine and feminine identities are the effects of a *rift* with nature; they are not natural in themselves. The phallus marks male and female bodies in sexually specific ways. While a number of feminists have justifiably accused Lacan of phallocentrism—the representation of *two* sexes by a single, masculine or sexually neutral model (for example, Irigaray, 1977; Gallop, 1982), he is also responsible for the insight of the subject's sexually specific construction.

3 Lacan grounds his conceptions of subjectivity not only in clinical practice or therapy, but also in the context of the history of philosophy, demonstrating that, within it, Freud's work is a moment of radical subversion. Freud shows the impossibility of identifying the knowing philosophical subject with the object known—a productive impossibility, founding and limiting the social sciences and humanities. Our direct access to reality, our capacity to know, our aspirations to objectivity are all frustrated.

4 He developed a primarily linguistic, semiological method of deciphering psychical symptoms. These are now clearly not innate or natural but are the consequences of the subject's symbolic production. This reformulation of Freud's work has helped make a number of psychoanalytic insights more palatable for and useful to feminists, in their attempts to theorise the inequalities and oppressive relations between the sexes. For example, penis envy can no longer be regarded as the literal envy of a biological organ. In substituting the phallus for the penis, Lacan has provided a socio-cultural and political analysis in place of an ontological and biological one.

5 Lacan's emphasis on language and the symbolic provides a map or grid of the requirements of a specifically patriarchal mode of social organisation. He pinpoints processes that are of strategic value for explaining the inculcation of patriarchal values, which may be capable of being undermined or subverted in feminist critiques. For example, his work may help explain why feminists have focused on questions related to infantile sexuality, the mother–child relation, the imaginary order and the acquisition of language in their attempts to transform patriarchy.

As a result of Lacan's rereading of Freud (and Althusser's rereading of Marx), Freud and Marx became crucial sources of academic feminism, whether negatively or positively. In the next section I will turn to Derrida, who seems to perform a broadly similar reading of the works of Nietzsche and semiotics.

Derridean deconstruction

Jacques Derrida is the final figure we will discuss in this broad survey of the sources and contexts of French feminisms. Along with Michel Foucault, Gilles Deleuze, Félix Guattari, Jean-François Lyotard, Jean Baudrillard and others, his name has been linked to postmodern and, particularly, poststructuralist politics and theory within a post-1968 framework. Insofar as his work is poststructural, his work can be located within a structuralist problematic. Yet he also moves beyond it in unpacking the structuralist presuppositions, and in developing internal subversions of its conceptual foundations. Like Foucault[13], Derrida utilises Nietzsche's denunciation of truth, objectivity and neutrality in the functioning of knowledges; and, like Althusser, he is interested in *reading texts* (although he does not share Althusser's passion for 'symptomatic reading', reading as symptomatic of an underlying or deeper structure), as well as in processes of the production of subjects through/as representation. However, unlike Althusser, he is unresolved in his relation to Marx[14] and implies that the very concept of ideology entails a problematic distinction between the real and representation, the latter being a distortion or inversion of the former. Such a dichotomy — between sign and referent, word and thing — is precisely the target of many of Derrida's deconstructive strategies. Like Lacan, he is interested in a latent or unseen discourse, a discourse at variance with consciousness. For Derrida, texts always contain their own undermining or subversion: these are irreducible textual elements — whether figures, literary devices, remarks, punctuation or other linguistic conventions. His object, like Lacan's, is thus a *textual* unconscious, a repressed materiality at work in all texts. Also like Lacan, he takes as his adversaries central texts within the history of philosophy, those associated with the 'proper names' of Plato, Aristotle, Rousseau, Mill, Hegel, Heidegger, Nietzsche, Freud, Saussure and others. Their metaphysical or *logocentric* form and ground is what he attempts actively to destabilise (Derrida, 1976).

Where Lacan subverts the idea of the unified subject, the subject-as-consciousness, Derrida takes the idea of unified, self-present knowledges and texts — logocentrism (logos = the word, knowledge) — as his object, posing the idea of the dispersed text, the text as *different from itself* in its place. Yet, where Lacan is clearly one of the methodological sources for Derrida's work. Derrida also claims that Lacan's work is itself logocentric or, rather, *phonocentric* (that is, governed by an opposition granting primacy to speech over writing). His claim, briefly, is that Lacan's dictum — the unconscious is structured like a language — presumes that language is identical to speech, whereas if he had understood Freud's formulation of a model for the unconscious in 'Note Upon a Mystic Writing Pad' (1925), he, too, could have seen that the unconscious is structured like/as writing. The unconscious is graphic rather than phonic.

Two aspects of Derrida's work are relevant here: his destabilisation of the structure of binary oppositions; and his use of Nietzsche in analysing the metaphor of femininity. Both involve some analysis of his understanding of difference and *différance*, which has become one of the pivots of contemporary French feminism.

Western metaphysics is structured in terms of binary oppositions or dichotomies. Within this structure the opposed terms are not equally valued: one term occupies the structurally dominant position and takes on the power of defining its opposite or other. The dominant and subordinated terms are simply positive and negative versions of each other, the dominant term defining its other by negation. Binary pairs such as good/bad, presence/absence, mind/matter, being/non-being, identity/difference, culture/nature, signifier/signified, speech/writing and man/woman mark virtually all the texts of philosophy, and provide a methodological validation for knowledges in the West. The first term is given the privilege of defining itself and of relegating to the other all that is *not it* (see Jay, 1981; Lloyd, 1984).

He shows that the positive term gains its privilege only by disavowing its intimate dependence on its negative double: far from identity or presence generating difference or absence through negation, they can be seen as vitally dependent on their opposites in ways that cannot be acknowledged. To recognise that identity depends on difference, and that presence relies on absence is to disturb the very structure of knowledges. Instead of difference or absence being the *deprivation* of identity or presence, difference and absence *can* be taken as the primary terms, and their opposites can be taken as the negative terms. If it is conceptually *arbitrary* which term has dominance, this is the effect of power relations, which entail that one set of terms always occupies the privileged position.

Western metaphysics is based on a series of assumptions about

27

the self-presence and transparency of concepts like truth, knowledge, being, reality, identity, etc. The fantasy of a self-certain and guaranteed truth, a truth unmediated by anything extraneous, haunts Western knowledge. This obsession with knowledge, so ably articulated by Descartes as based on certain and immediate foundations, signals an impossible ideal. This impossible but historically necessary ideal is a prime *logocentric* presupposition. Logocentrism presumes that being, language, knowledge are self-evident, neutral and transparent terms. Being can be known and experienced in its immediacy; language transfers meaning neutrally without interfering in the underlying thoughts it 'expresses'; knowledge undistortedly reflects reality in truthful representations. These beliefs retain the concept as a pure idea, existing independent of particular languages or forms of expression. Above all, philosophy as a body of knowledge has vested interests in regarding itself as above the 'mundane' questions of politics, language, materiality, untrammelled by the limits of its linguistic tools in the conceptual explorations it undertakes. Philosophy cannot acknowledge its *constitutive* dependence on language, on textuality, on the ambiguity and openness of all discourse. It cannot acknowledge that it is a material practice, like others, necessarily implicated in other practices and political networks. It cannot acknowledge its own (textual) corporeality. It conceives of itself as fundamentally *translatable*, capable of being expressed, ideally, in logical symbols to avoid any imprecisions or ambiguity, a language honed and purified of all its materiality, resistant to intention.

Deconstruction is one of Derrida's names for this process of problematising logocentric discourses. Deconstruction is not really a theory, method or device (in spite of claims made by Derrida's commentators, for example, Christopher Norris and Mark Cousins) but is spawned by logocentrism as its internal condition and its necessary byproduct. It is a series of close readings of particular philosophical and/or literary texts, seeking out the traces or remainders of textuality or materiality that are its central points, hinges, in a destabilisation of the text's explicit ideals. These metaphors, images, tropes, phrases, linguistic and technical devices are both necessary for the text to function (and are thus *untranslatable*, irreplaceable) but fall outside its logic and explicit goals. They resist the otherwise logocentric mobilisation of language. They signal blindspots, points of unrecognised vulnerability that can be exploited in, as it were, turning logocentrism inside out. They are points of paradox or excess, sites of difference, non-identity, where the text spills over its conceptual boundaries.

Deconstruction has also been called other 'names', among them, 'différence', 'supplement', 'trace', 'pharmakon', 'parergon', 'dissemination', 'grammatology', 'the science of writing' and, more problematically, 'Woman' (Derrida, 1979; 1981a:173–286). Each challenges the specific texts from which it is derived, and is an index of points of potential subversion in those texts.

These terms indicate a *supplement* (both lack and excess) in texts, a movement that escapes the logic of the self-present subject, considered as rational master of meaning. This excess eludes the subject, and demonstrates not the demise of meaning but its (potentially endless) deferral and displacement (Spivak, 1976; Derrida, 1981b).

Deconstruction involves a series of reading strategies to deal with dichotomous structures. Derrida devises a number of tactics to explain the force, the widespread nature and apparent inevitability of this mode of thought. At the same time he renders it problematic and attempts to displace its effects. If the dominant term within the binary structure gains its position by a kind of coercion or force, it would appear that the strategy most useful for revealing this domination is a reversal in the relative positions of the two terms. To overvalue the repressed term and devalue the dominant term, however, still preserves the binary structure. At best, it creates an inverted logocentrism. Reversal, however, remains *one* of the movements involved in a deconstructive reading, a necessary but not sufficient condition for its effectivity.

No challenge to logocentrism can tackle it from outside, for that leaves its operations intact. Deconstruction always operates from *within* logocentrism or from a position both with and without it—from a position on its margins. It is a movement internal to yet subversive of metaphysics, relying on its own commitments to subvert metaphysical texts. It is an attempt to open up the text to its exterior, to the terms, concepts, knowledges it must exclude or foreclose:

> *The movements of deconstruction do not destroy structures from the outside. They are not possible, nor effective, nor can they take accurate aims except by inhabiting those structures, inhabiting them* in a certain way, *because one always inhabits, and all the more when one does not suspect it. Operating necessarily from the inside, borrowing all the strategic and economic resources of subversion from the old structure, borrowing them structurally ... the enterprise of deconstruction always in a certain way falls prey to its own work. (Derrida, 1976:24)*

Deconstruction is always a *double* procedure, a 'double science' or writing, one that simultaneously occupies positions inside and outside the text. It is a duplicit procedure, doubled up on itself, using a theoretical system's own terms against it. The two undecidably dual procedures upon which it relies are a reversal of the dichotomous structure, and the simultaneous displacement of terms from their relative positions.

Merely to reverse the positions of binary pairs is to remain within logocentrism. The coercive force guaranteeing the primary position of the privileged terms is ignored and not adequately challenged. Simply asserting that difference has primacy over identity, or that the female is privileged over the male, remains merely wishful thinking, unless it can somehow combat the historically accumulated power and dominance that has preserved their hierarchical relation over centuries. Derrida's point is that in a culture and within a web of discourses where these kinds of values are ubiquitous, there is no counterforce, no equal or opposite power to reverse or displace. No strategy in itself can counterbalance the political investments in these logocentric structures.

For this reason, Derrida's reading strategies involve *both* reversal and displacement together: the dichotomy must be reversed (showing that the terms are not logically necessary or unalterable in their hierarchical relation); and the repressed term must be displaced, not *out of the structure altogether* but by positioning it within the core of the dominant term, as its *logical condition*. This makes explicit the unacknowledged debt the dominant term owes to the secondary term; moreover, it makes clear the fact that the dichotomous structure could be replaced by other conceptual paradigms — for although they have been *historically* necessary they are not *logically* necessary.

This duplicit reading makes clear the violence involved in the production of knowledge, in its creation of a new term, a third term, beyond the binary pair, confounding binary logic by participating in both terms. A third or 'hinge' term is sometimes taken from the texts Derrida analyses; or sometimes he coins neologisms to make explicit the kinds of subversion deconstructive readings imply. Included here are a number of terms now associated with Derrida's work — 'trace' (both presence and absence); 'supplement' (plenitude and lack); 'différance' (sameness and difference); 'pharmakon' (poison and cure); 'hymen' (rupture and totality). These terms are undecidable, poised over both binary categories, revealing that they are impossible or untenable. These hinge terms are the preconditions or 'raw materials' from which the binary terms are constructed; and are the excess or remainder, a leftover unrepresented by and uncontained in oppositional forms. They signal the 'origin' of these metaphysical terms and reveal a kind of space of free play not captured in the web of binary categories.

A useful example to illustrate Derrida's methods, and to link it more directly to the interests of French feminists, is the opposition between identity and difference. If identity is the positive, privileged term and difference is the absence of identity, Derrida argues that the primary term derives its identity from the suppression and curtailment of its opposite. *Both* terms are effects of an uncontrolled textual play. Sameness/identity and difference are *both* dependent on difference, but this difference is not the same difference as the oppositional term. To indicate this *different difference*, Derrida coins the neologism, *différance*. Différance is the condition of difference *and* identity. The term cleverly signals the primacy and displacement of a number of other binary categories as well: the primacy of writing over speech (the 'a' can only be read, not heard); of absence over presence (the 'a' only functions by virtue of the absent 'e'); of the matter over mind (the 'a' is the material difference generating conceptual differences); of the trace over the origin (as origin of the binary pair, it has meaning and strategic value only through their retrospective framing).

The play of différance is thus the condition of logocentrism and what logocentrism must disavow or deny. It is both (chronologically and logically) prior to the binary pairs and uncontained by them. It is also that which threatens to interrupt the normal, unquestioned use of dichotomous terms, for it indicates the impossibility of the priviledged term's self-representation. It designates a temporally and spatially impossible identity:

> *On the one hand, it indicates difference as distinction, inequality or discernibility; on the other, it expresses the interposition of delay, the interval of spacing and temporalizing ... [T]here must be a common, although entirely different root within the sphere that relates the two movements of differing to one another. We provisionally gave the name* differance *to this sameness which is not* identical. *(Derrida, 1973:129)*

Derrida's challenge to logocentrism, and the structure of binary oppositions on which it relies, has been recognised and utilised by a number of French feminists to provide a powerful series of reading techniques for undermining metaphysics or logocentrism in their generality, and also in challenging phallocentrism, a form of logocentrism in which the phallus takes on the role of the logos. Useful as deconstruction may be for various feminist projects, his position vis-a-vis feminist theory remains ambiguous and, one suspects, ambivalent. He remains controversial within feminist circles largely because of his use of 'Woman' as a metaphor for the unveiling of truth, particularly in his reading of Nietzsche (see Derrida, 1979; see also Spivak, 1983; Bartkowski, 1980; Burke, 1981). It is to this question we will now turn.

The implications of 'Woman' as a metaphor of texuality or 'style' is elaborated in a number of Derrida's texts (for example, Derrida, 1979; 1981a:173–286; 1982b; 1985), but is perhaps most thoroughly discussed in *Spurs: Nietzsche's Styles* (1979). Through his reading of a passage in Nietzsche's *The Gay Science*, Derrida is able to read 'Woman' as the *miming of truth*. 'Finally —if one loved them ... what comes of it inevitably? that they "give themselves", even when they—give themselves. The female is so artistic' (Nietzsche, 1974:317). Nietzsche's point seems to be that women impersonate orgasm, even on the point of orgasm itself. Derrida asks whether Nietzsche is not setting up another oversimplified opposition—between women's 'fake orgasms' and men's 'real' ones. Through his reading, three deconstructive 'moments' can be discerned in Nietzsche: in the first 'moment', truth and 'Woman' are seen as binary opposites—woman is seen as the liar, deceiver, false, in opposition to 'the credulous man, who, in support of his testimony offers truth and his phallus as his own proper credentials' (Derrida, 1979:97). In the second, the oppositional structure is reversed: instead of being on the 'other side' of truth, woman *is* truth, a truth that is not to be trusted, a dissimulation. As truth, woman does not believe in truth. Her truth is play-acting or sham. As Derrida makes clear, 'the woman, up to this point, then, is twice castrated: once as truth and once as untruth' (1979:97). In other words, both as untruth and as truth, woman is still defined phallocentrically, in terms of a privileged masculinity.

However, it is in the third 'moment' that Derrida's text turns in on itself, deconstructing itself:

> *Beyond the double negation of the first two [moments], woman is recognised and affirmed as an affirmative power, a dissumulatress, an artist, a dionysiac. And no longer is it man who affirms her. She affirms herself, and of herself, in man. Castration, here again, does not take place. And anti-feminism, which condemned woman only so long as she answered to man from the two reactive positions, is in its turn overthrown. (1979:97)*

Woman comes to act as the affirmation of the untruth of truth, the impossibility of identity or faith in reason. Neither the veil over truth (the first moment) nor truth as the unveiling of an absence (the second moment) but the unveiling which reveals only another veil.[15] Woman is the metaphor of truth's dissimulation: '... she engulfs and distorts all vestige of essentiality, of identity, of property ... There is not such thing as the truth of woman, but it is because of that abyssal divergence of the truth, because that untruth is "truth"' (1979:51).

'Woman' represents a resistance, a locus of excess within certain logocentric/phallocentric texts, functioning as a point upon which the text turns upon itself. Woman comes to be a metaphoric textual infrastructure that displaces, defers and delays the various logocentric commitments to an identity, substance or identity. This may explain why, in more recent work (1984; 1985), Derrida distinguishes two kinds of feminism, one largely *reactive* and negative, and the other atopic and 'maverick', deconstructive of the univocal singularity of metaphysical closure. If, on the one hand, 'there is a "reactive" feminism and ... a certain historical necessity often puts this form of feminism in power in today's organized struggles ... It is this kind of "reactive" feminism that Nietzsche mocks, and not woman or women' (Derrida, 1982:68). There is also a different kind of resistance that 'woman' represents:

Perhaps woman does not have a history, not so much because of any notion of the 'Eternal Feminine' but because all alone she can resist and step back (precisely in order to dance) in which revolution, or at least the 'concept' of revolution is generally inscribed ... Perhaps she was thinking of a completely other history: a history of paradoxical laws and non-dialectical discontinuities, a history of absolutely heterogenous pockets, irreducible particularities, of unheard of and incalculable sexual differences; a history of women who have—centuries ago— 'gone further' by stepping back with their lone dance, or who are today inventing sexual idioms at a distance from the main forum of feminist activity with a kind of reserve that does not necessarily prevent them from subscribing to the movement and even, occasionally, from becoming a militant for it. (1982b:68)

Derrida here follows Nietzsche's claim that there are two kinds of women: *feminists*, whose project is simply the reversal of phallocentrism, that is, who strive to be *like* men, to have a fixed identity, a natural essence and a place to occupy as subjects; and *women* who *differ from* rather than act as the opposites of the masculine, thus subverting and threatening to undermine masculine privilege. While clearly not mutually exclusive (women are not 'necessarily prevented ... from subscribing to the movement'), this distinction nevertheless involves a separation between those women who strive for identity (of whatever kind) and those who abandon the (phallogocentric) demand for a stable identity, and destabilise logocentrism itself.

In its most positive sense the metaphor of woman serves to disrupt a 'prescriptive order': 'It is that order that a problematics of woman, a problematics of difference, as sexual difference, should disrupt along the way' (1982b:72). Yet if this is feminism's most positive contribution, it is ultimately self-annihilating: its *telos* or goal would be to destroy male and female identities, and the binary structure dividing them—constructing a mixture of indeterminate positions where sexually identity is concerned:

> *I would like to believe in ... the multiplicity of sexually marked voices, this mobile of non-identified sexual marks whose choreography can carry, divide, multiply the body of each 'individual', whether he be classified as 'man' or as 'woman' according to the criteria of usage. (1982b:76)*

Derrida does not advocate the abolition of sexual difference. He raises the crucial question of whether sexual difference precedes or follows ontological difference (1982b:72)—an index of his recognition that the concept of sexual difference is not just one particular issue within a larger framework of logocentrism, but may be what underlies the virulence and the power invested in logocentric thought.

His recognition of the irreducible specificity of sexual difference is manifested in his commentary on Emmanuel Levinas (see Derrida, 1978:79–154; Cohen, 1986, especially the papers by Irigaray and Derrida). Levinas' work on the ethics of alterity—an ethics based on the obligation to respond to the absolute otherness of the other—the subject is put into question in the face of the excessive alterity of the other; yet at the basis of the meeting or encounter with the other, there must be a commonness, a humanity, to make ethics possible. For unless otherness is essential and originary, there can be no ethics (see Levinas, quoted in Derrida, 1982b:73).

While reading Levinas deconstructively, Derrida also voices his own concerns about the risky postulate of a neutral 'human' subject, prior to sexual determination. Levinas' position verges perilously close to an outright affirmation of phallocentrism, where

the human and the masculine are equivalent, originary and normative. Instead, Derrida suggests that 'the masculine should come,
like all sexual marks, only afterwards' (1982b:73). His own
project has turned to the analysis not of the metaphor of woman,
but to the masculinity invested in establishing certain metaphors
of woman and femininity.[16]

This is explicitly developed in *The Ear of the Other: Otobiography, Transference, Translation* (1985). In it Derrida explores
Nietzsche's coupling of philosophy and life in his use of his name
('he has perhaps been alone in putting his name—his names—
and his biographies on the line ...' (Derrida, 1985:6). The proper
name is 'always and a priori a dead man's name, a name of death'
(1985:7), the dead father). The autobiography is paradoxically
positioned between living/on and death, that is, between corporeality and the stasis of the proper name. Nietzsche positions
himself on the border between a paternal, symbolic death and a
maternal mortality: 'I am, to express it in the form of a riddle
[*Rätselform*], already dead as my father [*als mein Vater bereits
gestorben*], while as my mother, I am still living and becoming old
[*als meine Mutter lebe ich noch und werde alt*] (Nietzsche, quoted
in Derrida, 1985:15).

The proper name is double, divided between a dead man, and a
living mother ('this living on is the name of the mother' [1985:16]),
between a living 'mother tongue' and a dead scientific language
(1985:26), between a living umbilicus and the paternal state. The
deadness of the paternal—encrypted inside the subject, incorporated but undigested, a necessary locus for a kind of zombie
(the undead, the living dead), necessary for the autobiographical
signature—exists only with the burial, silencing the unnamed
mother and repressing femininity:

> *No woman or trace of woman, if I have read correctly—save
> the mother, that's understood. But this is part of the system.
> The mother is the faceless figure of a figurant, an extra. She
> gives rise to all the figures by losing herself in the background of
> the scene like an anonymous persona. Everything comes back to
> her, beginning with life; everything addresses and destines itself
> to her. She survives on the condition of remaining at bottom.
> (1985:38)*

Derrida's work remains controversial from feminist perspectives.
His position is highly complex, and given his methods (for example,
provisionally accepting what will eventually be deconstructed),
there is always a fine line between what he describes, what he

affirms and what he criticises. A number of feminists (for example, Irigaray, 1981; Jardine, 1984) have voiced their concern about Derrida's affirmative use of woman as a metaphor for truth — indeed, even feminists who remain overall sympathetic to his concerns express some alarm at his speaking *for* femininity (see Spivak, 1976, 1983 and 1985). As metaphor, 'woman' may well function as a disrupting, disturbing, unassimilable element in all logo- and phallocentric texts, but nevertheless it is also a name (albeit an 'improper' one) for women. To affirm the metaphor as subversive (which it undoubtedly is) may well, depending on who one is and the position from which one speaks, effectively silence women. Affirming the radicalising movement of 'becoming woman' seems to make sense only if one 'is' a man: it is a sexually specific project, an enterprise *for men*. It is clear that 'becoming woman' has a quite different meaning for those who are female!

> *If women have always been used as the instrument of male self-deconstruction, is this philosophy's newest twist? ... with respect, we cannot share in the mysterious longing [for woman]: for as simple as that the question of woman in general, asked in this way, is their question, not ours. (Spivak, 1983:183–4)*

If there is suspicion about his advocacy of 'becoming woman' and his use of feminine metaphors — 'hymen', 'invagination', etc. — these suspicions do not allay the usefulness of his work and the debt many feminists openly acknowledge to deconstructive readings. Spivak succinctly explains his ambiguous position in feminist and leftist political terms:

> *My attitude towards deconstruction can now be summarised: first, deconstruction is illuminating as a critique of phallocentrism; second, it is convincing as an argument against the founding of a hysterocentric to counter the phallocentric discourse; third, as a 'feminist' practice itself, it is caught on the other side of sexual difference. (Spivak, 1983:184)*

Derrida's undoing of philosophical oppositions cannot but be of some use for feminists involved in the social sciences, the so-called 'sciences of man', for it problematises precisely those oppositions constricting, confining and defining woman/femininity by giving primacy to masculinity. His interrogation of philosophical presumptions and power relations is openly acknowledged as a source for Hélène Cixous' quite different project, as she avows:

> *I do not answer the calling of philosophy even if I am in duet*

with something 'philosophical', yet all the while invoking all the liberties warranted or unwarranted of poetry. Insofar as philosophy is concerned, if I refer myself especially to Derrida, it is because he, of course, works on excess. How to exceed, not how to exit from, how to go out of, and exceeds without forgetting or retracting. (Cixous, interviewed in Conley, 1984:150)

We could summarise Derrida's contributions as follows:

1 His challenge to logocentrism parallels and refines feminist challenges to phallocentric discourse. Logocentrism is implicitly patriarchal: the oppositional structure on which it relies is governed by the division between men and women (that is, between men and non-men). Given the close cooperation between these 'centrisms', deconstruction and the play of difference it engenders are allied with feminist struggles within the production of discourses.

2 His stress on the materiality of reading processes confirms the productivity attributed to it by Althusser and Lacan. The production of discourses relies on coercion and is fundamentally political, not simply a matter of the use of an unquestionable *reason*. Derrida makes the powers at work in discourses (whether in knowledges, truths or fictions), powers that are clearly instrumental in the oppression of women, and others, explicit where they must normally function implicitly.

3 His development of the concept of différance has become emblematic of a powerful trajectory within feminist theory, distinguished from liberal struggles for equality. In recognising the limits of equivalences with the masculine (if masculinity is oppressive, why aspire to it as an ideal?), many feminists have instead directed their attention towards developing autonomous definitions of woman and femininity. This autonomy, at least for some feminists, finds a source in the Derridean notion of *différance*.

4 His focus on the irreducible textuality of discourses, their resistances to singular meanings and monological readings, confirms the interests many feminists have developed, not simply in women as the object of speculation and knowledges, but in the metaphors of femininity, excess, materiality and play in the production of knowledges — beyond the recognition of intellectual sexism to a recognition of phallocentrism. He helps make clear how these metaphors are necessary conditions for logo- and phallocentric texts to continue their dominance.

Between them, Althusser, Lacan and Derrida do not provide all the links and theoretical sources informing the works of Kristeva, Irigaray and Le Doeuff; a general milieu of shared proper names and texts infuses French philosophy over the last several decades. Mallarmé, Artaud, Bataille, Klossowski, Levinas, Blanchot, Barthes and Foucault should be included in any list of twentieth-century names stamping the character of French intellectual life. Yet Althusser, Lacan and Derrida serve here as convenient signposts, figures whose interests coincide with, and act as clear expressions of, a mood typical of the transition from pre-1968 to post-1968 politics. They are also useful in our context, insofar as their works are widely available and discussed in English, and so may act as a bridge for those unfamiliar with the feminist texts we will explore.

If it is possible to extract a few shared principles that help locate feminist theories, these three male theorists stress the necessary interlocking of two crucial concepts: language/representation, and the production of subjectivity. Language and systems of representation are vital elements of all social, political and interpersonal life: in the tradition of Saussure, they claim both an autonomy for signs systems, whether linguistic or non-linguistic, and their active, productive relation to what it is that they represent (whether 'reality' or 'ideas'). Far from the neutral transparency Cartesian philosophy assumes, Saussure's concept enables the materiality of discursive production to be affirmed. And, because of Lacan's intertwining of Saussure with Freud, language is also necessarily linked to the structure and forms of subjectivity.

Language and subjectivity need to be linked to power in order to understand the force of the 'French revolution' (to borrow from Turkle) of the 1960s and 1970s. Althusser explicitly links the forms of representation (ideology) to power, conceived in class terms. Lacan makes clear the socio-cultural and political investment subjects have in seeing themselves as unified beings in control of themselves and able to know themselves. Derrida, too, makes clear the political terrain on which all discourses function and have their effects. The three feminists we will discuss here need also to be located at the point of overlap of these three concepts. Each utilises and subverts the work of her male predecessors and colleagues. Each examines the relations between various kinds of discourse and an avowedly *sexual subject* within an explicitly recognised patriarchal socio-political framework.

2 Julia Kristeva and the speaking subject

I
F French philosophy characteristically explores the relations between language and subjectivity, French feminists are committed to a deeper analysis of the interrelations between language, conceived as phallocentric, and sexually specific types of subjectivity. Instead of focusing on *sexist language* — as Anglo-American feminists tend to in their investigations of *words*, grammatical and syntactical rules and conventions, the use of discriminatory phrasing, and in their concentration on language as an empirical object (for example, Casey Miller and Kate Swift; Dale Spender, etc.) — many French feminists question the underlying structure and prevailing forms of discourse. Language is not merely a system of naming, labelling or even communication. It is the threshold of all possible meaning and value.

Althusser claims that all systems of representation are effects of power relations (in his case, economic or class power), which remain unrepresented; Lacan sees language and representation as the crucial conditions of social subjectivity; and Derrida analyses the terminology, methods, conceptual categories and axiomatic assumptions within the traditions dominating philosophy. If, as these writers suggest, language is not simply a set of practices much like any other, but is the *condition for the meaningful existence of all other practices*, then analysing the structure of language may help make clear its crucial role in the functioning of power itself. Given the intense focus on questions about subjectivity, identity and consciousness in these *antihumanist* frameworks of subjectivity, language is a structuring device, a condition for the production of subjects.

Antihumanism asserts that there is no human essence and no pregiven, universal identity. These beliefs are the consequences of particular social/historical contexts and powers. If this is the case then the production of social subjects, and their internalisation and absorption of social ideologies and norms, needs explanation. Family-based socialisation practices play a crucial role in the processes of subject construction. But these models are plagued by the kinds of objections also levelled at behaviourism. Explaining the acquisition of sex-roles on a behaviourist model presumes the subject as pliable, plastic, manipulable and, above all, passive.

Behaviourist/learning theories cannot explain the possibilities of resistance to dominant practices and values. At best, resistance is the result of an inadequate, incomplete socialisation but cannot be regarded as a viable, active response to an untenable situation. Such models can only provide deterministic *causes* of social subjectivity but not *reasons* or explanations.

If behaviourist/determinist accounts cannot explain the subject's *interiority*, its production as a psychical and desiring being, they cannot adequately explain the production of *sexed* subjects within patriarchy. Learning theories, based on notions of stereotyping, 'conditioning' and determinism, explain how subjects conform to what is expected of them but not why subjects can resist these expectations. The antihumanist critique of the sovereignty of self-consciousness thus relies largely on psychoanalytic accounts of a decentred subject such as Lacan develops in his reading of Freud.

Psychoanalysis seems to provide one of the few possible accounts of the subject that can explain both the external pressure to conform and the psychical or lived desires and experiences of (sexualised) subjects. Lacan links together theories of the productivity of language with theories of the constitution of the subject. His conception of the necessarily split subject provides an alternative to humanist/Cartesian accounts; and his understanding of the materiality of language actively constructing the child's sexual drives and desires, organising the child's incipient unconscious, provides a necessary counterbalance to neutral, transparent, communicational models of language and theories of socialisation or learning.

Where Althusser argues that representational systems are ideological, governed by unacknowledged (class) values and interests, Derrida elaborates with considerably more sophistication how the very terms, central concepts, methods, definitions — the precise technical means of expression and the literary or textual devices necessary for texts to function and mean something — are also implicated in relations of power and domination. Unlike Althusser, for whom the power invested in representations is a reflected power, derived from elsewhere, in Derrida's work power relations are immanent in intellectual and textual practices. Texts, in short, have 'an unconscious', an unspoken, censored debt to terms whose repression guarantees the privilege of other, valorised terms. Inhabiting a text or position in order to push it to the limits of tolerance or intelligibility, forcing a text to approximate its own unconscious — these procedures become powerful *textual strategies* for (provisionally) undoing their domination.

Hegel, Althusser, Lacan and Derrida provide some of the conceptual materials Julia Kristeva's work utilises and develops. Her interrogation of the *speaking subject*, the subject of enunciation[1], brings together a Lacanian/Freudian conception of the split psychical subject (a subject of sexual drives and social inhibitions), with a Derridean notion of the text as different from itself. Kristeva places the speaking subject and the poetic text directly in a socio-historical and political context. In her earlier works (1984, 1974, 1976, etc.), she adheres closely to an Althusserian framework, whereby the subject is a function and effect of the socio-symbolic order. The speaking subject is not merely an individual producer of texts, an 'author', but is *symptomatic* of a social organisation: the ruptures and breaches in the ordered functioning of meaning and coherence mirror, even forecast, ruptures in social unities at the level of the State and ideological institutions. Textual analysis is thus simultaneously political and psychological in its implications.

In this and the following chapter, Kristeva's wide-ranging discussions of the speaking subject, signifying practices, avant-garde texts and social transgression will be examined. However, given the depth and difficulty of her work, and the changes it has undergone in the last twenty years, I will divide discussion into two phases, one chapter being based on her earlier and the other on her later writings. The dividing line between these two phases roughly dates from around 1980. The distinction between earlier and later stages is, of course, an arbitrary one — there is no clear dividing line between one 'phase' and another — but this may help organise her otherwise complex work into a more manageable form.[2]

The speaking subject

Virtually all of Kristeva's concerns converge on her notion of the speaking subject. She claims that traditional linguistic, literary and social theory is based on an unrecognised commitment to a concept of the speaking subject. No social or discursive function can be understood without some notion of the speaking being as the locus of textual production *and* deformation.

Traditional knowledges within the social sciences remain ignorant of the revolutionary upheaval in concepts of subjectivity effected by Freud's postulation of the unconscious, relying as they do on Cartesian/transcendental notions of a pre-formed, pre-linguistic subject. Psychoanalysis effects a rupture, a crisis in the rational self-certainty of the subject, the implications of which still need to be understood and unravelled in the social sciences. She forces these fields to confront Freud's Copernican revolution directly. Conversely, she forces psychoanalysis to confront its own often unrecognised commitments to an understanding of language and systems of representation — to the enrichment of both.

Kristeva is interested in exploring the region of overlap between linguistic/literary theory and psychoanalysis. She analyses the ways in which texts are able to confirm and stabilise subjectivity or to put it into question; and how the subject is able to transmit/ receive and deform meanings. She explores the contradictory tensions within and between the unified, rational subject and the coherent, meaningful text, revealing the wayward functioning of desire in both. She links subjectivity and textuality through a series of terms, including 'the semiotic', 'the symbolic' and 'the thetic'. These indicate sites and processes in human social development that provide the necessary conditions for representational and symbolic processes.

The semiotic

Kristeva uses the term 'the semiotic' idiosyncratically. It has resonances with Saussure's revitalisation of the term, which is derived from the Greek term *semeion*, 'sign'. In her usage it designates the contributions of sexual drives to signification. It must be opposed to the symbolic, understood in Lacan's sense as the law-abiding operations of socio-linguistic systems. All signifying practices and all social subjects are the effects of the interrelation of these terms.

The semiotic and the symbolic are the two energies or movements enabling the subject to signify, to produce and use sign systems, discourses and to engage in social practices, as well as in their potential subversion. These terms refer to two distinct but related orders — that of signification (the symbolic) and that of subject formation (the semiotic).

The semiotic is a *pre-signifying* energy, the order of the 'distinctive mark, trace, index, precursory sign, proof, engraved or written sign, imprint, trace [sic], figuration' (Kristeva, 1984). It is the material order of the textual/psychical trace or imprint. In textual terms it refers to the energies, rhythms, forces and corporeal residues necessary for representation. And in the case of the psychical it coincides with what Freud called the 'facilitation of neural pathways', that is, with the material inscription of the drive in the psycho-neurological networks (see Freud, 1895). The drive traces a pathway from sensation to perception and/or motility, and through the latter to satisfaction.

The semiotic consists in the dispositional and organisational structure of the drives (understood as not-yet-distinct oral, anal, scopic drives, drives in their polymorphous, undifferentiated state). It consists in the processes of dividing and organising the body according to the pleasure principle, that is, in terms of erotogenic zones. The semiotic also relies on the temporary stases and fixations of drives, particularly when invested in external love objects (including one's own body in primary narcissism).

In this sense the semiotic marks out the space or locus the subject-to-be will occupy as a subject. For Freud, this space and energy is dominated by the 'primary processes' (Freud, 1900), psychical processes directed towards obtaining immediate gratification of drives.[3]

The semiotic is composed of non-signifying raw materials. It is an anarchic, formless circulation of sexual impulses and energies traversing the child's body *before* sexuality is ordered and hierarchically subsumed under the primacy of genitality and the body becomes a coherent entity. These energies have no fixed aim, object or form. They animate the child's body in a series of rhythms, spasms, movements that predate its conscious corporeal control. They predate the distinction between subject and object and thus also the child's notion of thing or entity. They defy unification, distinctive boundaries and social regulation.

The semiotic thus precedes all unities, binary oppositional structures and hierarchical forms of organisation. It has clear affinities with Freud's notion of pre-oedipal drives; yet the concept is also broader insofar as it is anterior to the mirror stage. Although it is polymorphous, it is not yet auto-erotic; it precedes auto-eroticism insofar as it is pre-imaginary and pre-narcissistic. It is the symbiotic space shared by the mother's and child's indistinguishable bodies. It follows the 'organisation' of polymorphous perverse drives operating without respect for the reality principle, governed only by its own 'libidinal economy'. It thus coincides with the movements, sensations, perceptions, vocalisations *before* the child's acquisition of even the most minimal linguistic units (the phonemic oppositions, the minimal units of speech, only appear during what Freud calls the Fort! Da! game; see Freud, 1921). The movements which fragment the child's body (the Lacanian body-in-bits-and-pieces) and produce pleasure and/or pain are the elementary constituents of the semiotic.

Kristeva ascribes the semiotic to a space, a locus rather than to a subject because the semiotic precedes the acquisition of a stable subjectivity and identity. She locates it using a term derived from Plato's *Timaeus*, the *chora*. The *chora* is 'receptacle, unnameable, improbable, hybrid, anterior to naming, to the one, to the father, and consequently maternally connoted' (Kristeva, 1980:133). The *chora* is a function of the child's unmediated (imaginary) relation to the mother's body, even though the child does not, at this point, recognise itself as separate or distinct.

The semiotic involves both the inscription of polymorphous impulses across the child's body; and the *return* of these infantile inscriptions in adult form (her analogy is with Freud's concept of the symptom as the return of the repressed). They 'return' in the form of rhythms, intonations, melody accompanying all representation. They form a site, a threshold from which the earliest vocalisations, and eventually naming and language, can develop. The child's bodily processes (particularly its oral impulses) are ennervated by and respond to discontinuous or discrete rhythms and sensory inputs, of which one of the earliest and clearest expressions is *laughter*:

> *Oral eroticism, the smile at the mother, and the first vocalisations are contemporaneous ... During this period of indistinction between 'same' and 'other', infant and mother, while no space has yet been delineated, the semiotic chora ... relieves and produces laughter ... The chora is indeed a strange 'space': the rapidity and violence of the facilitations are localised at a point that absorbs them and they return to the invoking body without signifying it as separate; they stop there—impart the jolt—laughter. ('Place Names', Kisteva, 1980:284)*

Laughter is perhaps the most primitive instance of semiotic impulses harnessed in vocalisation. As such, it anticipates and pre-structures the child's later (symbolic) positioning in language as a speaking subject.

The thetic

If the semiotic consists in fundamentally unstable drives and impulses inscribed across and circulating throughout the child's body in an untrammelled way, there are strategic moments in the child's life when the unstable semiotic is (provisionally, temporarily) unified and harnessed to provide organisation, structure and order — the symbolic. The threshold between the semiotic and the symbolic — the *thetic* — is an anticipation of the symbolic from within the semiotic, as well as the residues of the semiotic in the symbolic. The thetic (from the term 'thesis', postulate or proposition) is Kristeva's name for those moments (in Hegel's sense), phases of unification, which organise the drives into symbolically amenable forms. Kristeva identifies them with the two crucial phases in the formation of a stable social identity. She correlates the thetic with the two moments Lacan identifies as pivotal to identity, the mirror stage and the oedipus complex/threat of castration.

Symbolic operations enabling the social subject to come into being are possible only because the mirror stage provides the child with a spatial location or position, an unstable identity as the mirror-double of the (m)other, a provisional and imaginary identity separate from the (m)other and capable of being located in space as a distinct identity.[4] Kristeva suggests that the subject's detachment from the immediacy of its lived experiences and its identificatory investments in images (including its own image in a mirror) provide the earliest divisions in its world, digitalising it by rendering its terms discrete — the condition for the signifier/signified opposition, and thus ultimately for signification. It produces the conditions necessary for 'holophrastic utterances' (Kristeva, 1984:43).

Through the mirror stage, the child can distinguish itself from the world, substituting images or representations for the immediacy of its lived experiences. The image stands in place of the felt experience. Its experiences, perceptions and sensations become the 'raw data' for a network of signifiers available to the child. Only with castration and the oedipus complex is the subject's definitive separation from the immediacy of its lived experiences secured: it is now able to designate and replace its experience with representations. If the mirror stage initiates the field of signifiers, marked by pure difference, the castration complex generates signs, which organise and render these signifiers meaningful:

Language learning can therefore be thought of as acute and dramatic confrontation between positing-separating-identifying and the motility of the semiotic chora. *Separation from the mother's body, the* fort-da *game, anality, orality ... all act as a permanent negativity that destroys the image and the isolated object even as it facilitates the articulation of the semiotic network, which will afterwards be necessary in the system of language where it will be more or less integrated as a* signifier.

Castration puts the finishing touches on the process of separation that posits the subject as signifiable, which is to say, separate, always confronted by an other: imago *in the mirror (signified) and semiotic process (signifier). (Kristeva, 1984:47)*

The mirror stage provides the barest differentiation between the signifier and signified, positing them as two orders within signifying practices. It establishes the relation between the image and the object. The thetic opens up the *gap* between lived experience and representation, and between reality and signs, which are the precondition of signification and the signified respectively.

The castration threat and resolution of the oedipus complex retrospectively restructure the rudimentary 'identity' posited in the mirror phase and the primitive vocalic systems established in the imaginary. They structure and regulate the primitive phonemic/conceptual oppositions according to the demands of coherence, meaning and sociality. They hierarchise signifying elements by submitting them to the requirements of double articulation (Jakobson) and grammatical/syntactic/semantic organisation. In agreement with Lacan, Kristeva asserts that this is accomplished through the child's assumption of a position, designated only with respect to the *phallic* signifier.

Kristeva asserts that the phallus is the crucial signifier in the subject's acquisition of an enunciative position. The phallus 'always refers outside itself', not only to another, but also to the Other, the locus from which language emanates. The law represented by the phallus requires the child's renunciation of the mother and its submission to an authority greater than itself or the (m)other — in other words, the symbolic father, the phallic law-giver.

This constitutes the child's first attempts to regulate and control lack by submitting it to the rigours of signification. In this process, the child transfers the energetic force of its pre-oedipal drives to the symbolic, signifying order through the processes of repression and sublimation:

... the phallus totalizes the effects of signifieds as having been produced by the signifier: the phallus is itself a signifier. In other words, the phallus is not given in the utterance but instead refers outside itself to a precondition that makes enunciation possible. For there to be enunciation, the ego must be posited in the signified, but it must do so as a function of the subject lacking in the signifier; a system of finite positions (signification) can only function when it is supported by a subject and on condition that this subject is a want-to-be [manque à être]. *(Kristeva, 1984:47–8)*

This primordial, ontological, lack-in-being, which the ego covers over and attempts to deny, implies that the child is fundamentally social: it needs the other for its survival. The child acquires a speaking position when it recognises the alterity of the other (from which it is prevented by its imaginary identifications) and when it accepts the law regulating the subject's exchanges with others. This hole or gap is the space of language, sociality and identity.

These thetic phases — the imaginary mirror stage and the symbolic castration complex — posit a unity and an organisation in the subject (based on the logic of imaginary identification and symbolic organisation respectively). They constrain the drives, forcing them to accept a compromise or partial satisfaction through acknowledgement of the reality principle. From this time on, the drive submits to the 'defiles of the signifier' (Lacan, 1977b). The thetic phases manage and structure the semiotic *chora*, dialectically superceding it through symbolisation. The thetic constitutes the limits, boundaries, forms and contours of the drive. The thetic provisionally orders the circulation of the drives, and redefines and renegotiates its relations to the imaginary, thus constituting the symbolic:

As a traversable boundary, the thetic is completely different from an imaginary castration that must be evaded in order to return to the maternal chora. *It is clearly distinct as well from a castration imposed once and for all, perpetuating the well-ordered signifier and positing it as sacred and unalterable within the enclosure of the Other. (1984:51)*

The symbolic

Unlike Lacan, for whom the symbolic severs the child's pre-oedipal attachment to its mother, for Kristeva, the symbolic is already anticipated in the thetic, and even in the illusory unity proposed by the mirror stage. The mirror stage provides the earliest outlines for the primal separation between subject and object, self and other and signifier and signified. The concept of lack has been introduced to and accepted by it. From this time a whole universe of binary oppositions is opened up.

The mirror stage provides a provisional identity and structure for pre-oedipal drives. It ties the child's desires for the mother to the circulation of sexual drives. Kristeva asserts that the imaginary, narcissistic structure of mirror-identifications linking mother and child is doomed by irresolvable projections, introjections and identifications that position it in a relation of crippling dependence on a singular other. There is no room for relations with others outside the imaginary dyadic structure. Each defines the other's identity and limits its own in relation to the other. This unmediated mother–child relation precludes the possibility of *exchange*, which requires the existence of a third term — the object exchanged, and a law regulating equivalences between exchangeable objects. The oedipus complex severs the child from its dependence on the (m)other by means of the castration threat, which pits the child's narcissistic investment in the integrity of its body against its desire for access to the mother's body. Only then can it gain a position within the socio-symbolic order, and the privileges associated with the Name-of-the-Father.

The symbolic organises the libidinal drives according to a phallic sexual economy, a normative and generative linguistic structure (including grammar, logic, syntax, and access to the shifter 'I', which gives the subject access to appropriating discourse as its own, as referring to itself), and a subjective and social identity. These various identities — sexual, linguistic, subjective — are provisional and threaten to dissolve when the thetic is chal- lenged and the semiotic transgresses its boundaries. These are moments of breakdown of identity (psychosis), meaning and coherence (poetry) and sexual identity (perversion, fetishism), instances privileged by Kristeva. Each demonstrates the usually repressed semiotic contributions to the symbolic by providing the semiotic with expression.

The symbolic is the domain of *positions* and *propositions* (1984:53), the order in which the object is *posited*, the proposition affirmed and the statement located so that truth (or falsehood) can be attributed to it. It is a stratified and stratifying system organ- ising drives and corporeal impulses, and coordinating them with the requirements of signification. It functions by hierarchical sub- sumption, using relations of logical and grammatical convention, and the distinctions between meta- and object-language to cohere and integrate the signifying elements provided by the semiotic. It is the sacrificial order, whose 'cost' is the repression of the semiotic and the pre-oedipal.

The semiotic and the chora are explicitly maternal and feminine in Kristeva's account, while the symbolic is paternal, bound up with the concepts of the symbolic father and the castrated mother. It is the order of naming (naming is possible only on the subject's assumption of the father's Proper Name), reference, meaning, enunciation and denotation. It harnesses and regulates the semiotic, providing energy and pleasure for the symbolic to sublimate and rechannel. For Kristeva, it is strictly impossible to calculate the contributions of the semiotic to the symbolic, which, because it predates the symbolic, is unrepresentable, being absorbed but unacknowledged by the symbolic.

In agreement with Derrida, Kristeva signals that reason, logic, grammar, syntax, univocal meanings — the so-called 'higher achievements' of civilisation — function only because of a some-times violent repression and sacrifice. The speaking subject must 'pay' for the unity and certainty of its position, its 'mastery', with the renunciation of its maternal pleasures and the sacrifice of its oedipal, incestual attachments. The symbolic is 'erected' only on the basis of repression of the maternal. As Freud argued, what is repressed is the feminine. Its silence is the condition of symbolic stability. Civilisation, the symbolic order, the coherent text, then, are possible only at the cost of the silencing, the phallicisation, of the maternal *chora*.

The symbolic and the semiotic are two heterogenous orders in the production of discourse, the constitution of the subject and in the regulation of social relations. Kristeva conceives of their inter-action as a dialectic, a confrontation between contradictory forces which enables change to occur. Taken together, they provide the energy, motility or impetus for all social and individual unities. The dominance of the symbolic is never guaranteed or secure. Symbolic components are liable to exceed the boundaries and limits imposed in them, thus bringing to a crisis point, and possibly to a point of revolutionary rupture, the previous stability which was secured only at the cost of the submersion of the semiotic.

Signifying practices

The subject is produced as such by the interaction of the semiotic and the symbolic, signifying systems and systems of meaning (linguistic or extra-linguistic), which imply the subordination of the semiotic to the symbolic. In her earlier works there is a direct correspondence between the heterogeneity of subjectivity and that of textual relations. She explains this interrelation in terms of a distinction between the *genotext* and the *phenotext*. The genotext is composed of a space or locus which, although it is pre-linguistic and pre-subjective, provides the *non-signifying conditions* of signification. It is the pre-textual arrangement of drives and pleasures, functioning in an a-signifying, pleasure-seeking rather than meaning-laden fashion. The phenotext, by contrast, is the signifying process or practice seen as a product rather than a process, the manifest text, the text as it presents itself to consciousness (Kristeva, in Moi, 1986:28).

> *What we will call the* genotext *will include semiotic processes but also the advent of the symbolic. The former includes drives, their disposition, and their division of the body, plus the ecological and social system surrounding the body, such as objects and pre-oedipal relations with parents. The latter encompass the emergence of object and subject, and the constitution of nucleii of meaning involving categories: semantic and categorial fields. (Kristeva, 1984:86)*

In animating the child's body, the semiotic transfers its particular characteristics onto signifying elements: phonemic units are produced from the energies and impulses of the drives, creating repetition, allusion, rhyme, intonation, rhythm and the other specifically and irreducibly material elements of representation. The genotext is closer to Freud's notion of primary processes than to Lacan's notion of the imaginary. It is a *topos*, a space which will later be occupied by the 'split unity' of the subject and the phenotext:

> *We shall use the term* phenotext *to denote language that serves to communicate, which linguistics describes in terms of 'competence' and 'performance'. The phenotext is constantly split up and divided, and is irreducible to the semiotic process that works through the genotext. The phenotext is a structure ... it obeys rules of communication and presupposes a subject of enunciation and an addressee. (1984:87)*

The phenotext relies on a pre-signifying *topos* which meaningful signification will take over. In metalinguistic terms, the phenotext represents an *algebra*, a set of functions which govern the combination of meaningful terms. The phenotext presumes a univocal, cohesive discourse, capable of transmission from a sender to a receiver, a communicational relation between subjects (1984:87).

Genotext and phenotext function together in any signification, just as the semiotic and the symbolic necessarily interact in any subject. But not all signifying practices draw on them in exactly the same way or to the same degree. There will always be a preference for one or other in any particular text. Kristeva claims that this is an effect of socio-political and historical constraints, which repress the processes of the *production* of signification by focusing only on the finite product, the text produced. The phenotext tries to minimalise genotextual intrusions disrupting and over-coding its desire for univocal communication. The text tries to obliterate its own materiality so that meanings, messages, can be transmitted without acknowledging the *inherent* polyvocity and plurality, the materiality, and ambiguity of all texts.

Kristeva speaks of the unified or thetic text as a conservative construct. It relies on already existing codes and conventions, necessarily confirming rather than questioning them. Within capitalist relations, which form the political framework of her earlier works (with little specification of the patriarchal forms of capitalism), there is only one general type of signifying practice that resists the constrictions and limits of symbolic coherence imposed on representation—the avant-garde text. This is her privileged object of analysis. It represents a politically transgressive discourse that challenges the limits of representation. Not usually explicitly political in its 'content', the avant-garde text is never-theless political in its capacity to shatter the norms and conventions governing signification.

Unity and process

Kristeva leaves behind the terminology of genotext and phenotext to turn to a series of different terms to describe the semiotic and symbolic components within representation. In her introduction to a collection of essays[5], she reformulates the genotext/phenotext distinction in terms of an opposition between 'unity' (phenotext, the symbolic) and process (genotext, the semiotic; see Kristeva, 1976).

The 'unity' or 'setting in place' of a signifying system involves the constitution of a stable social code governed by collective rules and shared conventions. Whether a social institution—like the State, the family, the Church or any other ideological State apparatus—or simply a representational system—painting, music, sculpture, poetry, film—it relies on the rule-governed, systematic coding of the energetic, disorganised, fragmented forces which Kristeva calls 'cutting through', 'traversing' or 'process':

> *The setting in place, or constituting of a system of signs requires the identity of the speaking subject in a social institution which the subject recognises as the support of its identity. The traversing of the sign takes place when the speaking subject is put into process and cuts across, at an angle as it were, the social institutions in which it had previously recognised itself. It thus coincides with moments of social rupture, renovation and revolution ... In any mode of production, signifying practice is that through which the mode of production signifies its stabilisation and its self-expenditure—the condition of its renewal. (Kristeva, 1976:64)*

Unity involves the establishment of limits, rules, procedures. *Preceding* and *exceeding* unity is process. It provides the preconditions and raw materials of unity. It also threatens to overflow the limits of unity. It is thus the unspoken, threatening condition of signification, unable to be signified.

These terms signal the marks or traces of the subject's necessary inscription in discourse, and conversely of language's constitutive relation to subjectivity. When unity and process are transcribed into subjective terms, they are the textual counterparts of the semiotic and the symbolic. Unifying processes, regulating them in order to create language, the symbolic has at best a tenuous hold over the semiotic and is subjected to the perils of overflow of identity, visible in socially disruptive moments, in a radical trinity of subversion which Kristeva attributes to 'madness, holiness and poetry' (1976:64). These are the three privileged domains in process or where the semiotic gains a position of dominance over unity or the symbolic. The semiotic explodes in an excessive, uncontrolled *jouissance* of madness (the madness of the psychotic or the fetishist, who refuse the father's law and retain their semiotic, pre-oedipal maternal attachments); of the 'holiness' of transgressive ecstasy (of which Lacan makes St Teresa of Avila the most striking example); and of poetry, which is at its most subversive in the writings of the avant-garde.

Unity denies the conflictual tension on which all signification is based. Kristeva cites the unifying instance of the State, which she claims functions only by disavowing the 'process of contradiction which traverses the forces and relations of production (1976:64). Similarly, the unity of the nuclear family covers over the contradictions posed by the mutually exclusive demands the family places on the child: the family engenders sexual drives *and* forbids their incestual expression. In the case of the unification posed by the institution of the Church, Kristeva also sees the reconstruction of a unity threatened with transgressions: it represents the unspeakable *jouissance* of process, the semiotic, by recoding and resymbolising it:

> *The unity, of state and family, is achieved at the price of a murder and a sacrifice—that of the* soma, *the drive, and the process. This is recognised by religion, which thus arrogates to itself the privilege of representing (i.e. unifying into the socio-symbolic ensemble the hitherto heterogeneous) and of speaking the infinite element which the ensemble oppresses and yet demands to be spoken. Religion here is that discourse (whether transcendental or not) which knows, as far as is possible, what is at stake in the relation between socio-symbolic homogeneity and the heterogeneity of the drives at work within and it restores their* other *to them, this religious discourse appears not only as the speculative (specular) form of what is unrepresentable in orgasmic (genital) pleasure and of what is uncapitalisable in expenditure (of productive power): it is also the privileged place of speculation and the place from which it represents its own signifying practice to itself—theory of language and of the function of language as communication or expenditure. (1976:65)*

Religion neutralises and homogenises the disruptive energies on which it is founded. It is thus complicit with other socio-psychical unities, though perhaps with a greater potential for social upheaval (given the precarious balance between sacred and perverse impulses it relies on). The symbolic coding of semiotic processes, such as the Church performs, is counteracted, in Kristeva's conception, by the transgressive eruptions of the semiotic in 'art'. Art problematises the limits of the socio-symbolic ensemble: it is both the 'companion' and the 'nearest enemy' (1976:65) of the sacred. Instead of affirming the necessity of sacrifice and renunciation, art celebrates the heterogeneity of drives and the disruptions of social cohesion they engender.

The unities of the State, the nuclear family and religion have been in a state of crisis since the end of the nineteenth century. The crisis of these social totalities is a crisis accompanied, indeed forecast, by the subversive breakdown of the unities that comprise art and signifying practices. It annihilates as well as constitutes representational identities—the identity posed by narrative structure in literature, the coherence of the sign in linguistics, and the coherence of the subject in psychical functions. These unities are unsettled, overthrown, by 'artistic' disturbances initiated through experiments in representation. Avant-garde practices hover on the borders of sense and nonsense, at the very limits of signification.

Art is a kind of index of social stability. Upheavals, transformations or subversions of artistic norms and canons do not exactly reflect or cause symbolic/social transformations; rather, they anticipate and accompany them. Kristeva refuses to reduce representations to the socio-economic order (as may occur in sociological readings of texts). Economic and social relations do not directly produce artistic transformations nor do artistic and representational upheavals incite social rebellion. This is to consider socio-economic relations in isolation from representations, as two distinct systems: one does not simply represent the other or act as its symbol or delegate. On the contrary, the mode of production necessarily implies the mode of sign-production (1976:64). Upheavals within representation are symptomatic of broader social instability, which may be highlighted through crises in representation, but which are most effectively worked on and transformed by directly political means. In this sense her work owes a considerable debt to the Russian formalists and to Mikhail Bakhtin, whom she, together with her countryman Tzevtan Todorov, introduced to French theory. The formalists (Jakobson, Tyanov, Vološinov, etc.) maintained the autonomy and integrity of the art object or text. Art and literature must be assessed only in their own terms, and not made to carry the weight of an entire social structure. Art *does not reflect life*; instead, it is an exploration of and experimentation with its own governing conventions. Yet, it is misleading to suggest that this was merely an aesthetic approach to art. The analysis of the techniques of signification is in itself already political. Analysing the literariness of the literary text, for example, is inherently political insofar as it examines the ways in which prevailing literary norms and canons are established and become dominant. If the text's literariness consists in its *estrangement* from conventions (see Hawkes 1977), its effects are political. They question prevailing representational norms, norms which also regulate the subject's libidinal economy. If literature is the capacity to estrange, shock and force re-evaluations, this cannot but have political effects. However, the politics invested in representations is not assimilable to corresponding social relations, nor is it a barometer of changes in social organisation yet to come. Social relations are representational as well as material.

For Kristeva, the text is thus not a gauge of historical events, nor a reflection of an author's intention. It is practice, a mode of 'production', a product, and a form of political intervention. It presumes a politics, not as a form of ideology, but in the production of subjectivity. This subject is not, however, the author of the text: the very concept of author presumes the author's existence prior to and independent of the text. The subjectivity to which Kristeva refers is constructed within the text. This discursive 'I' is not entirely distinct from the living social subject: the latter is to a large extent socially structured and positioned by the discursive construction of the 'I' in the symbolic.

The avant-garde and transgression

For Kristeva, avant-garde texts, especially those produced towards the end of the nineteenth century and early in the twentieth century, crystallise Freud's insight about the radically split subject. These texts (Kristeva's 'favourites' include Mallarmé, Artaud, Lautréamont and Joyce) liberate excessive, semiotic processes within symbolic production and within existing social unities:

> *It follows that the literary avant garde experience by virtue of its characterisation, is slated to become the laboratory of a new discourse (and a new subject) thus bringing about a mutation ... [It] rejects all discourse that is either stagnant or eclectically academic, preempts its knowledges where it does not impel it, it stimulates and reveals deep ideological changes that are currently searching for their own accurate political framework. ('How does one speak to literature?', in Kristeva, 1980:92–3)*

The avant-garde is a catalyst of social upheavals through its capacity to induce crises of representation, expressing and liberating the otherwise unarticulated *jouissance* of the semiotic. It captures and expresses libidinal, rhythmical impulses which threaten the symbolic with what it must repress, making explicit the social stakes vested in the repression and supercession of the semiotic by its own focus on openly semiotic elements.

> *Art — this semiotization of the symbolic — ... represents the flow of jouissance into language. Whereas sacrifice assigns jouissance its productive limit in the social and symbolic order, art specifies the means — the only means — that jouissance*

harbors for infiltrating that order. In cracking the socio-symbolic order, splitting it open, changing vocabulary, syntax, the word itself and releasing from beneath them the drives borne by vocalic or kinetic differences, jouissance works its way into the social. In contrast to sacrifice, what poetry shows is that language lends itself to the penetration of the socio-symbolic by jouissance, and that the thetic does not necessarily imply theological sacrifice. (Kristeva, 1984:80)

Art, then, serves to 'legitimise' non-phallic *jouissance* by giving symbolic expression to the semiotic. The avant-garde goes further than other artistic practices; not only does it introduce *jouissance* to the social; it makes *jouissance* exceed the socially tolerable boundaries of representation, problematising the very concept of identity:'Th[eir] musical rhythm bursts out in laughter at the meaningful and demystifies not only all ideology but everything that aspires to be identical with itself' (Kristeva, 1976:65).

The avant-garde thus explodes unity and identity, the thetic (subject and text); it refuses the unities or identities at the level of the sign, the proposition and the self. While creating fissures and ruptures within the symbolic, the energies liberated by the semiotic also have their own perils and dangers. They entail grave political risks, including: engendering totalitarianism or fascism on the one hand; and political cooption or recuperation back into mainstream capitalism on the other. They risk channelling what may be revolutionary socio-political forces into relatively harmless or positively dangerous expressive outlets, 'letting off steam' and strategically placing its subversive forces where they may be most subversive; or, in the case of recanalisation into fascist structures, the semiotic is tied even more firmly to a symbolic organisation brutal in its control of *jouissance*. Fascism is a 'canalisation of the drive process thus liberated in the direction of a totalitarianism...' (1976:65). It relies upon '... an appeal to violence against the traditional forms by which violence is sublimated' (1976:67). Stalinism, nazism, and its more contemporary forms, are the consequences of the semiotic upheaval of the symbolic law, rerouted through the structure of group psychology into an identification with the authoritarian figure of the law-giver and father (see Freud, 1921), or channelled into the corporeal, obsessional form of rigid 'character armour' so ably described by Wilhelm Reich.

Fascism and recuperation are the twin political dangers, opposites and extremes resulting from the breakdown of the symbolic's hold over the semiotic. Correlatively, there are two *psychical extremes* risked by avant-garde practices, risks that are sometimes borne out in the artist's/author's life. Kristeva compresses these psychical risks into two symptomatic extremes, fetishism and psychosis. Fetishism, in psychoanalytic terms, is the *disavowal* of maternal castration. In Freud's understanding, it is a response to the sight of the mother's genitals open only to the boy. (The girl has no motivation to sustain the fantasy of the maternal phallus as the boy has. He wishes to deny the possibility of his own castration, while in the girl's case she may well accept her own castration without acknowledging the mother's.)[6] Disavowal entails a *simultaneous affirmation and denial* of his observations. On the one hand, the boy accepts what he 'sees' — that the mother is castrated; while on the other, he denies it as well, by replacing the maternal phallus with a substitute, the fetish. The fetish substitutes for the missing maternal phallus and is put in its place in order to hide its 'absence'. In the sense that the phallus is missing, the boy accepts castration; and in the sense that he substitutes another object (the shoe, the raincoat, stockings, fur, etc.) for the phallus, he denies it. The fetish is the boy's way of both accepting the father's law (and thus gaining a social, symbolic and masculine position) and of retaining his pre-oedipal attachment to the (phallic) mother. It is his way of both renouncing and retaining his maternal attachments in the face of symbolic demands for renunciation. The fetishist thus acquires a place within signifying networks and gains access to articulation; yet at the same time he retains the pre-oedipal organisation of perverse sexual drives: 'fetishism is a displacement of the thetic onto the realm of drives' (Kristeva, 1984:64).

Fetishism affirms and libidinally invests the thetic in precisely the inverse form to signifying practice: instead of displacing the semiotic by means of the thetic and thereby organising it in symbolic terms, the fetishist 'regressively' turns the thetic back towards the maternal *chora*. This may also explain why

> *according to psychoanalysis, poets as individuals fall under the category of fetishism: the very practice of art necessitates re-investing the maternal* chora *so that it transgresses the symbolic order; and, as a result, this practice easily lends itself to so-called perverse subjective structures. (1984:65)*

Where avant-garde artistic practices *symbolise* the thetic, fetishism *semiotises* it. Yet they remain related insofar as each relies on the subject's capacity to repeat and represent the *chora* (by an object in the case of the fetishist, and by signification in the case of the poet). More extreme than fetishism is the risk posed by psychosis.

If the fetishist *disavows* maternal castration, the psychotic *forecloses* or *repudiates* it and, with it, the registration or representation of the father's law. Foreclosure is not only the denial or negation of observation (one of the two contradictory components of disavowal), it is the *failure to register* an observation. Denial, negation, disavowal and repression are defences involving the *registration* of a perception, for it is only on condition that something is registered that it can be denied or suppressed. By contrast, foreclosure is the refusal to register, the inability to signify, and thus to even negate, certain perceptions. Lacan claims that what is foreclosed — the father's symbolic name as represented in the castration threat — will return 'from the real', in hallucinatory form, as if it had come from outside the subject. What is psychically unrepresented nevertheless reimposes itself from 'outside', makes its reappearance in the real (see Freud, 1925).

Thus, where the fetishist *displaces* the maternal phallus, the psychotic *hallucinates* it (and, incidentally, the hysteric relocates it, from the 'normal' feminine phallicisation of the whole of a woman's body [Freud, 1914a] to a hysterogenic zone: Dora's cough reveals a phallicisation of the throat and oral cavity [Freud, 1905]). Where the fetishist has one foot in the symbolic, representational order and the other in the pre-oedipal maternal realm, he can operate in accordance with the symbolic (Freud claimed that fetishism is the most satisfying of the sexual perversions; see Freud, 1927). The psychotic, however, remains rooted in the imaginary, maternal space, a space based on the confusion of self and other, bound to the suffocating dialectic of identification with the (phallic) mother who is his imaginary double. The psychotic has no stable boundaries or borders, and finds his identity confused with that of the m(other). The fetishist strives to retain his libidinal attachment to the mother, the psychotic strives to *be* her, to experience no heterogeneity or alterity, and thus to be unlocated as a subject (see Lacan, 'The Subversion of the Subject..', in 1977a; Thom, in MacCabe, 1981; and Roustang, 1982).

The fetishist, the psychotic and the avant-garde artist rely on the support of a usually repressed or sublimated maternal in symbolic functions. The avant-garde maintains a fine balance between coherence (obedience to the symbolic) and transgression (the overflow of the semiotic) which could tilt in one direction (fetishism) or another (psychosis). The artist problematises the symbolic and therefore his own position as a subject in order to harness the pre-oedipal pre-signifying elements in signification:

> ... *these late 19th century texts, by virtue of the economics of their language and of their chosen signified itself, either fetishize the mother as inaccessible (mysterious support of the socio-symbolic edifice, raised to the level of cult object) or else perform an identification with it and themselves assume the place of the mother as repressed-unnameable: in the latter case they verge on psychosis, against which they can defend themselves only by erecting the orgasmic pleasure element, heterogeneous to the social system, as potent subject — thereby depriving it of the very heterogeneity it was originally supposed to express (Kristeva, 1976:70)*

The avant-garde artist faces the personal risk of fetishism and psychosis; and the political risk of recuperation and fascism. Only with these risks can the borders and limits of textual and represen-tational conventions be breached and transformed. Moreover, only by facing such risks can the social ensemble itself be questioned in any thoroughgoing fashion. Even if the mode of production is transformed, no change can be sustained in the long run without being accompanied by major upheavals in representation. At stake here are not simply a few obscure literary conventions but the very conditions of intelligibility, representability and meaning. This may help explain why Kristeva considers the avant-garde the revolutionaries of representation.

However much she applauds nineteenth-century avant-garde texts, Kristeva is critical of the tendency to evacuate content and to concentrate on formal conventions and experimentation with textual devices for the sake of experimentation alone. This seems to be her major criticism of their transgressions (and incidentally, her major concern about Derridean deconstruction as well. See Kristeva, 1984:140–1):

> *The texts of Lautréamont and Mallarmé do* not *proceed toward the knowledge of practice* ... *instead they set aside their rep-resentative 'content' (their* Bedeutung) *for representing the mechanism of rejection itself. Thus, although they expose the repressed material of philosophical knowledge and metaphysics — the secret of what they hold sacred — these texts are con-demned to be nothing but the complementary counterpart of philosophical speculation to the degree that they confine their*

*field of practice to the experience of heterogeneous contradiction.
(1984:188)*

While containing the conditions for social rupture, the nineteenth-century text falls short of its mark when it remains satisfied with internal textual self-reflection instead of mobilising the semiotic energies in the direction of the socio-economic totality.

Kristeva limits the kinds of 'poetic revolution' that are possible. It is significant that she uses the terminology of jurisprudence, for it points out a clear limitation to the political impact she accords to discursive or representational challenges. In conceptualising the symbolic as the *site of Law*, she understands resistance only on the model of a transgression. Avant-garde practices can lead to a transgression of the symbolic, that is, to the limits of signification, but they do not obliterate them. They are displaced and repositioned elsewhere. Representational ruptures cannot destroy socio-symbolic unities, for, on her understanding, this amounts to a dissolution of sociality itself.[7] Radical subversion is essentially reformist: as the order of language, the symbolic can only accommodate so much change at any given time. As Saussure pointed out, because the signifying structure (*langue*) is collective, it can adapt to change only within broadly recognisable parameters. Neologisms too far removed from the existing structure are not accepted by it. So, too, for Kristeva the avant-garde questions the limits of language only by pushing them further, not by eliminating them altogether.

The avant-garde can only speak through/as the symbolic, just as the unconscious can only speak through the discourses of consciousness. In this sense, there can be no 'pure' avant-garde, only a process already mediated by the symbolic, which, at the same time, problematises it.

Semanalysis

Semanalysis takes the processes by which discourses are put into question as its object. It analyses the confrontation between the unity required by the symbolic and the heterogeneity of the semiotic drives. It is the study of both the constitution and the 'deconstruction' of the text, of the *différance* within the text. Unlike Derridean deconstruction, Kristeva is interested in textual play in the interaction of discursive and subjective economies, their mutual dependence and problematisation. If (Saussurian) semiotics is the study of signs and sign-systems, semanalysis is the study of sign-deformation and its exorbitant processes and *excesses*, making signification both possible and questionable. In place of traditional presumptions about the unity of the sign, she poses its radical alterity, its fundamentally split, always open-ended, difference. In place of a structured, rule-bound sign system, she focuses on the becoming, of the processes involved in representation. Finally, in semanalysis, she coordinates these textual relations with the processes of subject formation, especially with the ways it constitutes and challenges personal identities.

Semanalysis is the analysis of the *remainder* or residue left over in sign systems or unincorporated by them, resistant to the unifications they impose. It is the production, not of meaning, but of textual *waste*:

> *We can now grasp all the ambiguities of* semanalysis: *on the one hand it demystifies the logic at work in the elaboration of every transcendental reduction, and, for this purpose, requires the study of each signifying system as a practice. Thus intent on revealing the negativity which Hegel had seen at work beneath all rationality but which, by a masterly stroke, he subordinated to absolute knowledge,* semanalysis *can be thought of as the direct successor of the dialectical method; but the dialectic it continues will be one which will at last be genuinely materialist since it recognises the* materiality — the heterogeneity — *of that negativity whose concrete base Hegel was unable to see and which mechanistic Marxists have reduced to a merely economic externality* ... *To rediscover practice by way of the system, by rehabilitating what is heterogeneous to the system of meaning and what calls in question the transcendental subject* ... *(Kristeva, in Moi, 1986:31)*

Taking her model from Hegel, Saussure, Derrida and Lacan, Kristeva differs from her sources insofar as she puts them into confrontational and antagonistic relations with each other. To Saussurian semiology, for example, she proposes Lacan's notion of the split subject; to the Hegelian dialectic and its play of negativity, she counterposes Saussurian 'pure difference' — a 'logic', unlike dialectics, with no teleological conclusion, no 'synthesis' arresting the tensions and contradictions which mark history and revolution in the Hegelian system. In relation to Lacanian psychoanalysis, she posits the idea of Derridean *différance*, a *différance* within as well as between subjects. And to all the philosophers and theorists on whom she relies, she raises the crucial question of politics and the effect (or lack of it) of their work on broader questions of social struggle and change. Kristeva's strength lies in her ability to take hold of disparate sources, frameworks, methods and to bring them together, not as incommensurable positions, nor as completely harmonious complements. She sets them to work against each other, while adhering to their insights. It may be this skill that enables one respected American academic[8] to proclaim that *The Revolution in Poetic Language* 'may someday seem a great summation' of intellectual and political life in the wake of 1968.

Kristeva's conception of her own project has changed between the publication of *The Revolution in Poetic Language* and *Tales of Love*. Her earlier semanalytic preoccupations centre on the scientific analysis of an ideological realm of representation. Kristeva is committed to semanalysis as a scientific analysis of the production and subversion of the text. Sciences generate their own objects of analysis, and for Kristeva, semanalysis generates its own peculiar understanding of the text (as an intrusion of the semiotic in the symbolic). Kristeva's work is politically motivated, and her various analyses are directed towards rupturing certain conservative values (those embodied in the evaluation of identity over difference) and, through this rupturing, the creation of new modes of reading, assessing and valuing texts. As we will see in the following chapter, these are no longer her current concerns. Her critique of individualism and humanism remains powerful, but her desire to establish a scientific methodology and subordinate her analyses to a broader conception of (class) politics is now less obvious.

In *Powers of Horror* the question of the scientific status of her work seems less relevant: she is concerned there with elaborating an historical, concrete set of experiences (the abject) with a body of writings (that of Céline). Here it is not the extraction and formulation of laws, rules, structures that concern her (as they seem to in her earlier works) but the detailed specificity of her theoretical object. The abject, for example, is examined from a number of non-reducible perspectives — psychoanalytic, theological, anthropological and literary — instead of her earlier ambition, which is to develop a more or less complete and systematic (meta-)theory that incorporates all these inputs into an overarching, higher-order totality.

If her aims have changed in the last decade, there remain a number of central themes and objects that continue to haunt her writings and inspire her choice of analytic objects in the present. If her adherence to marxism and to an account of ideology is loosened, her commitment to psychoanalysis becomes firmer and more dominant. And if the polyvocity and plurality of textuality remains a central focus today, her understanding of textuality has itself been modified. If anything, the psychical preconditions and effects of discourses and representations provide more of a framework than in her earlier work. For the remainder of this chapter we will discuss her understanding of the position of women, the feminine and maternity, for these (especially the latter) become more and more central to her endeavours. This section may thus also serve as an introduction to her more recent publications.

Women, mothers and femininity

While Kristeva's commitments to marxism are clear in her earlier texts, her relations to feminist issues and feminist struggles against patriarchal power relations are more obscure and ambiguous. She does briefly raise feminist issues but she is difficult to locate in feminist terms. She seems to hover between sceptical distance and affirmation. She denounces a number of feminist groupings — especially the *des femmes* collective (not without good reason) — but her own positive commitments to feminism remain unspecified. This does not mean that her work is not useful to feminist researches; nor that it is antifeminist. Simply it means that her feminism is highly idiosyncratic and has a number of problems, which will be discussed in the next chapter.

Her position is unclear in feminist terms mainly because of the absence of *women* from her central concerns. She does discuss women in two narrowly circumscribed contexts — in her account of her visit to China (in *On Chinese Women*); and in her discussions of maternity. But in her textual analyses, her use of Lacanian and Freudian, as well as Kleinian frameworks, she is uncritical of her sources and affirms their various misogynistic, phallocentric presuppositions. This is particularly problematic in her use of psychoanalytic models, which rely on the correlation of femininity and the maternal with castration.

The absence of women is most noticeable in her discussions of poetic language and semiotic transgressions. She rarely mentions women writers, and when she does it is generally either disparagingly or in terms inferior to comparable works by men.

On her understanding, women write in one of two ways, either to reproduce/mime the familial and maternal roles: 'Women generally write in order to tell their own story. When a woman does not reproduce a real *family* of her own, she creates an imaginary story through which she constitutes an identity; narcissism is safe ...' (Kristeva, in Marks and de Courtivron, 1981:166). Or else they write 'hysterically', a submerged, silenced speech, muted in its

innovations, the speech of 'underwater bodies', muffled and partially obscured, never in joyous, celebratory, carnivalesque forms
she attributes to an exclusively male avant-garde. Woman's
discourses are subdued, subordinated, derivative. It is particularly
significant that when discussing the avant-garde she makes no
mention of women artists, writers and poets. Strikingly absent, for
example, is any mention, let alone discussion, of Gertrude Stein's
work, which, by rights, should find some place in her analyses.

Women's writing (*écriture féminine*) is, for her, a disturbing
category. It essentialises woman and attempts to provide her with
a fixed identity. Although she may be well justified in questioning
some views of 'women's writing' prevalent in French feminisms[9],
she seems generally hostile to writings by women, rather than
writing specifically oriented to expressing a repressed femininity.
She directs some of her most critical remarks unexpectedly to
Virginia Woolf's writing. She may here be contesting feminist
evaluations of Woolf's work but it is curiously antagonistic:

> *In women's writing, language seems to be seen from a foreign
> land; it is seen from the point of view of an asymbolic, spastic
> body. Virginia Woolf describes suspended states, subtle sen-
> sations and above all, colours — green, blue — but she* does not
> dissect language as Joyce does. *Estranged from language, women
> are visionaries, dancers who suffer as they speak. (Kristeva, in
> Marks and de Courtivron, 1981:166, emphasis added)*

This remarkable statement entails a number of questionable presumptions, including: the claim that women's writing (writing
by/for women as women) implies taking up a position outside of
language; writing which is self-consciously feminine or feminist is
'asymbolic' (does she mean presymbolic? or extrasymbolic? —
there is a crucial difference!); that the female body from which it
emanates is 'spastic'; that Woolf *uses* but does not *dissect*
language; and that women write *hysterically* when they write as
women. These beliefs may also explain her reluctance to discuss
Getrude Stein's writings.

Stein's avant-garde position is not representative of *women's*
writing in the sense that it is 'about women' or markedly written
'by a woman'. It consists in writing about writing. Classification of
Stein's work as 'homosexual', as that of a woman suffering from a
'masculinity complex', might be inferred from Kristeva's general
position. The 'masculinity complex' occurs when the woman
disavows sexual difference. The oedipal girl refuses to accept that
she is castrated, and clings to the belief that, although her genital

is 'small', someday it will grow. She disavows being a woman or, at least, she denies being castrated. Such a woman would, presumably, not write 'as a woman' but as a man! But if Stein's avant-garde experiments are like those of men, Kristeva's neglect of her work is, even on her own terms, unjustified.

Although she avoids writings by women, let alone self-consciously women's writings, she invokes woman and femininity as a metaphor for a more general and diffuse struggle against identity per se. In this respect her work remains close to Derrida. Women, particularly feminists, represent a semiotic, negative dialectical movement, a transgressive challenge to the symbolic; but they, it seems, are not the most powerful or effective agents in subverting the symbolic. Ironically, this is reserved, in her view, for the texts of the (male) avant-garde.

By avoiding the specificity of women's writings, she also uncritically accepts and affirms the psychoanalytic conception of women and femininity. She affirms some of the more misogynist stereotypes of feminists. She never questions the Freudian adoption of the model of the boy's development as a paradigm for the girl as well. The pre-oedipal child is bisexual, polymorphous, but also neutral with respect to sex differences. The sexual identity of the subject can only be raised from the point of view of an oedipal overlay. Moreover, she accepts Freud's and Lacan's privileging of the phallus as the condition of sexual difference, representation and the symbolic order. Above all, she accepts Freud's patriarchal reduction of women to a *telos* of maternity.

The polarisation of the poet and the hysteric, and the opposition she invokes between woman as being and man as representing, are recurrent themes in her work. In 'The Novel as Polylogue' (1980), her ostensive object is Philippe Sollers' writings. A contemporary avant-garde novelist (also her husband and one of her co-editors on *Tel Quel* and, since its demise, on its replacement, *L'Infini*), she again sees women and femininity on a psychoanalytic model, one shared with Sollers:

I think that for a woman, generally speaking, the loss of identity in jouissance [which is Lacan's understanding of female sexual pleasure, see 'God and the Jouissance of Woman', in Mitchell and Rose, 1982] demands of her that she experience the phallus that she simply is; but this phallus must immediately be established somewhere: in narcissism for instance, in children, in a denial/hypostasis of the other woman, in a narrow-minded mastery, or in fetishism of one's 'work' (writing, painting, knitting, et cetera). Otherwise, we have an underwater, under-maternal drive: oral regression, spasmodic but unspeakable and savage violence, and a denial of effective negativity ... The problem is to control this resurgence of phallic presence; to abolish it at first, to pierce it through the paternal wall of the superego and afterwards, to reemerge still uneasy, split apart, asymmetrical, overwhelmed with a desire to know more and differently than what is encoded-spoken-written. If a solution exists to what we call today the feminine problematic, in my opinion, it too passes over this ground.

I believe two conditions are necessary if this course is to be followed. The first is historical; it involves throwing women into all of society's contradictions with no hypocrisy of fake pro-tection. The second condition is sexual ... it involves coming to grips with one's language and body as others, as heterogenous elements. (1980:164–5)

Kristeva suggests that disentangling women's self-definition from the domination of the phallus requires two conditions: first, women should be thrown into society's contradictions not by patronising but by positioning them in the same ways as men; and by experiencing a heterogeneity, not between one (sexually specific) body and another, but between oneself and one's body or oneself and one's language.

She assumes that there is a general category of subject in our culture, a subject whose internal distinctions and ruptures are more significant than any differences *between* subjects. The subject remains a neutral term and the phallus refers equally to both sexes, submitting both sexes to the same law: '... castration applies not to this or that individual or to that person, but specifically to each individual in recurrent fashion. It applies to him as he experiences his phallic fixation; to her as she accedes to it, and the other way around, interchangeably' (1980:165).

Her destabilisation of the unity of the otherwise heterogeneous speaking subject has an uneasy relation to feminist politics. It is by no means clear that women's struggles are compatible with her position; many feminists object to her reduction of feminist strug-gles to a generalised dissolution of identity, for it makes no contribution to the overthrow of women's specific oppression. She advocates an ironically phallocentric program whereby women's cultural and representational specificity is neutralised by a uni-versal model based in men's specificity. In this regard her remarks about feminism and feminist struggles are revealing.

She sees feminist struggles as purely negative or reactive. Their function is temporary and provisional, and is ultimately bound up with negativity. Feminism is about saying 'no' to various oppressions. But above and beyond the elimination of obvious inequalities or acts of discrimination, it should aim at the transgression of the binary codings of male and female, and at the dissolution of male and female identities:

> *Women's practice can only be negative, in opposition to that which exists, to say that 'this is not it' and 'it is not yet'. What I mean by 'woman' is that which is not represented, that which is unspoken, that which is left out of naming and ideologies. Some 'men' know something of it too, it is what those texts [the avant-garde] signify. (1981b:166)*

In 'Women's Time' (1981c), she distinguishes three generations of feminists. The first is recognisably a liberal or egalitarian feminism, where women strive to be the same as men. This position is most notably represented by de Beauvoir. The second generation is what is today called a 'feminism of difference' and is represented by Irigaray and Cixous; while the third position is her own. It no longer seeks either an identity like men's, nor one different from men's, but the dissolution of all identities. She seeks, not sexual differences distinguishing subjects from each other, but a sexual differentiation *internal* to each subject.

Given that transgression is always the shifting of lawful boundaries, it makes sense that transgression can only occur from a position within the law or the symbolic. Given also the psychoanalytic account of the resolution of the oedipus complex and the definitive assignment of each sex to a masculine or feminine position, in which the boy is able to resolve his oedipal relations by his abandonment of the mother, repression of incestual wishes and identification with the father's law, and given Freud's uncertainty about how or even whether the girl is able to resolve her oedipal complex, it is not clear how or if the girl does accede to the symbolic. Insofar as she speaks, insofar as she works, woman is part of the symbolic; yet she is not positioned there in the same way as the male. For one thing, where he is positioned in the symbolic with the attributes of active, subject and phallic, she is positioned as object, passive and castrated. The symbolic (that is, masculine) subject is the subject who can say 'I' of himself; it is never clear that in saying 'I' the feminine subject is not in fact referring to a (masculine) 'you'.

If women are subjects in the symbolic at all (and not simply objects for other subjects), they are not subjects in the same ways as masculine subjects. If transgression implies a position from which transgression is possible, this may explain why Kristeva does not accord the feminine, or women, the subversive position of the avant-garde. Only men can transgress the symbolic because only they are subjects with a position to subvert. Only some men are able to retain a position in the symbolic as enunciative subjects *and* an attachment to an archaic maternal *chora*; it is only those men who can put their symbolic position in jeopardy through their investments in a subversive *chora*. While women can retain their maternal attachments, they do not gain a stable position in the symbolic. And where they gain a stable speaking position, it is through masculine identification, and consequently her specificity as a woman is effaced. For woman the only socially recognised, validated position in the symbolic is as mother.

To conclude, then, a brief summary of the key issues raised thus far is necessary:

1 There is a parallel between three orders or realms of social existence in Kristeva's work: the (speaking) subject, signifying practices and the socio-political ensemble.

2 These orders are structurally homologous — the unities secured at the level of one serve as a support for the operations of the others.

3 Within (and between) each of these orders, a dialectic between semiotic/process and symbolic/unity is played out.

4 In this dialectic the ordering, organising movement of the symbolic must gain a precedence over the more chaotic, libidinally oriented semiotic in order to maintain any stability or regularity.

5 At best, this primacy is provisional, for the unified, symbolic system cannot guarantee a permanent and irrevocable supercession of the semiotic. On the contrary, in times of crisis the semiotic overflows its symbolic boundaries and transforms the character of the symbolic unities themselves.

6 These are moments of revolution and transformation which, although they cannot be articulated in or by themselves, transgress the limits of the symbolic and thus regenerate it in a different form.

7 Using psychoanalytic theory, these two systems can be coded in terms of the distinctions between pre-oedipal and oedipal, primary and secondary processes, unconscious and conscious, feminine and masculine and maternal and paternal respectively.

8 Thus although these movements are correlated with sexual characteristics, they are not readily coded in terms of male/female sexual *identities*. Rather, within each subject and each social and signifying practice, there is a play of masculine and feminine, a play not of sexual difference but of differentiation.

9 Upheavals at the level of the State and the social ensemble consist in revolutionary transformations; at the level of the subject they consist in unconscious eruptions, that is, in symptoms, ranging from dreams to psychoses; and at the level of signifying practices they consist in the transgressions effected by the avant-garde.

10 Given the constraints on semiotic eruptions, where transgressions are always defined with respect to law, it follows that only those with a secure position in the symbolic may have access to its transgression. Systems cannot be transgressed from outside.

11 This may explain why Kristeva accords a transgressive status to those avant-garde texts produced by men, even though there are many women who may also fit into this category. This may be because, in not occupying a phallic position in the symbolic, women can only imitate men, act in ways that are modelled on men's behaviour.

3 Julia Kristeva: Abjection, motherhood and love

K RISTEVA'S concern with the distinction between a maternal semiotic and a paternal symbolic, her notion of the symbolic as the site of semiotic ruptures and upheavals, and the transgressive position of the poetic or avant-garde text remain central in her more recent investigations. Even if her work does not undergo a dramatic shift in interest, there is an inflection and reorientation of her earlier preoccupations. She seems less concerned with the scientific status of her work, less committed to the framework of the notion of ideology; and less influenced by marxist issues and more concerned with the psychical components of signification. Her commitment to psychoanalysis seems to have grown in inverse proportion to a widening distance from Althusserianism. She also remains fascinated with privileged moments of symbolic transgression — 'madness, holiness and poetry' — and their interruptions and subversions of psychical and signifying unities. Her focus is now explicitly directed towards the structure of the pre-oedipal mother–child relation: the mobilisations of drive energies; the thetic moments; the semiotic, pre-linguistic conditions of symbolic functioning; and the unspoken moments of faltering, instability and breakdown in the subject and the text are all themes anticipated, if underdeveloped, in her earlier works.

In this chapter I examine three of Kristeva's current interests — abjection, maternity and love. These are not unrelated but are intimately connected through her concept of the pre-oedipal or semiotic phase. This phase is crucial to her concept of abjection, which is the subject's reaction to the failure of the subject/object opposition to express adequately the subject's corporeality and its tenuous bodily boundaries; second, it is crucial to her notion of the maternal, considered as pre-oedipal, corporeal and semiotic, the privileged condition of representation in religious and artistic discourses; and third, to her understanding of romantic love relations and the discourses on love, which are also symbolic expressions of an archaic semiotic maternal attachment. The centrality of the maternal to all of Kristeva's investigations provides a framework for examining the contributions of women, femininity and female specificity to symbolic functioning. Her psychoanalytically 'heretical' concept of the 'imaginary father' and 'his' role in abjection, and her understanding of romantic love will also prove useful in explaining and assessing her most recent theoretical developments.

Abjection

Her notion of abjection sketches the peculiar space and time (given that we cannot yet talk of a subject) marking the threshold of language and a stable enunciative position. In *Powers of Horror: An Essay on Abjection* (1982), Kristeva claims that the delimitation of the 'clean and proper' body is a condition of the subject's constitution as a speaking subject. Abjection attests to the always tenuous nature of the symbolic order in the face of a series of dispersing semiotic drives.

The genesis of stable subjectivity and coherent articulation are possible only because sexual drives and bodily process become enmeshed, bit by bit, in signification. When images, perceptions, sensations become linked to and represented by signifiers or delegates, the child has the psychical prerequisites for taking up a position of enunciation, participating in the production of discourse. Understanding abjection involves examining the ways in which the inside and the outside of the body are constituted, the spaces between the self and the other, and the means by which the child's body becomes a bounded, unified whole — the conditions under which the child is able to claim the body as its own and, through its 'clean and proper' body, gain access to symbolisation.

In *Powers of Horror* Kristeva analyses the ways in which 'proper' subjectivity and sociality require the expulsion of the improper, the unclean and the disorderly. This is not a new insight but a variation of Freud's position in *Totem and Taboo*, where he claims that civilisation itself is founded on the expulsion of 'impure' incestual attachments (see also Freud, 1930). What is new is Kristeva's assertion that what is excluded can never be fully obliterated but hovers at the borders of our existence, threatening the apparently settled unity of the subject with disruption and possible dissolution. It is *impossible* to exclude these psychically and socially threatening elements with any finality. The subject's recognition of this impossibility provokes the sensation Kristeva describes as abjection.

The abject is a condition of symbolic subjectivity; and is also its unpredictable, sporadic *accompaniment*. It is the underside of a stable subjective identity, an abyss at the borders of the subject's existence, a hole into which the subject may fall when its identity is put into question, for example, in psychosis. The subject needs a certain level of mastery over the abject to keep it in check, at a distance, to distinguish itself from its repressed or unspeakable condition.

If, as Lacan claims, the ego and the object are correlates, supporting and providing each other with stability, the abject is neither the subject nor the object. It is a recognition of the impossible, untenable identity the subject projects onto and derives from the other. If the object is the external support of the subject, the abject is more the fading, instability or even the disappearance of the subject, its precarious, imaginary hold on the object. The abject is that part of the subject it attempts to expel, but which is refused the status of object. It is the symptom of the object's failure to fill and define the subject.

Abjection involves the paradoxically necessary but impossible desire to transcend corporeality. It is a refusal of the defiling, impure, uncontrollable materiality of a subject's embodied existence. It is a response to the various bodily cycles—incorporation, absorption, depletion, expulsion—a cyclical movement of rejuvenation and consumption. Abjection is the result of the child's bodily boundaries being structured by the circulation of drive energies, themselves based on the cycles of incorporation and evacuation, processes that are indistinguishably psychical and physiological. These incorporated/expelled objects—food, faeces, urine, vomit, tears, spit—designate the various zones of the body, later to become erotogenic zones—mouth, anus, eyes, ears, genitals. According to Lacan, sexual zones are structured as a *rim*, a space in between two surfaces that can be seen as the boundaries between the body's inside and outside (Lacan, 1977b). It is a boundary that must be traversed by the incorporated object, which is neither entirely within nor without the rim.

The abject is understood on the model of Lacan's notion of the *objet petit a*, the object of the drives (Lacan, 1977b). The *objet a* is a part of the subject which the subject considers detachable. It confronts the subject as alien and external. The erotogenic rim seeks a satisfaction in which the object ideally stops up the lack.

Lacan stresses that the *petit a* is not a thing or object but a movement, an activity, the taking in or introjection of the object, its absorption into the subject. This produces satisfaction and leads eventually to the object's expulsion. Abjection occurs when the object does not fill the rim; a gap emerges, a hole, into which the subject, through lack of an anchor in the object, is propelled.

For Kristeva, the abject is a condition of the unified, thetic subject, yet is intolerable to it. Even at times of its greatest cohesion, the subject teeters on the brink of a yawning hole which threatens to draw it into it. This abyss marks the place of the genesis *and* the obliteration of the subject, for it is a space inhabited by the death drive, Hegelian negativity, the indistinct space occupied by mother and child in symbiotic dependence.

Abjection is what the symbolic must reject, cover over or contain. The abject is what beckons the subject ever closer to its edge. It insists on the subject's necessary relation to death, corporeality, animality, materiality — those relations which consciousness and reason find intolerable. The abject attests to the impossibility of clear borders, lines of demarcation or divisions between the proper and the improper, the clean and the unclean, order and disorder, as required by the symbolic. Symbolic relations separate the subject from the abyss that haunts and terrifies it.

> *We may call it a border; abjection is above all ambiguity. Because, while releasing a hold, it does not radically cut off the subject from what treatens [sic] it — on the contrary, abjection acknowledges it to be in perpetual danger. But also, abjection itself is a compromise of judgment and affect, of condemnation and yearning, of signs and drives. Abjection preserves what existed in the archaism of pre-objectal relationship, in the immemorial violence with which the body becomes separated from another body in order to be — maintaining that night in which the outline of the signified thing vanishes and where only the imponderable affect is carried out.*
> *(Kristeva, 1982:9–10)*

She distinguishes three broad forms of abjection, against which social taboos and individual defences are erected: abjection in relation to food, to waste and to sexual difference (roughly corresponding to oral, anal and genital forms of sexuality). The individual's defensive reaction to these abjects is visceral and psychical. Usually expressed in retching, vomiting, spasms, choking, that is, in disgust, they demonstrate and produce bodily processes and zones 'rational' consciousness is unable to accept or deny. They represent a body in revolt, the body as a disavowed condition of consciousness.

Abjection is a byproduct of the traversing of bodily zones and sensations, those which need to be unified and harnessed in the constitution of the subject according to the norms and rules of a given culture. The abject cannot be readily classified, for it is necessarily ambiguous, undecidably inside and outside (like the skin of milk), dead and alive (like the corpse), autonomous and engulfing (like infection and pollution). It disturbs identity, system and order, respecting no definite positions, rules, boundaries or limits. It is the body's acknowledgement that its boundaries and limits are the effects of desire not nature. It demonstrates the precariousness of the subject's grasp of its own identity. The subject may slide back into the chaos from which it is formed. Abjection is one of the few avowals of the death drive, an undoing of the processes constituting the subject.

Oral disgust is the most archaic form of abjection. Kristeva illustrates this using the example of disgust at the skin of milk. This skin is repulsive, inducing the subject to retch and choke, because it is the subject's skin, the boundary between it and the world which the child wishes to expel. The subject chokes on its own limits, its own mortality. The desire to expel food, to refuse to take it in, is its refusal of the very stuff signifying parental/ maternal love. In expelling it, the parents' demands are also refused: ' "I" want none of that element, sign of their desire, "I" do not want to listen. "I" do not assimilate it, "I" expel it' (1982:3).

In refusing food the (m)other offers it, the child is not only rejecting, refusing the mother, but ultimately itself as well: 'But since the food is not an "other" for "me", who am only in their desire, I expel *myself*, I spit *myself* out. I abject myself within the same motion through which I claim to establish myself' (1982:3).

Oral disgust is the refusal of the limits of the self. Using Mary Douglas' work on purity and defilement (1966), Kristeva claims that oral abjection has its social equivalent in the broad-ranging social taboos surrounding unclean foods. Clearly these are culturally specific. Yet *some* form of taboo, some mode of inclusion and exclusions of what is considered edible and what is prohibited seems universal.

The abominations and taboos cited in *Leviticus* surrounding various foods are based on the prohibition of animals which are not readily classifiable into clear-cut categories. Only those animals inhabiting their 'proper' environment can be consumed. That is, only birds that fly, fish that have fins and gills, and animals that walk on all fours, chew their cud and have cloven hooves are considered clean. Animals crossing the boundaries of habitat, and especially whose modes of locomotion are at variance with their 'natural' environment, are not to be consumed. This is why, for example, the snake, which *slithers* indeterminantly on land or in the water, is not regarded as pure. Only those animals living and moving in their *proper place* can be considered pure.

The personal disgust and the various social taboos associated with *waste* also attest to a psycho-social horror at what transgresses borders and boundaries. Bodily fluids, wastes, refuse — faeces, spit, blood, sperm, etc. — are examples of corporeal byproducts provoking horror at the subject's mortality. The subject is unable to accept that its body is a material organism, one that feeds off other organisms and, in its turn, sustains them. The subject recoils from its materiality, being unable to accept its bodily origins, and hence also its immanent death. For example, faeces signifies an opposition between the clean and the unclean which continually draws on the opposition between the body's interior and exterior. As internal, it is the condition of bodily existence and of its capacities for regeneration; but as expelled and externalised, it signals the unclean, the filthy. Each subject is implicated in waste, for it is not external to the subject; it *is* the subject. It *cannot* be completely externalised.

The most extreme case of abjection in the face of waste is the near-universal horror of confronting the corpse. In Kristeva's view, the corpse,

> *the most sickening of wastes, is a border that has encroached upon everything. It is no longer 'I' who expel, 'I' is expelled. The border has become object ... The corpse seen without God, and outside of science, is the utmost of abjection. It is death infecting life. Abject. It is something rejected from which one does not part, from which one does not protect oneself as from an object. (1982:3–4)*

The corpse is a concretisation of the subject's inevitable future. It is intolerable because, in representing the very border between life and death, it shifts this limit or boundary into the heart of life itself. The corpse signifies the *supervalence* of the body, the body's corporeal recalcitrance to will or consciousness. The cadaver poses a danger to the ego in questioning its solidity, stability and self-certainty.

If the corpse poses a threat to the very foundations of the ego, then the third category of abjects, disgust at the signs of *sexual difference*, is probably the most widespread of all 'objects' of social taboo. Where the corpse threatens the ego from *outside*, sexual difference challenges the ego from *within*:

> *Excrement and its equivalents (decay, infection, disease, corpse, etc.) stand for the danger to identity that comes from without; the ego is threatened by the non-ego, society threatened from its outside, life by death. Menstrual blood, on the contrary, stands for the danger issuing from within identity (social or sexual); it threatens the relationship between the sexes within a social aggregate and through internalisation, the identity of each sex in the face of sexual difference. (1982:71)*

The incest taboo is the cultural correlate of the individual's oedipus complex. In Freud's conception, the oedipal interdict introduces the child to the concept of sexual difference. The reduction of sexual difference to the opposition between phallic and castrated, accepted by Kristeva as readily as by Lacan, means that menstruation is likely to become a prime 'abject', resulting in personal horror and social prohibition. The prohibitions surrounding incest and menstruation are effects of the inclusion and exclusion of subjects in categories (phallic and castrated, active and passive, etc.).

As Kristeva readily acknowledges, the horror of menstruation is *not* straightforwardly connected to the ambiguities of sexual *difference*. In fact, menstruation does not differentiate female from male.[1] Rather, it marks the difference between men and *mothers*. The horror of menstruation serves to tie women into a (presumedly natural) maternity without acknowledging women's *sexual* specificity, a residual femininity unrepresented by maternity.

The horror of menstrual blood, the living matter which helps to produce and sustain life, is a refusal of the expelled link between the mother and the foetus, a border, as it were, between one existence and another that is not the same as nor yet separate from it. In psychoanalytic theory this is perhaps too easily explained by women's castration rather than seen as a threatening boundary or threshold between life and non-life, between male and female. It marks the site of an unspeakable debt of life (an 'umbilical' debt) that both the subject and culture owe to the mother but can never repay.

For Kristeva, abjection testifies to a break (between the subject and the corporeal) and a merger (of self and other). It is a resistant, dangerous merger/rupture within symbolic psychical identity which can never be adequately covered over. Castration definitively binds and distinguishes categories whose otherwise ambiguous obscurity threatens the subject with engulfment. She locates abjection in the space and time preceding binary divisions, social order and naming:

> *The non-distinctiveness of inside and outside [is] unnameable, a border passable in both directions by pleasure and pain. Naming the latter hence differentiating them, amounts to intro-ducing language, which, just as it distinguishes pleasure from pain as it does all other oppositions, founds the separation inside/outside. And yet, there would be witnesses to the pervi-ousness of the limit, artisans after a fashion who would try to tap that pre-verbal 'beginning' within a word that is flush with pleasure and pain ... Poetic language would then be, contrary to murder and the univocity of verbal message, a reconciliation with what murder as well as names were separated from. It would be an attempt to symbolize the 'beginning', an attempt to name the other facet of taboo: pleasure, pain. (1982:61–2)*

If abjection is an unnameable, pre-oppositional, permeable barrier, it requires some kind of control or, failing that, some mode of exclusion to position it at a safe distance from the symbolic. A number of rituals marking the boundary between the sacred and the profane perform this function. Kristeva's trio of 'revolutionary' terms, 'madness, holiness and poetry', establish particular relations to the abject which breach, yet also confirm symbolic conventions. She claims, for example, that religion func-tions to wrest the subject away from the abyss of abjection, to *displace* abjection. Socialisation, the acquisition of a symbolic place must *repress* the abject (which, for her, is the true 'object' of primal repression [1982:10–11]). Literature, poetry, the arts, re-present more or less successful attempts to *sublimate* the abject.

Each relies on the expulsion or disavowal of the archaic debt to corporeality and *jouissance* marked by abjection. It is a personal and cultural horror of the subject's (and culture's) finitude and material limits. The abject is thus a pre-signifying psycho-visceral response and an occasional accompaniment of an oedipalised consciousness. It is an effect of the paradoxical nature of the ego and its self-deluding conception of its own capacities and identity. Although the ego is formed through a recognition of its body in the mirror phase, it recoils from the idea of being tied to or limited by the body's form. The body's parts, its energies and flows structure the ego's boundaries. Abjection is a sickness at one's own body, at the body beyond that 'clean and proper' thing, the body of the subject. Abjection is the result of recognising that the body is more than, in excess of, the 'clean and proper'.

These boundaries are constituted *and* blurred in the mother-child dynamic. The symbolic must territorialise this space in order to reproduce itself. Abjection is thus a social danger against which taboos, forms of social rejection, inoculation and marginalisation are erected. The abject is the space of struggle against the mother, 'the earliest attempts to release the hold of *maternal entity*, even before ex-isting outside of her ...' (1982:13). At the same time it is a desperate attempt to be her, to blur the divisions between the child's identity and the mother's.

The semiotic, the maternal *chora* and the abject are all placed on the side of the feminine and the maternal, in opposition to a paternal, rule-governed symbolic. And, as in her earlier works, Kristeva suggests that certain writers (such as Proust, Joyce, Artaud, Borges and Céline) make strategic use of the archaic maternal abject.[2] The feminine, the semiotic, the abject, although inexpressible as such, are articulated within symbolic represen-tations by those (who happen to be men) who risk their symbolic positions in order to plunder the riches of the unspoken maternal debt. These men, if they are to avoid complete psychical/signifying disintegration, remain anchored by some threads of identity to the symbolic, even if only by the most precarious ones—Céline, through antisemitism[3]; Dostoyevsky, through an appeal to paternal authority.[4] They are able to maintain their imperilled hold on the symbolic only by naming the abject, naming the space of the undivided mother-child. By naming it they establish a distance, a space to keep at bay the dangers of absorption it poses. To speak (of) the abject is to ensure one's distance and difference from it.

Motherhood

Maternity is probably the most central and sustained object of Kristeva's investigations. Concepts like the semiotic, the *chora* and the abject are linked to the pre-imaginary symbiotic indistinction between mother and child. The mother's body, her desire, and her status, meaning and power within culture are of central importance to any discussion of the socio-symbolic, signifying order. 'She' remains the *necessarily* unspoken underside of social and psychic order.

Kristeva's discussion of the maternal can be divided into two components, one describing the space of gestation (pregnancy), and the other defining the space of subjectivity (motherhood).

The maternal body

The maternal, for Kristeva, designates both a space and a series of functions and processes. But it must not be confused with a *subject*, for maternity is a process without a subject. While pregnancy is something that 'happens' to a woman (Kristeva never, incidentally, states this explicitly), it does not involve *agency* or identity. If anything, it is their abandonment. The process of 'becoming-mother' is distanced from subjectivity and identity. Pregnancy occurs at the level of a fusion and movement of the organism (not the subject). Nurturing occurs at the level of the subject:

> *Cells fuse, split, and proliferate; volumes grow, tissues stretch, and body fluids change rhythm, speeding up or slowing down. Within the body, growing as a graft, indomitable, there is an other. And no one is present, within that simultaneously dual and alien space, to signify what is going on. 'It happens, but I'm not there.' 'I cannot realize it, but it goes on.' Motherhood's impossible syllogism. (1980:237)*

Pregnancy has no subject. Inhabited neither by one nor two beings, it is more a *cipher*, a filter, than an act of will or the decision of an agent. To claim that pregnancy is the act of a (woman-)subject, she suggests, is to claim a master (the fantasy of the phallic, omnipotent mother), which may impel the subject into a psychotic identification.[5] This is to make the mother everything, and thus for the child to be engulfed by her. Yet to deny that there is anything there in pregnancy is to be unable to anchor oneself anywhere as a subject: 'every speaker would be led to conceive of its Being in relation to some void, a nothingness asymmetrically opposed to this Being, a permanent threat against its mastery, and, ultimately, its stability' (1980:238).

Like the abject, maternity is the splitting, fusing, merging, fragmenting of a series of bodily processes outside the will or control of a subject. Woman, the woman-mother, does not find her femininity or identity as a woman affirmed in maternity but, rather, her corporeality, her animality, her position on the threshold between nature and culture. Her 'identity' as a subject is betrayed by pregnancy; and undermined in lactation and nurturance, where she takes on the status of the part-object, or breast for the child. She is the 'subject' to whom part-objects, including the phallus,

79

are attributed. In a sense 'she' is a screen onto which the child's demands and requirements are projected, and from which images are introjected. 'She' does not exist as such.

Kristeva argues that maternity satisfies a desire originally directed towards the mother's mother (the pre-oedipal desire to give/bear her mother a child): in this sense maternity functions on a 'homosexual–maternal' axis (1980:239). The baby comes to represent the mother herself, and she, her own mother, in a vertiginous identification that brings the mother into a corporeal contact with her mother's maternity.[6] On the other hand maternity also connects the mother to a 'symbolic–paternal' axis, in which her body is marked as phallic and/or castrated of the male attribute.

Based on her own pre-oedipal and oedipal attachments, the woman-as-mother remains divided. She produces the 'social matter' that, in being subjected to the father's law, provides subjects for the social formation. On the other hand maternity is also a breach in the symbolic, an unspoken *jouissance* whose form is always reduced to but never exhausted by the symbolic; except perhaps in art (1980:240). Moreover, if the maternal body provides the means by which the child acquires a symbolic place (even if only by abandoning her), the child in turn provides the conditions under which the woman-mother has indirect access to the Other.

A relation with an other/alter-ego who is also not another, the obliteration of an identity that strives for affirmation, maternity is the source of the semiotic and the precondition of the symbolic. It is the site that must be territorialised, marked by a proprietorial name, contained by it, for the father's law to be accepted by the child. She must be recognised as his, and regulated by his law — hence the castrating brand etched on her body.[7]

Like her understanding of femininity, maternity is not the action of a *woman*, of women; it is organic, a-social, pre-signifying. Although material, it is disembodied and abstract. It cannot be attributed to woman, for 'woman' is precisely that which 'does not exist'. 'Woman' is, for Kristeva, an essentialist category — unlike Lacan's conception where 'The Woman' who does not exist is man's projection of his own perfection through The Woman (see 'God and the Jouissance of The Woman', in Mitchell and Rose, 1982):

> *[W]omen cannot be: the category woman is even that which does not fit in to being. From there, women's practice can only*

be negative, in opposition to what exists ... Certain feminist arguments seem to resuscitate a naive romanticism, believing in an identity (the opposite of phallocratrism). (1980:166)

Kristeva problematises the concepts of 'man', 'woman' and 'identity', seeing them as residues or manifestations of the metaphysics of presence. At the same time, unlike many other feminists, she concedes the relevance of biological, physiological, chromosomal and genetic factors to the analysis of the subject. She is content to attribute an irreducibly biological and genetic 'nature' to maternity, even though she refuses to characterise it as specifically female on essentialist grounds!

While we may concede that pregnancy is not the act of an agent but a series of (largely biological) processes a woman undergoes, this does not entail refusing women the status of agents in nurturance and socialisation practices. In refusing to accord a *sex* to the maternal body, Kristeva readily accepts an essentialist account of *maternity* as a process without a subject:

the childbearing woman ... cathect[s], immediately and unwittingly, the physiological operations and instinctual drives dividing and multiplying her, first, in a biological, and finally, a social teleology. The maternal body slips away from the discursive hold and immediately conceals a ciphering of the species, however, this pre- and transsymbolic memory ... make[s] of the maternal body the stakes of a natural and 'objective' control ... it inscribes both biological operations and their instinctual echoes into this necessary and hazardous program constituting every species. The maternal body is the module of a biosocial program. (1980:241)

In her view the maternal provides the space–time of an archaic 'phylogenetic' inheritance, teleologically governed by the species' requirement of reproduction. Kristeva's resistance to attributing *any* female identity to maternity becomes ludicrous, in view of her willingness to describe maternity in biological and physiological terms. Reluctant to ascribe any psychical identity to the female body on the grounds of essentialism, she happily attributes maternity to an equally essentialist and biologistic explanation.

Kristeva claims that maternity is the unspoken foundation of all social and signifying relations, 'origin' of all heterogeneity, source and primal object of archaic *jouissance*. It needs to be tightly controlled — ideally by repression and sublimation — in order that unity, stability and identity are possible. Yet Kristeva gives women no special link to the maternal body—either in infancy (which Kristeva subsumes under the oedipal model of sameness with the boy—the little girl is, for Freud 'a little man'!), or in her position as mother. The female is both *too close* to and *too distant* from the maternal (too close because she never really resolves her oedipal relation to establish a relation with the mother; and too far because, when she does acquire a distance between herself and the maternal body, she does so as a pale or inadequate reflection of the male, who, by this fact, is more able to represent the complexities of the infant–maternal relation).

It is consistent with Kristeva's claim that certain men, in the privileged moments of the rupturing of their oedipal and symbolic unity, are able to name, evoke, reinscribe the maternal space–time and pleasure where women cannot. The feminine and the maternal are 'liberated', expressed and articulated most strikingly in two kinds of discourse, the analysis of which are Kristeva's current preoccupations: the poetic text (her abiding object) and religious discourse. Her detailed discussion of the latter includes some of her most useful insights about the maternal function. It is for this reason I will now turn to her discussion of religious representations of maternity, especially of the Virgin Mary.

Holy mothers

In her earlier works Kristeva claims that religious discourses are in a unique, privileged position to recognise the *cost* of symbolic organisation. It is the system by which the renounced *jouissance* of the drives is recuperated back into the symbolic order. Religious ecstasy is neither repressed nor sublimated, religion being one of the few social unities that tolerates, indeed encourages, the expression of a normally unspoken (sexual, pre-oedipal) pleasure. As the privileged site of the symbolic, the space where it can 'elaborate a theory which represents its own signifying practice to itself' (1976:65), it is a highly condensed, rich object of speculative investigation for her researches on the speaking subject's debt to repressed maternity. Religious discourses make clear what is at stake in the interface between the social and the discursive, and further, they act historically as a major force in the proliferation of certain conceptions of femininity and maternity lived by women in the West.

Kristeva focuses more or less exclusively on a Christian religious tradition rather than on its more archaic Judaic predecessor. Christianity has '... in a magisterial way, been orchestrated around this amorous space which ... is the support of all possible subjectivity' (1984d:20). At the outset of her analysis of the Virgin Mary[8], she notes that the Christian cult of the Virgin occurs throughout the nineteenth century, culminating only in the 1950s (the dogma of the Assumption dates from 1950, see 1984d:20 — certainly a politically well-timed pronouncement). It is, she claims, the consequence of a culturally convenient mistranslation of the Hebrew legal term for single woman by the Greek term *parthenos*, a moral term denoting virginity.

The Virgin Mary's uniquely sinless position, as many have noted (for example, Warner), is opposed to the other major female figure in the Bible — Eve. Two sides of the same coin, Mary and Eve represent woman as the coupling (for man at least) of sexuality and death: in the case of Eve, the temptation of Adam, the expulsion from Eden and the mortality of humans are the consequence of Eve's 'wayward desires'. In the case of the Virgin Mary, she remains virgin even though she is mother (the oedipal son's ideal!). She does not die but is 'taken' to heaven (Dormition). Mary is represented entirely in the light of, and as complement to Christ, first, by the 'recursive', retrospective attribution of virgin birth to the Virgin mother (medieval scholars debated Mary's own 'sinless' birth, seeing it as a condition of Christ's [1986:166]); second, although she is the mother, progenitor of the son, the son himself is the model on which the mother is based; in a sense he is her mother and she, his daughter; and third, she is represented as Christ's bride or beloved (1986:169), never outside nurturing or quasi-sexual terms (for example, in descriptions of love in the 'Song of Songs').

She is the receptacle of those socially necessary attributes — humility, self-abnegation, modesty — which are marks of compliance ensuring acceptance of the status quo amongst the oppressed and downtrodden. On the other hand she also evokes an archaic, primal shelter, the protective maternal harbour. The representation of maternity through the cult of the Virgin in the discourses of Christian theology is an attempt to smooth out and cover over the contradictory status and position of maternity in the symbolic, a maternity both 'respected' and unrecognised, both sexless and fully eroticised:

A skilful balance of concessions and constraints involving feminine paranoia, the representation of virgin motherhood appears to crown the efforts of a society to reconcile the social remnants of matrilinealism and the unconscious needs of primary narcissism on the one hand, and on the other the requirements of a

*new society based on exchange and before long on an increased
production, which require the contribution of the superego and
rely on the symbolic paternal agency. (1986:183)*

Her point is that there is an unrepresented residue in maternity
which has not been adequately taken up in religious discourse, a
residue that refuses to conform, as Christianity requires, to masculine, oedipal, phallic order. This residue of maternity is occasionally touched upon by discourses of the sacred and is
experienced as religious ecstasy, in bliss, in surrender of a most
corporeal kind (it is no surprise that saints — St Teresa, St Joan,
St Catherine and others — could, in another terminology, be defined
as hysterics!). Among the facets of maternity that the Marian
symbolism necessarily leaves unrepresented, Kristeva cites the
unresolved tension, the 'war', of mother–daughter relations (after
all, although she is herself a 'daughter', Mary has no daughter);
the passionate attachments of one woman to another, which is
posited on the mother–daughter model; and the possibility of a
'repudiation of the other sex (the masculine) ... to lead to an
acknowledgement of what is irreducible, of the irreconcilable
interest of both sexes in asserting their differences, in the quest of
each one — and of women, after all — for an appropriate fulfilment'
(1986:184). These active possibilities are not adequately represented in Christianity's image of woman.

Kristeva's continuing fascination with religious discourses is
directly related to her interest in the poetic text. The religious and
the poetic are inverted reflections of each other: poetic discourse
challenges, traverses or transgresses the present 'bounds of sense';
its open-ended deferral of meaning and its refusal to congeal into
a symbolic identity is the converse of the sacred. Where the poetic
text signals a language to come, the sacred text attempts to
stabilise a situation in decay or breakdown; where the poetic
engenders a semiotic breach of the symbolic, the religious is a
semiotic recoded in symbolic terms; where the poetic is naming,
speaking the unnameable *chora*, the religious is its 'revelation'.
Religion is the recoding of what is becoming uncoded in the poetic
or the revolutionary.

*When I spoke about love and stressed Christianity, for me that's
not nostalgia. It's more a questioning about the discourse that
can take the place of this religious discourse that is cracking now.
And I don't think political discourse, the political causality
which is dominant even in the human sciences in universities
and everywhere is too narrow and feeble ... If we stay with only*

*a political explanation of human phenomena we will be over-
whelmed by the so-called mystical crisis, or spiritual crisis —
that happens, it's a reality ... So my problem here is: how,
through psychoanalysis or something else like art, through such
discourses can we try to elaborate a more complicated elaboration, discourse, sublimation of these critical points of the
human experience which cannot be reduced to a political
causality. (1984c:25)*

The imaginary father and love

Underlying Kristeva's fascination with religious discourses and the
figure of the Virgin Mary is her increasing preoccupation with the
concept of love. Love is understood psychoanalytically: it is a
transference, based on infantile narcissism and primary (imaginary) identifications.[9] In other words love provides another perspective and framework from which to illuminate the enigmatic
pre-oedipal, semiotic period. Her discussion is mediated by the
particular role played by a third party to the mother/child dyad *in*
the pre-oedipal period itself, which she designates as the 'imaginary
father'. In introducing the third term pre-oedipally, she departs
from Freudian and Lacanian orthodoxy, which claims the third
regulating term is the symbolic father or phallus.

This concept is derived from Freud's position in *The Ego and
the Id* (1923), where he outlines the most primitive and archaic
sources of the ego-ideal in the figure of the pre-oedipal rather than
the castrating, oedipal father. Freud claims that the ego-ideal is
the result of the child's earliest (narcissistic) identifications with
this father figure:

*Whatever the character's later capacity for resisting the influ-
ences of abandoned object cathexes may turn out to be, the
effects of the first identifications made in earliest childhood will
be general and lasting. This leads us back to the origin of the
ego ideal, for behind it there lies hidden an individual's first and
most important identification, his identification with the father
in his own personal prehistory. (Freud, 1923:31)[10]*

The pre-oedipal father is a sexually undifferentiated, imaginary
father, the father as other, not Other. While agreeing with a
number of Lacanian pronouncements about the pre-oedipal,
Kristeva also questions his equation of the imaginary with the
advent of the mirror phase. For her, by contrast, the semiotic and
the functioning of 'primary repression' are anterior to mirror-stage

identifications (in this sense she remains closer to Melanie Klein's position on the oedipus complex than to Freud's and Lacan's). Narcissism, for Kristeva, relies on a non-oedipal triangular relationship which lacks the stability or organisation of the symbolic or oedipal structure. The first term in this relation is the narcissistic ego, the ego based on identifications with one's own mirror image; Kristeva, following Lacan, claims that the second term is 'the void':

'Narcissism' would, then, be a protective formulation of this void [vide] that designates for me the displacement of the drive into the psychic (from motion to representation): in other words, it is the very locus of the emergence of what will be a speaking subject. (1982c:36)

The third term completing the narcissistic triad is left over from, unrepresented by, the ego's attempts to cover over the void, the abject, the neither-subject-nor-yet-object. Kristeva represents the primal constituents of infantile narcissism in the following diagram (from 1982c:36):

Figure 3.1

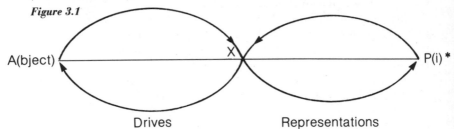

A(bject)   X   P(i)*

Drives   Representations

Note: *P(i) is Kristeva's formula for 'un Père imaginaire', an imaginary Father; and also, 'l'identification primaire' primary identification.

This is a remarkably compressed diagram: on the one hand it is a 'translation' of Lacan's famous diagram of the genesis of the ego, 'Schema L' (see Lacan, 1977; Gross, 1976), in which the other or *autre* is understood as the mother/mirror-image. In Kristeva's representation it is the imaginary *father* who provides support for the child's identificatory relations with the other. The diagram is also an echo of Saussure's famous representation of the sign, which Lacan formulates as 'signifier over signified', represented by the following diagram (see Figure 3.2) (see Saussure, 1974:66):

Kristeva's diagram (Figure 3.1) thus represents the structure of signification, the internal relation between the sign's constituents,

Figure 3.2

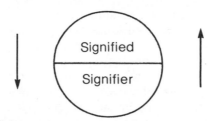

and the relation between one sign and other signs. Moreover, as doubled, each circle acts as a mirror for the other, representing the narcissism of one of the parents relative to the other, thus locating the subject, marked by the X, at the point of their convergence. This double-looped structure situates a space the speaking subject will come to claim as its own through the expulsion of the abject and the resolution of the imaginary by the symbolic:

> *The two circles constitute themselves as such, so that this alteration, this void (which, for the subject, activates the splitting, and, for the sign, the bar and arbitrariness), from their overlap can ... folded up, represent the two parents' narcissisms. That each of the two generators [geniteurs] reflect him/herself in the other, in order to take themselves for the other ... all this thanks to their offspring—this surprises no-one. Still, it is necessary that this mirage be entwined in this way so that the two instances, A and P(i)—the abject and the imaginary Father—keep each other at bay, differentiate themselves and allow within the fields of two narcissisms, a third party being lodged: the speaking child. (1982c:36–7)*

If the child's relation to the pre-oedipal, phallic mother is pre-linguistic, unspoken and unrepresentable, its relation to the imaginary father provides the first displacements of the drive's absorption by and formation through signification. It involves the first fixing of mnemic traces to signs. 'He' functions to provide the child with 'a substitute for the satisfaction of the drive in a *constructive interpretation*. Constructive ... of sense and meaning at the same time as the drive and never the one without the other' (1982c:37, emphasis added). The imaginary father is a kind of link or bridge between the maternal *chora* and the symbolic father, the bearer of the castration threat. 'He' is the 'relay' between narcissism and the oedipal. The imaginary father, as source of the ego-ideal, also bears the weight of what will, through oedipal interdicts, become the superego: the internalised authority of the symbolic father.

As the key to acquiring a symbolic position through oedipalisation, the imaginary father is not the stern, judgmental, prohibiting
father Freud evokes in *Totem and Taboo* — the God of Protestant-
ism. The latter is the symbolic representative of law. Kristeva
instead evokes the loving father, an image of the father rarely
represented in the Bible (she gives one counter-example, that of
David and Bathseba's sexual encounter, *Samuel* 12:24—5). His is
a qualitatively different love from a proprietorial seizure by the
phallic, masculine subject, or the passion for the 'chase' that is
Don Juanism. Rather than *eros*, it is *agape* ('brotherly' love,
Christian charity), a love which, instead of seeking its own satisfaction and consummation, transfers love onto a third term, the
Other. As such, it is represented, outside the Christian God, in the
pederastic love Plato (in *The Symposium*) deemed necessary for
the acquisition of the love of knowledge. Like 'platonic' love
(rarely has there been such a misnomer in popular culture), it is a
love that binds the boy and, Kristeva insists, the girl to 'higher
accomplishments' of civilisation; that is, it binds the child's homosexual libido to the naming of drives and their modes of representation (1982c:38).

If *eros* 'tries to achieve something that is placed above ... tries
to go beyond the possibilities of the person he loves; it aspires to
power...' (1984c:25), that is, if it is coded as phallic and is based
on *idealisation, agape* is different from *eros* insofar as it is an
excessiveness or profusion: 'it comes to you from outside, you
don't need to merit it, it's a sort of profusion, it's the love of
parents for their children, for instance, when it happens which is
not very often' (1984c:25). This love, it seems, is not easy for the
mother. Her relation to the child is 'too close' and the love it
produces vacillates between two poles: a fusional, overwhelming
image of the mother (the phallic mother of psychosis); and
abjection, the abandonment by the object/other. The love the
symbolic father offers is, by contrast, abstract and judgmental, a
love that must prove its worth. It is only love that is founded on
the relation with the imaginary father that enables the child to
move on, to displace, to signify, to love others outside the family
structure.

The imaginary father should not be confused with the biological
father or with any concrete empirical male subject. The imaginary
father is the term within the child's imaginary and identificatory
relations: it is represented by the *position* the father occupies in
the mother's desire — that is, the mother's desire for the phallus.
Insofar as the child represents the satisfaction or product of this

desire, the full weight falls onto the child without being mediated. But insofar as some third term takes on this role for the mother, the child accedes to its patriarchal and symbolic heritage:

If for a mother the child is the meaning of her life, it's too heavy. She has to have another meaning in her life. And this other meaning in her life is the father of pre-history. And it's the guarantee of a love relationship between the mother and the child. If it doesn't exist, it produces a clash which produces all sorts of inhibitions, and also difficulty to even accede to language. (1984c:23).

The imaginary father *qua* third term or mediator is thus the forerunner of the sign, and, more generally, of the symbolic order. 'He' is the social mediation of dual psychotic/nascissistic relations. The heir to his mediating position is language and representation — but only on condition that it adequately expresses and contains the impulses and energies originating in the dual imaginary relation. When it does not succeed they return, rupturing, dismantling and unsettling any unities based on their subsumption. The *jouissance* provisionally contained by the symbolic is the energetic basis of a number of specific social relations/products. It provides the raw materials for all signifying relations, all ideological institutions and even economic relations. It also forms the basis of adult norms of sexuality, wishes, values, judgments and beliefs in accordance with specific frameworks and presumptions; and interrelations — sexual, erotic, loving, exchanging — between individuals.

Heretical ethics

Her abiding commitment to analysing literary and poetic practices and her philosophical and psychoanalytic reflections on the speaking subject have led Kristeva away from 'scientific marxisms'. Her interests are all detectable in her earlier works although her emphasis has changed. She reformulates earlier conjectures using different terminology. Her political interests, while not oblivious to marxism and critiques of imperialism, are located more at the level of the individual, even the intrapsychical relations within individuals. It is significant that in moving from an economic conception of politics to an understanding of the politics internal to the operation of systems of signification and subject formation, instead of becoming closer to a feminist 'politics of the personal', she remains distant from identifiably feminist positions. She prefers psychoanalytic explanations. Coupled with her deepening commitment to psychoanalytic methods and insights, Kristeva seems to replace (or displace) her marxist/Maoist political orientation with what could be described as an *ethical* (in Spinoza's sense) framework. This is perfectly consistent with her use of psychoanalysis, with which it shares a concern to elaborate what persons are and how they should behave.

The ethical seems to be the 'natural' heir to the libidinal excess that has thus far been left to religious discourses to express. The crisis of current religion (even if it is not a crisis in numerical terms, it is a crisis of relevance), needs to be replaced, not by political analysis but, she claims, by ethics. And not by *any* ethics but, in her terms, an 'herethical ethics', an heretical ethics, an ethics of heresy (her/ethics?). The breakdown of the authority of religious discourses in the Enlightenment is matched, she believes, by the upheavals initiated by the Symbolists in the late nineteenth century which are still with us today. We are today facing a crisis of representation that inherits its form from religious texts.

> *The crisis of representation in contemporary art could be ... an attempt at* nominating this narcissism *that haunts us ceaselessly, tragic and delectable fantom, bedrock of our identity, that we attempt to resolve ... in our loves. The crisis of representation is* a discourse of love: the wager of naming the imaginary Father. *An exorbitant pretension to name or nominate everything, at the price of an avowal: that this naming or nomination is not everything, but that it is possible only through distance — separation, void, silence. (1984c:39, my emphasis)*

The discourse of love is a discourse of/from the imaginary father, borrowing from and relying on the resources of the maternal *chora*, but harnessing them through the given structures of symbolic organisation. The imaginary father is 'he' who enables discourse, the speaking of love, replacing the maternal 'umbilical' bond with representation. The discourses of love, directed towards the maternal body, gain their orientation through the imaginary father, and their terminology and enunciative positions from the symbolic father. It is redirected towards the Other: towards God in religious discourses: towards beauty in Art; to meaning and narrative in literature; and copulative sexual union in the sexual sphere. Yet, Kristeva seems to suggest that the crisis of representation, which poses a crisis also for love, needs to be examined in *ethical* terms.

The discourses of love are difficult to articulate because their object, motherhood, remains unspoken.[11] Ethics becomes necessary, for Kristeva, insofar as the maternal debt *needs to be spoken*. But such an ethics is not 'feminine' or feminist in any sense (indeed, a feminine or masculine ethics per se makes no sense —ethics being, at least on a number of accounts, most notably, Levinas', the encounter with alterity, with the other); rather, it is an ethics that ranges over sexual differences and differentiations. An ethics appropriate to maternity is necessary:

> ... *if ethics amounts to no avoiding the embarrassing and inevitable problematics of the law but giving it flesh, language and* jouissance—*in that case its reformulation demands the contribution of women. Of women who harbour the desire to reproduce (to have stability). Of women who are available so that our speaking species, which knows it is moral, might withstand death. Of mothers. For an heretical ethics, separated from morality, an* herethics, *is perhaps no more than that which in life makes bonds, thoughts, and therefore the thought of death, bearable: herethics is undeath* [a-mort]; *love* ... *(1986:185)*

Women, feminism and the feminine

Kristeva is consistently critical of 'feminists'. She uses every opportunity to distance herself from feminist positions. Yet, she sees herself as a feminist in some broad sense of the term, though her position is different from other, more standard feminist positions. This is clearly indicated in her discussion of feminism in her paper on the topic, 'Women's Time' (1986). Here she places herself *within* (but also going *beyond*) a feminist heritage. She believes that her position is the logical conclusion of this feminist tradition. She brings to it the wideranging critique of metaphysics associated with Derrida, seeing in it the culmination and the end point of women's struggles.

Kristeva distinguishes between women, feminists and the feminine. In her understanding, woman is a metaphysical term, the binary opposite of man. It is an essentialist and biologistic category that ignores a heterogeneity of positions and differences amongst women. She positions women on the side of subversion, even if she believes that women react to their lived and socially sanctioned positions of subordination in one of two ways: either they aspire to the phallic status attributed to men—that is, they suffer from a 'virilising' 'masculinity complex' (Kristeva, in Marks and de

Courtivron, 1981:166); or, on the other hand, they shun all that is phallic in an opposite extreme: 'we flee everything considered "phallic" to find refuge in the valorization of a silent underwater body, thus abdicating any entry into history' (Kristeva, in Marks and de Courtivron, 1981:166). Both positions, Kristeva points out, involve the unquestioned given value of the phallic—one by affirmation, the other by denial.

She considers 'women's struggles' to be reactive, negative, rather than productive. This description, however, *entails* that, when women break social codes, they are able to do so through negativity. Their contributions as women are not productive. This sharp separation of critique from theoretical construct is itself a conventional way of excluding women's academic researches from being recognised as original (after all, the history of philosophy is marked by texts that taking preceding texts as the object of their critiques; these critiques and the positive accounts they may have developed are not clearly separable. See Le Doeuff, 1977; and Gatens, 1986).

In this case they are aligned with a basically radical, revolutionary rupture; but when the time comes for replacing the old order with a new one, women fall on the side of conservativism:

> *If women have a role in this on-going process, it is only in assuming a negative function: reject everything finite, definite, structure, loaded with meaning, in the existing state of society. Such an attitude places women on the side of the explosion of social codes: with revolutionary moments. But women tend to move immediately to the other side—the side of symbolic power. Women can become the most solid guarantee of sociality because they can make decisions concerning procreation (in the 'developed' countries and as the final arbiters), and because they tend to identify with power after having rejected it. (Kristeva, in Marks and de Courtivron, 1981:166)*

Her position in enigmatic insofar as it acknowledges a tendency to conservativism in (some) mothers, and does not affirm the opposite tendency, also present in maternity, and as easily affirmed *as a generality* as Kristeva's claim. Moreover, it is not clear why it is women, and not the oppressed of all kinds, who 'identify with power after having rejected it'. Is this women's particular response? If it is not, then in what sense can her claim be understood—as description (of oppression), as prophecy, as an innate characteristic?

Women, considered neither as mothers and nurturers nor as lovers and wives, but in their relations to other women, are not theorised as such by Kristeva. Even in lesbian relations, Kristeva does not see a relation between two women, but a relation between a woman and her (fantasised) mother. Woman's womanly love, a love outside of and beyond the maternal love, is the one category missing from *Tales of Love*.

In psychoanalysis, lesbian desire cannot be conceived except as an imitation of masculinity; Kristeva's position implicitly confirms this without presenting any criticisms or developing a distance from it.

Woman remains a blank term, a formula for a locus of resistance to symbolisation. Kristeva confirms Lacan's view that women and especially the unique sexual pleasures they experience 'beyond the phallus', are unable to speak about or to know their pleasure. The experience precludes symbolisation, intellectualisation or reflection. This is because the phallus is the signifying threshold of representation. To be 'beyond the phallus' is thus to be beyond representation, to be unsayable, ineffable. To be, precisely the *condition* of representation. Representing no 'content' of its own, this 'blank term' is the space filled in by any content/meaning.

If women are untheorised and unrepresented in Kristeva's work, her comments on feminism and feminists seem oversimplified and puzzlingly hostile. Clearly there may be a number of points of major disagreement between her position and that held by other feminists. What is puzzling about her position is the desire to distinguish herself from feminists rather than making connections, even critical ones, with their researches. She does not, for example, seem to share the general recognition of women's oppressed social positions and the need to transform prevailing models of sexual valuation — minimal feminist conditions. Because one does not agree with some or even all feminists does not imply that feminism is itself irredeemably problematic. Her political disengagement from feminist struggles and issues can readily be interpreted as an *anti*feminism rather than non-feminism. Indeed, even her closest feminist supporters seem reluctant to describe her position as feminist (for example, Moi, 1985:167). If Kristeva had specified *which* feminists and feminisms she disputes, her position could have been regarded as an *internal* critique. Instead it is readily seen as an external critique, a critique which begins from premises different from, even alien to, feminist ones.

Kristeva acknowledges that feminist struggles render questionable many of the common presumptions of power, ideology and representation which ignore the concept of subjectivity and sexuality. But insofar as feminism is the outcome of a recorded symbolic order, it must remain locked into many of the presumptions that it aims to challenge. Ultimately, this is why she maintains the necessity of 'deconstructing' feminist as well as patriarchal positions:

> *The Women's Movement ... by its negativity, indicates to all the institutions of the right, and of the left, what it is that they repress: for example that 'class consciousness' cannot exclude the unconscious of the sexed speaker. The trap for this potential demystifying force ... is one of identifying with the power principle that it believes itself countering: the hysterical saint plays her* jouissance *against the social order, but in the name of God. A question: who is God for contemporary feminism? Man, or his replacement, Woman? Any liberation movement (feminism included) as long as it has no analysis of its relation to the instance of power, or until it has renounced all belief in its own identity, is recuperable through power and through spiritualism ... it is indeed spiritualism's last chance. (1981b:167)*

Her position seems extremely ungenerous to the positions of other feminists. A number of her French colleagues clearly share her concern about essentialism, metaphysical identities and logo-centric categories. Many are as virulent about metaphysical identities as she is (for example, Cixous, Irigaray). It is not clear that when Irigaray or Cixous refer to women or women's 'identities', they do so from a Hellenic and Christian metaphysical context. They are as aware as she is of Lacan's decentering of the subject and his problematisation of an identity based on the pretensions of the ego. The identities they attribute to women are not, it seems to me, metaphysical. Differences between the sexes, like the differences between signs, undermine the concept of identity presumed by them both. The relations between the sexes may be based on a non-metaphysical identity, an 'identity' that is relative rather than absolute, based on a Saussurian rather than a Cartesian framework.

Kristeva's question—who is God for feminism—will prove crucial in assessing feminist attempts to resolve and move beyond phallocentric representations. She pre-empts an answer by suggesting two of her own: first that man remains God, ideal for woman to emulate. Here she seems to regard feminism as a quest for equality, a levelling of the two sexes by making women indistinguishable from men within secular humanism. Her other suggestion is more alarming: feminists, she implies, remove Man from his post-Enlightenment position as God only to position Woman in his place. Here she seems to have in mind a rather puerile and simple-minded anti-patriarchalism some feminists claim in adopting a 'non-patriarchal' position at will, and in that guise developing a feminism that is the exact reverse of patriarchy (and is thus its repetition). While these no doubt describe two *possible* feminist attitudes, they are not exhaustive. They affirm a singular, sexually specific God: but there is no mention of the feminist equivalents of agnosticism and atheism; or, as we will see in examining Irigaray's work, reconceiving the very idea of God in different terms.

She attributes a number of attitudes to feminism and to feminists that seem to me to be either inappropriate or out of date. In her more recent work she charges that feminists have naively accepted a fantasy of the (phallic) mother instead of attempting to undo patriarchal representations of maternity. As a consequence, she claims, feminists remain unduly critical of maternity, without seeing that such a maternity is only one possible form it may take:

> ... *when feminism demands a new representation of femininity, it seems to identify motherhood with [an] idealized misconception, and because it rejects the image and its misuse, feminism circumvents the real experience that fantasy overshadows. The result?—A negation or rejection of motherhood by some avant-garde feminist groups. Or else an acceptance—conscious or not—of its traditional representations by the great mass of people, women and men. (1987:161)*

Out of a variety of possible positions, Kristeva's strategy is to define two that are opposed and to take them as representative of all feminisms. In this case she divides feminist attitudes to maternity into a naive, uncritical acceptance of patriarchal representations of maternity or an outright rejection of maternity, as if feminists had no choice but to accept or reject a position. She ignores those texts in French feminisms (notably, Cixous' and Irigaray's) where a different understanding of maternity may be possible.

Her critical attitude to feminist texts is, I suggest, a function of the slippage she effects from the concept of woman to that of the feminine, a displacement of the question of identity by *differentiation*. This remains the most troublesome of her various contentions regarding feminist theory and politics. By means of this manoeuvre, she is able, on the one hand, to evacuate women of any privileged access to femininity, and, on the other, to position men, the avant-garde, in the best position to represent, to name or speak the feminine.

Unlike male and female, she claims that masculinity and femininity are not binary oppositions. The latter are not mutually exclusive, but coexist in each individual, whether male or female, founded on the constitutional bisexuality of the child. Infantile polymorphous perversion, the indeterminacy of the sexual aims and objects of the pre-oedipal period, and the child's inability to understand sexual difference provide a backdrop to Kristeva's disembodiment of masculine and feminine, and her refusal to see the *sexed body* as the site of the inscriptions of masculine and feminine attributes. (On the problems of such a sex-gender opposition, see Gatens, 1983.)

She distinguishes her postulate of bisexuality from androgyny (which is more like a higher-order union of a heterogeneous masculine and feminine than like an unsuperceded heterogeneity). Her interest, as she now states it, is the *individual*, who necessarily contains both masculine and feminine qualities in varying proportions. Because of his or her preformation in the space of the maternal semiotic, because of his/her identification with and introjection of the mother's body, each subject is considered as 'feminine', where feminine = passive. Children of both sexes must overcome or repress their pre-oedipal dependence to acquire an autonomous identity. Yet insofar as the mother is construed as phallic, in a world where there is no sexual difference, in a world where the libido is considered masculine, the young child is presumed masculine. Or indeterminate.

The speaking subject is able to tap into and thus articulate this maternal, semiotic space and energies, and, by that fact, touches upon an archaic femininity repressed in most subjects. He—for it is only the phallic subject who definitively acquires a symbolic position—is able to say what she (the mother, the infant) experiences. Though a risk to his masculine, phallic identity, he can evoke the *jouissance* he experiences with her in a way that she cannot. He can transgress the boundaries of the symbolic, while she exists at its presocial margins. He can speak the *jouissance* which overwhelms her 'identity'.

The pre-eminence she grants to the avant-garde text in rupturing social and psychical identities is correlated with her attempt to neutralise feminist struggles, subordinating them to the critique of humanism. She puts feminism in the provisionally revolutionary position of destabilising the norms and expectations, inequalities and discriminations rendering one sex oppressed. But in her view this is merely one specific step in a more generalisable struggle against *all* identities. Feminism can be considered 'as but a *moment* in the thought of that anthropomorphic identity which currently blocks the horizon of the discursive and scientific adventure of our species' (1981b:211).

Feminism, for her, is not really a movement about a category, class or caste of *women* at all: it is a movement about the collectivity of individuals with unique specific combinations of masculine and feminine, a movement about *the liberation of the subject*:

> ... *political struggles for people that are exploited will continue, they have to continue, but they will continue maybe better if the main concern remains the individuality and the particularity of the person ... [I]f the feminist movement is a movement of individuals I think it's a good political answer to what I called the political religion which can erase the individual. (1984c:27)*

Her advocacy of the (male) avant-garde as spokesman for a repressed femininity and lost maternity, coupled with her call for a feminism that is not confined to sexual differences but analyses and confronts the question of sexual differentiation, the existence of masculine/symbolic and feminine/semiotic elements within each subject, imply the annihilation of women's struggles for their sexual specificity and autonomy. This is treated *a priori* as the quest for a metaphysical identity, whether this is an essential identity or a constructed, discursive one (such as Irigaray develops).

To summarise, then, some of the key elements of Kristeva's position:

Her work seeks out the interlocking relations constitutive of the unities of subjectivity, sociality and signification: in each case, these operations can be formulated in terms of a dynamic and conflictual relation between semiotic and symbolic energies and constraints.

The symbolic provides the semiotic with its only possibilities of expression; in turn, the semiotic provides the symbolic with its raw materials and its energetic impetus. Social order or unity is possible, at the levels of the subject, culture and representations, only if the semiotic is hierarchically subordinated to the symbolic.

The semiotic, however, erupts and overflows its symbolic boundaries in certain 'privileged' moments of 'rupture, renovation and revolution'. Kristeva situates these ruptures under the headings of 'madness, holiness and poetry': neuroses and psychoses signal its eruption in the subject's psychical economy; religious ecstacy and jouissance indicate its expression in religious discourses; and avant-garde experimentation in all of the arts point to its disruption of the rules of signifying practice.

As a (re)evocation of the abandoned maternal body, semiotic interventions into the ordering of the symbolic mark the reappearance of a repressed femininity into the operations of a phallic and paternal sexual, social and representational economy. The semiotic thus provides the energy for social and signifying upheavals which transgress the limits of the symbolic, reorganising them into other, different forms of totality and unity.

The locus of the maternal body is thus both unrepresentable as such, and the necessary condition of all representations, the unspeakable debt that culture, language and sociality owe but cannot express without violence. The function of the imaginary father is to mediate between this potentially overwhelming maternal body and the universality of the symbolic father's law, providing the child with a base for its (narcissistic) identity and an anticipation of its symbolic position.

The ruptures effected in 'madness, holiness and poetry' are thus the result of the attempt to render the maternal debt representable. The revolutionary speaking subject must be positioned in the symbolic order (in order to pose the threat of its internal subversion) yet must also retain some access to the semiotic. This subject must be a masculine subject, able to speak and represent by being positioned as a speaking being in the symbolic, but a subject who has refused to abandon all residues of his attachment to the maternal body. He places the security of his masculine identity at risk in returning to the resources of the semiotic. The avant-garde artist is thus a masculine subject, whose masculinity is placed into question by his refusal to abandon a feminine, preoedipal, semiotic attachment.

The avant-garde artist's position as an exemplary revolutionary force in representation becomes, in Kristeva's conception, a model of the kinds of upheavals to which feminism should direct itself: feminism, for her, is not a struggle for women's attainment of an identity — this simply extends a logocentric and metaphysical term to women, without adequately questioning its implications. Feminism is, in her view, fundamentally negative or anti-sexist rather than productive of a new social order; it is to be superceded in more far-reaching struggles against the very notion of identity.

Kristeva's project, then, does not simply involve the destabilisation of the norms of representation and the structures of sexual identity. She questions the long-term effectivity of feminist goals of claiming a recognised social position and value for women as women. This places her work in a tense and contradictory relation with Luce Irigaray's work, which is the object of analysis of the next two chapters. Through a comparison of their positions, we will see what is at stake in the contentious question of sexual difference.

4 Luce Irigaray and sexual difference

O NE of Kristeva's most articulate contemporaries is Luce Irigaray, who is also a psychoanalyst, philosopher and feminist theorist. They share a number of striking similarities, which is not altogether surprising given their similar training, background, orientation and interests. But less noted in the secondary literature on French feminisms are the major *differences* and disagreements that place them on opposing sides in a number of theoretical controversies and political issues. In analysing Irigaray's contributions to French feminist theory, the similarities — and differences — will need further elaboration. While both rely on a series of shared terms and theoretical frameworks (including the work of Lacan and Derrida), the similarities are largely superficial. Identifying them too closely obscures political and intellectual differences, differences in 'styles' of writing, in objects of investigation, in methods of analysis and in overall objectives.

Irigaray is perhaps best known outside France as the most active and vocal advocate of the concept of *sexual difference*. Given her training in Lacanian psychoanalysis and her interest in Saussurian, structuralist and poststructuralist linguistics and language[1], her position seems close to and compatible with Kristeva's understanding of sexual difference. Indeed, both are commonly described as feminists of sexual difference.[2] Yet, as outlined in the last two chapters, Kristeva's understanding of sexual difference entails the dissolution of all sexual identities and converts the feminist aspiration of establishing an identity for women into a dispersed process of sexual differentiation relevant to both sexes. Rather than seek a notion of women's sexual *autonomy and specificity*, as Irigaray does, Kristeva aims to uncover women's (repressed) masculinity and men's (disavowed) femininity through the acknowledgement of a repressed semiotic, sexual energy or drive facilitation on which both male and female 'identities' are based and to which they are vulnerable. Where Kristeva challenges or deconstructs the notion of sexual identity, Irigaray actively affirms a project challenging and deconstructing the cultural representations of femininity so that it may be capable of representation and recognition in its own self-defined terms. She insists on precisely the notion of women's *sexual specificity* which Kristeva seeks to undo.

In this chapter I will examine Irigaray's earlier works, those published before 1979, particularly *Speculum of the Other Woman* (1985a) and *This Sex Which Is Not One* (1985b), to see what is at stake in her disagreements with Kristeva. What are the implications and effects of advocating sexual difference rather than sexual differentiation? In what ways do the concepts of difference and differentiation differ?

Irigaray's writings are extremely difficult to write about. They are exceptionally elusive, fluid and ambiguous — the moment one feels relatively confident about what she means in one context, one loses grasp of other related passages which seemed comprehensible when they were read. Her writing, her 'styles', involve new forms of discourse, new ways of speaking, a 'poetry' which is necessarily innovative and evocative of new conceptions of women and femininity. Her writing varies from text to text. For example, she claims that in a number of her more recent texts, she has self-consciously sought different styles, according to content and context.[3] Her writings reproduce the rhythms of spoken French; her sentences are frequently 'unfinished', half-said, as they might occur in conversation. Grammar and syntax are consciously stretched, sometimes to their limits. Yet they are never meaningless. On the contrary, they resonate with ambiguities that proliferate rather than diminish meanings, although they defy attempts to pin them down definitively. Her writing is thus very different from Kristeva's erudite but dry and 'serious' 'style'. Irigaray has none of Kristeva's reverence (for systematicity, for science, for precision, for 'fair' representations of other texts, etc.), nor her commitment to an ongoing, fundamentally totalising and systematic *world view* or overarching explanatory framework. Kristeva in turn has none of Irigaray's irreverence, her playful mockery and her sense of outrageousness.

More fragmentary and less purposively goal-directed, Irigaray does not, for that matter, lack rigour. Like Derrida's, her texts are readings of other texts, exercises in intertextuality. Like Cixous' writings, they are festivals or celebrations of female specificity in discursive forms. Irigaray's texts are thus simultaneously 'serious' philosophical critiques of phallocentric discourses; and experiments in new conceptual and representational practices, carried out within *and* beyond phallocentric constraints. Thus where Kristeva's writings are 'critical' (in both senses: that is, are critiques of various positions, and are commentaries or secondary texts on or 'about' other texts), Irigaray presents 'constructive', poetic, exploratory texts capable of multiple readings and different associations. No two readings, even by the same reader, are identical. Her writings perform what they announce.

Because her writings are richly poetic and highly ambiguous, and because they are fragmented and often elliptical, my analysis will provide a more systematic organisation and structure than Irigaray's own writings. My justification for the imposition of order onto her polyvocal texts is pragmatic: given the limitations of space here, and, more seriously, given the difficulties of analysing/reading Irigaray in an Irigarayan mode, her project is exceptionally difficult to re-present convincingly.[4]

Kristeva and Irigaray

Both Irigaray and Kristeva are interested in articulating the hitherto unexpressed debt that a patriarchal symbolic order (including relations of economic, textual and representational production) owes to femininity, and particularly to maternity. Each seeks out the buried maternal, pre-oedipal bedrock which underlies the paternal, phallic, symbolic law (that is, the oedipus complex or the Name-of-the-Father). Each conceptualises the subject's experiences of corporeality (including its *jouissance*) in terms of psychoanalytic theory—in order to avoid biologism and essentialism. While relying on a psychoanalytic framework to establish their own works, each goes well beyond the role of faithful disciple in order to develop a position distinctively her own, positions which may be unpalatable for Freudian or Lacanian orthodoxy. They are not apprentices who will carry on the master's trade in his name. They refuse many of the canons and norms of psychoanalysis, each developing a position related to but different from it. Kristeva uses psychoanalysis to understand the constitution of the speaking subject; Irigaray uses it to articulate a culturally (rather than psychically) produced unconscious, a repression in texts, knowledges and institutionally regulated practices.

Although both are trained in and committed to psychoanalysis, the kinds and degree of commitment differ considerably. Kristeva accepts the oedipal structure and its necessary organising role in the acquisition of culture without seriously criticising Freud. Irigaray, on the other hand, is scathing about Freud's views on the oedipal structure as an asymmetrical regulative principle of sexual organisation. She continually draws attention to Freud's and Lacan's notion of sexuality or drives as masculine and their attribution of an *a priori* privilege to masculinity and its qualities.

Kristeva will use basically unquestioned psychoanalytic tools to explain the way 'texts' of all kinds function; while Irigaray will focus more on the analogies between psychoanalytic interpretations of symptoms and knowledges, and 'truthful' discourses which necessarily contain a repressed or unconscious 'feminine' element.

Kristeva remains committed to psychoanalysis as an overarching framework or theoretical paradigm. While there are a number of details she questions, alters or refuses to accept, there is no question of the necessity of something like psychoanalytic models of the unconscious and sexual drives. By contrast, Irigaray's commitment seems more strategic and provisional. Although she uses psychoanalytic methods in a number of her most well-known texts, unlike Kristeva she has grown away from psychoanalysis, and from psychological accounts more generally, to turn her attention to key philosophical texts and frameworks, in which Derrida, Levinas, Heidegger and Nietzsche figure as crucial texts and methodological frameworks. She does not *abandon* psychoanalysis even in her most recent texts; instead, its strategic usefulness for her purposes varies considerably from one project to another and so is utilised in some contexts and is irrelevant in others. Rather than adhere to its overall framework, she is content to utilise it or replace it with others.

If Lacanian psychoanalysis provides a first point of similarity, Derridean deconstruction is a second shared commitment. Once again, however, the apparent similarities are superficial. Deconstructive readings have provided a powerful source of inspiration for virtually all of French thought in the 1970s and afterwards. Few contemporary French intellectuals are untouched by or indifferent to Derrida's interrogations of key texts from the history of philosophy. Kristeva and Irigaray are no exceptions. Once again, however, their common interests in Derridean readings and conceptions of textuality are directed to different elements of Derrida's writings and possibly incompatible uses of his work.

Both Kristeva and Irigaray make considerable use of Derrida's reading of difference through his concept of *différance*. Yet, there is hardly a point of overlap, convergence or common usage.

Kristeva will use the concept of difference, as Derrida does, to render problematic key logocentric presumptions within knowledges, particularly those which imply some kind of metaphysical *identity* (including that of establishing a sexual identity for women). Opposed to identity or sameness, difference signals a semiotic movement of 'cutting through' social identities to reveal a debt to a pre-oedipal energy which underlies and is repressed by symbolic identity. Kristeva uses this concept to criticise feminist attempts to attain a social, linguistic, political, intellectual identity for women. Irigaray, by contrast, uses Derrida's concept of difference to clear a space in which women's self-description in terms other than those which define men's self-sameness becomes possible. Where Kristeva uses it to designate the difference *internal* to each subject, Irigaray uses it to refer to the differences *between* one sex and another. For Kristeva, Irigaray's project is logocentric and steeped in a metaphysical tradition; for Irigaray, Kristeva's position is antifeminist and phallocratic.

They seem to occupy positions that are the *distorted reflections* or inversions of each other: not identical, but twins nonetheless, similar enough to be mistaken for each other by those who do not know them well. This may explain why they are so regularly discussed together (in English at least) and why it is commonly assumed that their positions are compatible if not complementary. In fact, however, their positions are extreme poles apart when judged from a feminist point of view. We will now turn to Irigaray's critique of the phallocentrism of psychoanalysis.

Phallic sameness

Irigaray uses psychoanalysis without being committed to its fundamental presuppositions. Her position is ambivalent: she is clearly critical of Freud's presumptions and conclusions insofar as they cast women into a secondary, dependent position *by cultural necessity*; on the other hand she continues to use psychoanalysis — in spite of its recognised problems — as a critical tool in the analysis of other texts from the history of (phallocentric) philosophy. Psychoanalysis is a particularly pertinent and revealing discourse insofar as it states *explicitly* the various presumptions and beliefs usually left unspoken by other texts. Like Rousseau or other openly misogynist philosophers (see Lloyd, 1984; Gatens, 1986), Freud makes clear what is at stake in patriarchal knowledges which deny their production from sexually specific discursive positions. In other words, psychoanalytic theory can itself be read as a *symptom* of a broader, underlying cultural and intellectual misogyny.[5]

Given the wishes, desires and needs of the oedipalised male subject, Freud *deduces* (rather than observes) a femininty that complements male development, and satisfies men's needs. In other words, Freud develops a model of human subjectivity that represents all the variations of subjectivity only according to a singular (Western, capitalist, white, Eurocentric) male model. Femininity is always represented in some relation of dependence on this model, a lack or absence of the qualities characterising masculinity. On Irigaray's reading, this institutes a phallic economy, an economy based on sameness, oneness or identity with the masculine subject — an '*a priori* of the same'. His position, in short, is *phallocentric*. Phallocentrism is not simply, as Ernest Jones defined it, the primacy of the phallus (or, more precisely, the privilege of the male organ, the penis), but can be identified with a more general process of cultural and representational *assimilation*. Phallocentrism is the use of *one* model of subjectivity, the male, by which all others are positively or negatively defined. Others are constructed as variations of this singular type of subject. They are thus reduced to or defined only by terms chosen by and appropriate for masculinity. Irigaray's aim, among other things, is the recategorisation of women and femininity so that they are now capable of being autonomously defined according to women's and not men's interests.

Phallocentrism is a subtle and not always easily identifiable representational system. It has three distinct forms, which, if taken together, describe the historically varied positions that have been socially acknowledged for women in patriarchal cultures: whenever the two sexes are conceived as *identical*, as *opposites* or as *complements*, one of the two terms defines the position of the other. This is clear in cases of personal or sexual identity (as occurs in universalist and humanist conceptions): one term is taken as the norm against which the other is measured. When the one conforms to the other — when the two are 'equal' — an identity is posited. In complementarity (such as the advocates of androgyny, on the one hand, and conservative proponents of the sanctity of the nuclear family, on the other hand, illustrate), one term is taken as given, in need of completion or complementarity, while the other is regarded only insofar as it serves to satisfy this need. The case of dichotomous opposition is more difficult and is worth a rather lengthy digression, for this is the most pervasive form of theoretical misogyny, and the one onto which Irigaray focuses her critical attention.

In her paper 'Gender and Dichotomy' (1981), Nancy Jay provides a persuasive account of the oppressive effects of the structure of binary oppositions. She demonstrates that they are as much political weapons as intellectual categories. Jay claims that:

1 The two terms in a dichotomous structure are contradictory, and thus mutually exclusive. There is no possible mediation between them for they are strictly discontinuous.
2 The two terms are also mutually exhaustive — there is no third term, no middle ground between them. There are no other possible terms. The two binary terms cover every situation and possibility (the logicians' 'law of the excluded middle').
3 Within the binary structure, only one term has positive value. The second term is defined as the negation of the first: it is simply the absence or privation of the defining attributes of the first. It is thus not recognised as possessing any characteristics or value of its own.
4 Although the first term is amenable to clear and precise formulation, the negative, secondary term becomes amorphous and includes everything other than the first term (the process in logic known as the 'infinitisation of the negative').

For Jay, the problem with the oppositional structure (which she represents as a relation between A and −A) is that it is frequently represented as if this were a reciprocal relation between two autonomous terms, that is, a relation of *difference* (represented by the relation between A and B), a relation that is neither mutually exhaustive, nor composed of one term and its negation. In logical terms, it is a relation of contrariety, not contradiction.

In spite of her reservations about psychoanalysis and her recognition of its clear privileging of the phallic and the masculine, Kristeva takes Freud's model of psychical functioning as universal. This may be because, alongside of his phallocentrism, Freud also provides a profoundly unsettling critique of the primacy of consciousness through his postulate of the unconscious. The unconscious, that 'other scene' beyond conscious awareness and control, demonstrates the existence of another logic or 'reason', another mode of pleasure and organisation than that which consciousness takes for granted. Using this insight, Irigaray suggests a close resemblance between the unconscious in its relation to consciousness and women in relation to patriarchal social relations. She accepts Freud's identification of the repressed with femininity but goes one step further: if what is repressed is the feminine, she claims, it is possible to regard women, not as *having* an unconscious, but as *being* it (for men, for the phallic, for patriarchy). Freud's concept provides a dazzling metaphor of women's simultaneously repressed/oppressed social position and the permanent possibilities of resistance—the threat the unconscious poses to civilisation in its symptomatic 'return'.

Instead of faithfully adhering to orthodox interpretations of Freud, Irigaray is left free to develop a position cognisant of the details of psychoanalysis yet distant enough from it to develop a critical, independent view. The more problematic elements of Freud's position, for example, the centrality of the oedipal structure, are used by Irigaray as a description and explanation of *male* rather than human sexuality. On the other hand she uses Freud's notion of the unconscious as a metaphor for the *cultural* position of femininity. In short, the whole of Freud's endeavour, which, of course is not readily divisible into these separate components, is subtly displaced by her reading. She could be seen as psychoanalysing psychoanalysis itself, seeking out the repressed or negated elements upon which it has been based, searching for its blindspots and disavowed conditions of existence.

Woman as castrated other

In the face of Freud's phallocentrism, Irigaray's audacious claim is that women are represented only on models that are masculine. We live in a resolutely *homosexual* culture, a culture based on the primacy of the male, the *homme*, who can function only with others modelled on himself, others who are his mirror reflections. The problem with this libidinal structure of masculine desire is that it leaves no space for woman as such. Women can be represented only by means of a violence that contains them, and their differences, within masculine sameness:

> ... *Freud discovers*—*in a blind reversal of repressions*—*certain variously disguised cards that are kept preserved or stored away and that lie beneath the hierarchy of values of the game, of all the games, the desire for the same, for the self-identical, the self (as) same, and again of the similar, the alter-ego, and, to put it in a nutshell, the desire for the auto* ... *the homo* ... *the male, dominates representational economy. 'Sexual difference' is a*

deviation from the problematics of sameness, it is, now and forever, determined within the project, the projection, the sphere of representation, of the same. The 'differentiation' into two sexes derives from the a priori assumption of the same, since the little man that the girl is, must become a man minus certain attributes whose paradigm is morphological — attributes capable of determining, of assuring, the reproduction-specularization of the same. A man minus the possibility of (re)presenting oneself as a man = a normal woman. (Irigaray, 1985a:26–7)

Even the sexual binary polarisation is determined by the logic of sameness: as Irigaray observes, in psychoanalysis the female development is only conceptualised in three ways: in the pre-oedipal period, Freud describes the little girl as a 'little man'; her libido is masculine whether directed to male or female love objects; and her sexuality is 'phallic'. In other words, the pre-oedipal girl is seen as *the same as* or *identical with* the boy. He oedipus complex transforms this fundamental identity or phallic sameness into negation and binary opposition. The girl is confronted with the 'fact' of her castration, her 'lack' of the organ which empowers men, giving the boy active access to the mother and to social sublimation. Her 'castrated' position is correlative with his valorisation as a phallic subject. Her 'lack' creates and confirms his phallic position. She is deprived of the very attribute that grants him a position as an active, desiring, anaclitic subject; consequently, she is relegated to the position of castrated, passive object, who seeks, not (actively) to desire, but (passively) to be desired. Oedipalisation converts her phallic sameness into a logical *opposition*. As a result of the 'resolution' of the female complex, her position becomes *complementary* to the man's attributes. When, and if, she reaches an acceptable, that is, feminine, resolution of the complex, Freud suggests that she develops several specifically 'feminine' characteristics — among them, a recognition and acceptance of her castration; the substitution of the desire for the phallus for the desire for the mother; the transfer of sexual focus from the clitoris to the vagina; the acquisition of the skills of seduction and the traits of narcissism, masochism and exhibitionism — which mesh in apparently complementary harmony with the characteristics of masculinity.

Freud makes a particularly convenient target for Irigaray's critique of philosophical phallocentrism. His model of the oedipus complex, which separates the pre-oedipal, infantile forms of sexuality from their adult forms, encapsulates many ingredients of this conceptual history. Freud is strategically positioned at the point of intersection of a psychological and a philosophical analysis of subjectivity. He thus provides the most innovative psychological explanations and is the culmination point of a patriarchal history of philosophy, the last flowering of an (idealist) history of conceptions of human 'nature'.

In opposition to Freud's containment of women in men's self-reflecting representations, yet, at the same time recognising it as an account of what patriarchy requires of women, Irigaray attempts a feminist deconstruction of psychoanalysis. Her project is both to undo the phallocentric constriction of women as men's others and to create a means by which women's specificity may figure in discourse in autonomous terms. Her challenge revolves around two central themes: that of the cultural debt to maternity, the creation of a means of representing the mother's relations to the child beyond the orbit of the symbolic father's authority; and that of adequately representing and constructing an autonomously conceived female sexuality, corporeality and morphology. Each requires more than a reorganisation and equalisation of socialisation and child-rearing practices (as feminists like Chodorow, Dinnerstein et al. proclaim); they imply a profound and difficult reorganisation of the forms and means of representation—a reorganisation of language itself.

Irigaray aims to break out of the phallogocentric circuit in which women function only as objects (of consumption or exchange) between and for men. In the first instance, this means that representational systems marking women's bodies as lacking, dependent, oriented towards the phallus, etc., need to be problematised. Such systems are incapable of posing women in woman-oriented terms. Irigaray thus seeks out the *residues*, the remains or traces of female eroticism and corporeality which exceed patriarchal representations, those points of recalcitrance or what she has described as the 'blind-spot of an old dream of symmetry' (see Part 1 of *Speculum* ...). They indicate points of 'repression' and sites of symptomatic eruption of femininity which can be exploited in critical feminist analyses of Freud's and other's texts.

Changes in social organisation, in institutional ensembles, in economic and exchange relations as well as in interpersonal, experiential or erotic relations are also required to achieve women's autonomy. But these are unable to attain their goals if language and representational norms are left untransformed:

109

It appears to be impossible, at least in any profound and lasting way, to modify social relations, language, art in general, without modifying the economic system of exchange. They go hand in hand. Sometimes the one predominates, sometimes the other, but changes in both are indispensable for any social mutation. We can neither decide nor hope to liberate ourselves from a given order without changing the forms of that order. The one demands the other. (1986b:12)

She aims, then, to represent woman and femininity *otherwise* than in phallocentric terms. To re- or de-form language, discursive structures and representational systems, she must clear the representational space thus far taken over by patriarchal representations as well as formulate alternatives, discourses and models that can re-occupy that space and accommodate women's specificity. To reconceive of women and femininity in terms independent of men and masculinity requires a major reorganisation of sexual, linguistic and socio-symbolic systems, and indeed of desire itself. More specifically, it requires reconceiving the female body as a positivity rather than a lack.

Language, power and bodies

Irigaray's discussion of the female body and feminine pleasure must always be situated in the context of the prevalent (misogynist) texts in the history of phallocentric representations. She develops a displacing, threatening alternative to their various images of woman. Her strategy is to seek out the blindspots, the points of textual excess that all texts rely on yet disavow. In her understanding, this occurs most commonly where phallocentric discourses pose the question of femininity, female sexuality and the maternal function. Philosophical texts, including psychoanalysis, render themselves vulnerable to deconstructive readings of their notions of femininity.

It must be stressed that her work is not a *true* description of women or femininity, a position that is superior to *false*, patriarchal conceptions (truth, after all, is engaged in precisely the relation of doubles, or mirror reflections that is the hallmark of phallocentrism[6]). Her aim is quite different: it is to devise a *strategic* and combatative understanding, one whose function is to make explicit what has been excluded or left out of phallocentric images. Unlike truth, whose value is eternal, strategy remains provisional;

its relevance and value depend on what it is able to achieve, on its utility in organising means towards ends.

Irigaray posits an *isomorphism* between male sexuality and patriarchal language, an intricate mirroring and entwining of phallocentric discourses and oedipalised forms of male sexuality:

> *All Western discourse presents a certain isomorphism with the masculine sex; the privilege of unity, form of the self, of the visible, of the specularisable, of the erection (which is the becoming in a form). Now this morpho-logic does not correspond to the female sex: there is not 'a' sex. The 'no sex' that has been assigned to the woman can mean that she does not have 'a' sex and that her sex is not visible nor identifiable or representable in a definite form. (1977:64)*

This isomorphism, this correspondence of form or shape between phallocentric representational systems and phallic male sexuality, in spite of what a number of her critics have suggested[7], is not a product of nature, anatomy, a male 'essence' or a neutral, transparent, reflective or 'objective' language. Her concepts of the body and corporeality refer only to a body that is structured, inscribed, constituted and given meaning *socially* and *historically* — a body that exists as such only through its socio-linguistic construction. She renders the concept of a 'pure' or 'natural' body meaningless. Power relations and systems of representations not only traverse the body and utilise its energies (as Kristeva claims) but actively constitute the body's very sensations, pleasures — the phenomenology of bodily experience.

Whether male or female, the human body is thus already coded, placed in a social network, and given meaning in and by culture, the male being constituted as virile or phallic, the female as passive and castrated. These are not the result of biology, but of the *social and psychical meaning of the body*. It is for this reason that Irigaray carefully refers to the *morphology* and not to the anatomy of the body: 'We must go back to the question not of the anatomy but of the morphology of the female sex' (1977:64). The lived body, the experience of corporeality, is a *social* body: but it should not be reduced merely to a sociological phenomenon, the consequences of socialisation and learning. In a rather more complex fashion, systems of language and representation must be internalised, taken on as one's own, in order that speech and language are possible, and that the subject's perceptions and experiences acquire meaning and thus value within its terms. The body is organised and structured as unified, cohesive, controllable through psychical development and is specularisable or representable only through the acquisition of signification.

There is, in short, a parallelism, an isomorphism between patriarchal power relations, the structure of dominant or socially recognised discourses, and the socially produced phallic male body. This isomorphism is not the result of male conspiracy.[8] It is not based on men's *psychological* need to dominate, nor is it an effect of a '*natural*' impulse (whether genetic, hormonal or physiological). Irigaray makes no suggestion of a causal connection between men's bodies and dominant representations, although it is not uncommon to see commentators assert that she directly links patriarchal domination to men's 'natures'.[9] It is not the anatomy of the male body which seeks its own image in dominant discourses. Rather, the pre-existence of patriarchal social relations relies on the *production* of a specific form of male sexuality through internalisation of images representations and signifying practices. In other words, men do not form discourse in their own image(s); rather, phallocentric discourses form male sexuality in their image(s).[10]

In her understanding, languages and discourses do not reflect a pre-existing material reality; they function to actively constitute the world and human experience as meaningful or representable[11], an effect of forces and relations of power. Each relies on and implicates the other. Power and language function not simply through coercion or ideology, but also through the active construction of a meaningful reality. Bestowing significance on 'things', constructing them as things, presenting them as natural, enticing and inciting are among the more insidious effects of the cooperation of discursive and political structures.

Bodies are not conceived by Irigaray as biologically or anatomically given, inert, brute objects, fixed by nature once and for all. She sees them as the bearers of meanings and social values, the products of social inscriptions, always inherently social. *Speculum* ... and *This Sex* ... need to be read in the light of this mutually defining cluster of terms. Her emphasis on morphology in place of anatomy indicates that she has stepped from the register of nature into that of social signification.

Toril Moi, for example, dismisses Irigaray's use of the term with a simple wave of the hand: she simply equates it with anatomy although the only thing she acknowledges about the concept is its difference from anatomy! 'Irigaray's *theory of "woman"* takes as its starting point a basic assumption of analogy between women's psychology and her "morphology" ... which she rather obscurely takes to be different from her anatomy' (Moi, 1985:143).

Moi articulates probably the most common objection to Irigaray's work. *If* morphology is reduced to biology, the charge of *essentialism* seems well justified. *If* men's *biologically given* bodies are isomorphic with the structure of dominant discourses, this becomes simply a 'fact of nature' that must be accepted, not a political move that can be countered. The reduction of morphology to biology occurs only on the crudest of misreadings and a *wilful* ignorance on the part of the critics.[12]

A detailed analysis of Irigaray's images and representations of feminine morphology thus needs to be undertaken, not only because this occupies a central place in her writings, but also because it constitutes the most densely invested and heatedly contested area of her work.

Morphology and anatomy

If psychoanalysis reduces women to an identity or sameness with men — by posing identity, opposition or complementarity as women's only possibilities — one of Irigaray's major concerns is to free the conceptual space left by phallocentric discourses for a more adequate representation of woman. Contrary to Moi's assertion that she aims to develop 'a theory of "woman"', Irigaray's main concerns up to 1979 are largely negative: to place phallocentrism 'on trial', not to oppose it or reject it once and for all (which is in any case both phallocentric and utopian), but to devise a series of tactics which *continually* question phallocentrism, destroying its apparently naturalistic self-evidence and demonstrating the possibility of alternatives. Instead of devising a 'theory' of women's oppression, Irigaray's aim is largely methodological and tactical. Indeed, she refuses either to define woman or to present a theory about women (which she sees as politically problematic insofar as one voice then represents all others in an insidious representationalist politics).

Her deconstruction of phallocentric representations of women and female sexuality relies on psychoanalytic theory to provide both a deconstructive 'tool' and as a major object of her criticisms. Like the Derridean 'double science' of deconstruction, her work is duplicit, double-dealing: she must use the language of prevailing discourses against their explicit pronouncements and claims (see Derrida, 1978). This is a perilous but necessary task, for it thereby risks the reproduction of an unrecognised phallocentrism, insofar as the critique relies on what it criticises; yet it could not be otherwise insofar as there are no non- or anti-phallocentric terms free of patriarchy which could be used in their place. The point is, as Gayatri Spivak observed (1984/5), there is no pure position outside of phallo- or logocentrism. Irigaray thus uses psychoanalysis to criticise itself and other phallocentric texts; and to provide a starting point in the positive construction of other images and representations.

In Freud's work female sexuality is conceived in one of two ways: when he describes the pre-oedipal girl, he presumes a clitoral (that is, phallic) form of sexuality; and, as the consequence of her oedipus complex, the girl converts her active sexual aims into passive ones, transferring sexual intensity from the clitoris to the 'female organ proper', the vagina. Like Kinsey, and Masters and Johnson, Freud sees female sexuality in disjunctive terms. In defining it, he assumes it is either clitoral or vaginal. But, as Irigaray argues, it is just as misleading to valorise the clitoris as the 'real' or true source of female sexual excitement and the site of women's sexual liberation from patriarchy, as a number of feminists have, as it is to valorise the vagina.

Both clitoral and vaginal models are phallocentric. They privilege a phallic, masculine model of sexuality. For example, clitoral conceptions of female sexuality consider the clitoris homologous to the penis, 'only smaller'. The vaginal conception, while not *similar* to male sexuality, is the complement to the penis, its 'completion' and harmonious counterpart, always defined with respect to the primacy of his organ, not in its own terms:

> *Female sexuality has always been conceptualised on the basis of masculine parameters. Thus the opposition between 'masculine' clitoral activity and 'feminine' vaginal passivity, an opposition which Freud—and many others—saw as stages, or alternatives, in the development of a sexually 'normal' woman, seems rather too clearly required by the practice of male sexuality. For the clitoris is conceived as a little penis ... and the vagina is valued for the 'lodging' it offers the male organ.*
> *In these terms, woman's erogenous zones never amount to anything but a clitoris-sex that is not comparable to the noble phallic organ, or a hole-envelope that serves to sheathe and massage the penis in intercourse: a non-sex or a masculine organ turned back upon itself, self-embracing. (1985b:23)*

Both conceptions conform to the logic of male identity, as analogue of male sexuality, as its opposite or complement. The question for which these are 'answers', 'where is female sexuality to be located?', already posits women in male terms. Indeed, that it is a question of speculation, debate and controversy at all signifies the degree of mystification surrounding female pleasure considered in its own terms. The question implies an answer specifying *one* place, one pleasure and one sexual organ between which women (and male experts) are to choose. Whatever alternative is chosen, the other term is relegated to the position of 'secondary' sexual organ, part of 'foreplay', preliminary to 'real' sexual, that is, genital, copulative relations (a phallocentric notion if ever there were one!).

If Irigaray's concept of female pleasure is based on Freud's account of pre-oedipal polymorphous sexuality, she diverges from his presumption that it is a masculine phase for both sexes. As Freud himself noted, the girl remains in contiguity with the pre-oedipal period in ways that are barred for boys. For boys, there is a singular and momentous break with the pre-oedipal and the maternal. The boy's first acts of repression must definitively separate him from the mother. In the case of the girl, there is no clear-cut division between the pre-oedipal and the oedipal; she occupies an oedipalised position only gradually and unsurely. Her oedipal complex may persist indefinitely or fade because of disappointments, rather than end through a dramatic repression. She thus remains *in touch* with the pre-oedipal maternal continent, even if she can express her maternal attachments only through her relation to the father, and later through father substitutes.

For Irigaray, feminine pleasure is not singular, unified, hierarchically subordinated to a single organ, definable or locatable according to the logic of identity. This is consistent with Freud's position, although he himself is not so explicit. It is neither vaginal nor clitoral but *more*. It is *both*, not because there are two identities which can be added together, but insofar as its identity is undecidably one and two. Irigaray constructs an image or model to represent female sexuality which indicates the phallocentrism invested in both clitoral and vaginal alternatives. Her image stresses the multiplicity, ambiguity, fluidity, and excessiveness, of female sexuality; it evokes a remainder or residue of *jouissance* left unrepresented in a phallic libidinal economy.

Female sexuality could be positively represented by the metaphor of the 'two lips'. The two lips are never one, nor strictly two. They are one and two *simultaneously*: where one identity ends and another begins is never clear. (The idea of 'one lip' seems absurd!) This image defies binary categories and forms of classification, being undecidably inside and outside, one and two, genital and oral.[13]

This image, it must again be stressed, is in no way a 'true' or accurate description of women. Its function is not referential but combatative: it is an image to contest and counter dominant, phallomorphic representations. Its purpose is to reveal the implicit assumptions, and the sexual positions constituted and affirmed in dominant representations, and to ease their hold over the terrain, so that different representations may be possible. It does not designate a female essence or anatomy but subverts the dominant male conceptions of women's essence:

> *So woman does not have a sex organ? She has at least two of them, but they are not identifiable as ones. Indeed, she has many more. Her sexuality, always at least double, goes even further, it is plural ... Indeed, woman's pleasure does not have to choose between clitoral activity and vaginal passivity, for example. The pleasure of the vaginal caress does not have to be substituted for that of the clitoral caress. They each contribute irreplaceably, to women's pleasure. (1985b:28)*

The 'two lips' is not a truthful image of female anatomy but a new emblem by which female sexuality can be positively *represented*. For Irigaray, the problem for women is not the experience or recognition of female pleasure, but its representation, which actively constructs women's experience of their corporeality and pleasures. If female sexuality and desire are represented in some relation to male sexuality, they are submerged in a series of male-defined constraints.

Contrary to the objection that she is describing an essential, natural or innate femininity, unearthing it from under its patriarchal burial[14], Irigaray's project can be interpreted as a contestation of patriarchal representations *at the level of cultural representation itself*. The two lips is a manoeuvre to develop a *different* image or model of female sexuality, one which may inscribe female bodies according to interests outside or beyond phallocentrism, while at the same time contesting the representational terrain that phallocentrism has hitherto annexed. This image reveals the interests — normally hidden under the claim to 'neutrality' — of phallocentric systems in upholding masculine privilege: it demonstrates the unnaturalness, the political motivations, lying submerged in prevailing definitions of femininity. It accords women activity, satisfaction, and a corporeal self-sufficiency usually denied them in heterosexist cultures. It presents women as both active *and* passive, able to find pleasure in intercourse with men or making love with women (or in masturbation or celibacy) according to their desire. Irigaray's metaphor makes clear the limited alternatives that the clitoral/vaginal debate imposes on women's pleasure. The 'two lips' is an indecidable image that is both genital and extragenitally polymorphous.

She has produced a powerful metaphor for women's potentially excessive pleasures to hold up against the confining representations granted them in dominant discourses. As strategic, it makes no claim to eternal, transhistorical or transgeographical truth (which, of course, is not to say that it is false either — it is neither true nor false, for it is not within the realm of truth at all). Her purpose is to displace male models, rather than to accurately reflect what female sexuality *really* is. In other words, her writing always refers to other texts or discourses, not to a non-discursive or 'real' corporeality, experience or pleasure. It is an *active*, creative coding or inscription, a positive marking of women's bodies, which may produce a female body whose sexuality is lived in other, different terms than the limiting possibilities available to women in patriarchy.

In her understanding, patriarchal knowledges represent (male) sexuality by a solidity, stability and identity congruent with the kind of identity constructed for the boy by his oedipus complex. Her aim is to reveal the *fluidity*, the polymorphous multiplicity of the pre-oedipal which underlies and precedes it. This is not a nostalgic celebration of a lost, irretrievable past, nor the romantic utopian desire for a polymorphous, 'liberated' future — for it is neither a memory of the past nor a blueprint for the future. On the contrary, Irigaray aims to insert this polymorphous fluidity into synchronic, adult forms of sexuality. Phallic genitality is and always remains tenuous insofar as it relies on the repression of the pre-oedipal yet must, as Kristeva claims, utilise its energies. Because repression banishes and yet preserves what it expels, the repressed is liable to return through its re-evocation in current, often chance or contingent events which recall it and may act as catalyst for the emergence of symptoms. The fluidity of pre-oedipal maternal pleasures is *always already there* in any adult sexual pleasure (men's as well as women's).

The self-understanding of male sexuality is based on a 'mechanics of solids'. This metaphor enables her to evoke an alternative 'mechanics' capable of characterising female sexuality. It also provides a metaphor of women's containment in phallocentric models. The solidity sought by masculinity is the result of congealing a feminine fluidity. The fluid has no given form on its own but it can, of course, be given a form: when placed within a constricted space, it takes on the shape of that space. Fluids have the capacity to mingle with other fluids without clear-cut boundaries or distinctions (a striking metaphor of the mother–daughter relationship):

One must know how to listen otherwise than in good form(s) to hear what it says. That it is continuous, compressible, dilatable, viscous, conductible, diffusible ... that it allows itself to be easily traversed by flow by virtue of its conductivity to currents coming from other fluids or exerting pressure through the walls of a solid; that it mixes with bodies of a like state, sometimes dilutes itself in them in an almost homogeneous manner, which makes the distinction between one and the other problematical and furthermore that it is already diffuse 'in itself', which disconcerts any attempt at static identification. (1985b:111)

Not having *one* identity, *one* location, *one* organ or *one* orgasm, female sexuality has been understood as *no* identity or sexuality. Irigaray accepts the phallocentric image of woman as 'not one' but reverses its meaning: if woman is 'not one', she is *more than* one. The two lips, fluidity, are a plenitude, a form of auto-erotic self-containment. They require nothing external to be satisfied. The penis *may* be the object of women's desire but need not be. The forcible entry of the unwanted penis is clearly a violation, in action and/or representation. Lips can be opened or closed. Opened lips embrace, take in.

Male sexuality is itself not *inherently* violent or aggressive either: the process of oedipalisation produces male bodies as virile, phallic, active and aggressive, and restricts male pleasures to a singular, goal-directed, genital and orgasmic form. The price paid for his identification with the phallus is the abandonment of his corporeality:

In the system of production that we know, including sexual production, men have distanced themselves from their bodies. They have used their sex, their language, their technique, in order to go further and further in the construction of a world which is more and more distant from their relation to the corporeal. But they are corporeal. It is necessary therefore for them to reassure themselves that someone [a woman] is indeed the guardian of their body for them. (1981a:83–4)

Men must renounce a certain hierarchical mastery, control and propriety over their bodies in order to remain in contiguity with their possibilities of pleasure. This involves the decentralisation of the phallus, the exploration of the body's other zones and the encounter or confrontation with an otherness that is acknowledged as other. There must be room in the sexual relation for women, and not just men's fantasies of a femininity that conforms to their (oedipal) needs. There must be a space for women *as* woman. And in turn, for Irigaray, this implies a renegotiation of the mother–daughter relationship, for until the mother can be seen as a woman, the daughter does not have the basis for a feminine identity.

Mother–daughter relations and the genealogy of women

In Freud's understanding, the girl's oedipus complex must ensure that she relinquishes her primary libidinal attachment to the mother in order eventually to take her father as love object. Her passive yet amorous, seductive relation to him inherits the structure of her prior maternal attachment, and is itself the mediating or transitional phase between (homosexual) maternal attachment and non-incestual heterosexual attachment. Although she must abandon the mother, the girl must retain an identification with her in order to acquire the appropriate feminine attributes. The daughter, however, must abandon not the woman-in-the-mother but a *phallic mother*. And later, she must identify with the *castrated mother*, the powerless mother who has submitted to and acts as a representative of the symbolic father. Her alternatives are thus to love a (phallic, masculine) mother or to identify with a (castrated, powerless) mother. Neither provide the girl with an adequate basis for autonomous identity.

Central to Irigaray's concerns is a re-exploration of the prevailing images of the mother–daughter relation and the construction of different, positive models. Prerequisite to the attainment of an autonomous position (if not identity) as a woman is the represen-tation of woman as, and beyond, her maternal function. This may also provide the basis of *a genealogy of women*, a history of maternal connections and relations that have been effaced in the functioning of the patronym. Her project involves reconceptualising the woman which any mother is, and reclaiming for her a history and context that have been covered over and destroyed by her burial in maternity. Maternity has functioned to elide the specifi-city of women's identities and social positions by equating femi-ninity always and only with reproduction and nurturance.

This is not to claim, along with de Beauvoir or Firestone, that women must free themselves of maternity; rather, it is the assertion that even (and especially) for those women who are mothers, the maternal function must be prevented from strangling their existence as women. She shows that being a woman is always excessive to maternity. The woman in all mothers, a woman not reduced to the preservation and care of others, must be conceived if women are to assert their particularity. Freud presumes a masculinised model of the oedipal triangle, in which the child is male and the mother is construed in masculine terms (either as phallic or as castrated). In Irigaray's view, this means that the child does not have an adequate understanding of the *two* sexes, for it only has experience of two variations of the one sex. Women are reduced to being only a mother:

> It is indispensable that the child, girl or boy, have a represen-
> tation of the *two sexes* ... But in the traditional conception of
> the family in fact, he or she doesn't have this. Because if the
> mother is uniquely mother, the child has no image of woman,
> and thus of sexual difference. (1979a:44)

Unlike earlier feminists, for Irigaray there is no disjunction between maternity and feminism, or maternity and politics (see de Beauvoir, 1972:705). They are not mutually exclusive choices women must make. Motherhood itself must be reconceptualised so that it can be seen as pre-eminently political. For Irigaray, women's containment in maternity must be rethought, even for those women who are not mothers. Their relations to their own mothers must no longer be seen in terms of the old rivalries dividing women.

If the child's pre-oedipal relation with the mother is 'the dark continent' of psychoanalysis, then the mother–daughter relation must be 'the dark continent of the dark continent, the most obscure area of our social order' (see 1979b). Shedding some light on this dark cultural space would then pose a threat to the social order which so resolutely ignores the debt that children, men and culture in general owe to the maternal.

For example, the son is unable to accept the debt of life, body, nourishment and social existence he owes the mother. An entire history of Western thought is intent on substituting for this debt an image of the self-made, self-created man. One could go even further and suggest that the idea of God itself is nothing but an elaborate if unconscious strategy for alleviating man's consciousness of and guilt about this debt. As man's self-reflecting Other, God usurps women's creativity and their place as the source of the terrestial. God (and through Him, man) becomes the creator or mother of the mother.

Born of woman's body, man devises religion, philosophy and true knowledges not simply as sublimations of his desire, but as forms of disavowal of this maternal debt:

> ... *in order to become men, they continue to consume ... [the mother], draw on her resources and, at the same time, they deny her or disclaim her in their identification with and their belonging to the masculine world. They owed their existence, their body, life and they forget or misrecognise this debt in order to set themselves up as powerful men, adults busying themselves with public affairs ... (1979a:44)*

The restriction of women to a phallocentrically constrained maternity is crippling for both mother and daughter. For the mother, it implies the severe limitation on her possibilities of self-definition and autonomy, her subjection to the Law of the Father, her subsumption under the patronym, her renunciation of an identity as a woman and a sexual being. As the silent unrecognised support — the 'mute substratum' — of culture, she must remain unacknowledged, confined to a predesignated reproductive function. As mother, her material and economic possibilities are severely limited. Cut off from social and sexual recognition, she becomes either the mother who gives *too much* of herself (the suffocating mother, represented in Woody Allen's film *Interiors*); or the mother who gives *too little* (the selfish mother represented in Ingmar Bergman's *Autumn Sonata*). These represent the two extremes of maternity in a culture which refuses to acknowledge the woman who is (and is more than) the mother.

With no access to social value in her own right, she becomes the mother who has only food (that is, love[15]) to give the child. Unable to give the child language, law and exchange — the phallus — she has only nurturance, and its most tangible manifestations — eating, defaecating — through which she may gain social recognition and value. She risks choking or smothering the child with an excess that fills it to the point of freezing, or leaves it starving for more. This love is powerfully articulated in Irigaray's short text *Et l'une ne bouge pas sans l'autre* (1981b), where she outlines the paralysis and suffocation the child experiences in being over-nurtured. She describes a suffocating maternal bond which it must sooner or later attempt to flee in order to have any identity.

Irigaray uses as her 'textual' reference the Italian film *Maternale*, in which the polio-stricken daughter is fed, nurtured and over-protected by a mother who finds her only satisfaction and identity in mothering and taking care of her daughter. Inevitably, when the daughter turns from her mother to her father, rejecting her mother's food in the process, the mother finds herself in the dependent position:

> *You have made me something to eat. You bring me something to eat. But you give yourself too much, as if you wanted to fill me all up with what you bring me. You put yourself into my mouth and I suffocate. Put less of yourself in me and let me look at you. I'd like to see you while you are feeding me. Not to lose my/your sight when I open my mouth to you. And that you should still remain close to me while I am drinking you. But continue to be on the outside, as well. Keep yourself, and keep me just as outside, too. Do not swallow yourself up, do not swallow me down in that which flows from you to me. I'd like it so much if we could be there, both of us. So that one does not disappear into the other, or the other into the one. (1981b:11)*

It is not the mother's *lack*, her castration, as Freud implies, which produces a constricted mothering, in which the child is equivalent to the mother's phallus, but an excess or plenitude of love that can find no other form of expression than through tending the child. This excessive generosity defines the 'good' mother, and its negative counterpart is the 'bad' mother, the mother who never gives enough, who keeps the child clamouring for more (love/food/attention/desire). This is not an effect of nature nor is it a social necessity but is the result of women's submersion in maternity and thus her eclipse as woman. It is an effect of a social organisation which induces guilt in those women-mothers who assert themselves as women, as autonomous, sexual beings, independent of the child or its father:

> *More of us have suffered from over-protection by our mothers which paralysed them, as their own mothers were already. Because this investment corresponds to a guilty and prescribed motherhood, abstract function whose power is then without limits ... Whence the threatening fantasms attached to the maternal function. The fear of being engulfed by an abyss, of sinking into darkness. (1979b:12)*

Maternity under patriarchy curtails the mother's ability to act as a woman. It also implies an 'exile' for the daughter, for she is cut off from access to the woman-mother; and thus from her own potential as a woman. She has no *woman* with whom to identify. She can take on the socially validated place as a mother herself only by replacing her mother, by 'killing' her: 'Women are torn from their first desires, their sexuality. And they never find a substitute for the mother, except by taking her place. By suppressing her to take her place' (1979a:43).

The girl must renounce her earliest maternal, homosexual attachments in order to be initiated into the symbolic order, to take up a place in relations of sexual exchange between men. Her (pre)history is erased, and her primal relations to the love object, and thus to her own sex, are renounced. This is an exile from the maternal continent: 'A woman, if she cannot in one way or another, recuperate her first object, that is the possibility of keeping her earliest libidinal attachments by displacing them, is always exiled from herself' (1977:76).

Irigaray does not contest the accuracy of Freud's model (for it *is* relevant to the ways our culture functions), but its necessity. It leaves no space for restructured relations between women, or for reinventing a body-to-body and a woman-to-woman relation with the mother.

Among the strategies Irigaray harnesses in attempting to displace the father's central place in the oedipal triangle is her call to establish an impossible yet necessary genealogy of women, a history that has been thus far rendered invisible by the burial of women under the patronym and within a patrilocation: 'Withdrawn into proper names, violated by them. Not yours, not mine. We don't have any. We change names as men exchange us, as they use us, use us up' (1985b:205).

The project of (re-)creating a lost past does not simply consist in excavating those women 'forgotten' in history (a project which may leave the phallocentric presumptions of traditional historical research intact where women are simply added to the list of men's historical events); nor is the reorganisation of one academic discipline — history — sufficient to engender such a genealogy. To be able to trace a female genealogy of descent entails new kinds of language, new systems of nomenclature, new relations of social and economic exchange — in other words, a complete reorganisation of the social order. If the woman's maternal genealogy is made difficult by the covering of woman's 'family' name with her husband's, it is made impossible by a history of representations and knowledges surrounding women's 'nature', social roles, function in the divine order, etc. Irigaray's desire, her wish, for such a genealogy is not an announcement of her future work, but a paradoxical and impossible call. In revealing this lack, this impossibility, she makes explicit the ways in which maternity is ignored and actively effaced in culture.

A genealogy of women is made impossible not only because the mother bears the father's name, but also because, even if she retained her (father's) name, the woman who is the mother (let alone the woman who is not) is made invisible. At best, a genealogy of *mothers*, not women, could be created.

If Irigaray suggests the tactic of a genealogical exploration of women's histories and interconnections through different generations as a means of loosening the bonds linking women — mothers and daughters — to the father's domination, she also poses a second tactic for acknowledging the autonomy of women in relation to, and beyond, men. She makes explicit the ways in which not only the father and husband exploit from and profit by the mother's burial in maternity, but also how the daughter is implicated in the reproduction of patriarchy. In this respect, Irigaray suggests that it may be necessary for the daughter to give up the mother as haven, refuge and shelter. In exchange for this apparent loss, the daughter may, for the first time, be able to relate to the mother as a woman.

This clearly involves a loss for both of them, insofar as maternity is one of the few socially and interpersonally legitimated functions women are granted; and one of the few sites where women have some respite from the circuits of sexual, political and social exchange. The mother must abandon maternity insofar as it suffocates her possibilities as a woman. The daughter must abandon her sheltered protection by the all-powerful mother, a phallic mother who is bound to disappoint her, in order to see the mother — and thus herself as well — as a woman. These amount to a real loss for both if the mother–daughter relation is transformed without accompanying social upheavals in the workforce and in the structure of the nuclear family. But this transformation in the mother–daughter relation also implies a rejuvenation, a rediscovery of the identities mother and daughter share which may enable the daughter — and the mother — to resist the circuits of patriarchal exchange within which they function as objects. Instead of being the objects exchanged between one man and another, Irigaray advocates the two women taking on an active subject-to-subject relation. It is for this reason that she suggests the mother must give the daughter more than food to nourish her, she may also give her words with which to speak and hear. The gift of language in place of the suffocation and silence imposed by food. This gift of words will always be reciprocated as food can never be: it is 'returned' to the mother 'with interest', in the daughter's new-found ability to speak *to*, rather than *at* her mother:

> *to talk to one's mother as a woman presupposes giving up the idea of maternal omnipotence ... To accept that one's mother is not all protective, the ultimate amorous recourse, the refuge against abandonment. Which then allows us to establish with her ties of reciprocity, where she could eventually also feel herself to be my daughter. (1979b:13)*

Restructuring the mother–daughter relation, then, means that the fantasy of the *phallic mother*, the fantasy of a mother capable of satisfying all needs, is given up; and that the mother ceases to be buried under and represented by the father's or husband's name and place. It requires a new mode of language, in which both mother and daughter can be represented as self-referential subjects and not merely as exchangeable objects for men. And it means a reorganisation of desire itself, so that the lost object that founds desire — the object whose loss begins the chain of substitute metonymic objects of desire — need not be given up or lost. Identity need not be seen as definitive separation of the mother and child; the loss of the mother implies the daughter's loss of self-representations.

In turn, these imply the rejection of rigid dichotomous characterisations of the two sexes, and the corresponding oppositions between subject and object, self and other, inside and outside, active and passive. Unlike the object-relations orientation so common in American feminist theory, Irigaray's aim is not to ensure the attainment of an identity for the daughter or son independent of the mother, nor does she maintain the symbiotic closeness between them. She explores an undecidable fusion with and differentiation from the mother which defies patriarchal logic.

Such a possibility is lyrically evoked in the concluding chapter of *This Sex ...*, 'When Our Lips Speak Together'. Here Irigaray provides the first articulations of a different relation between mother and daughter, a relation superceding the paralysing symbiosis and abandonment she evoked in 'And One Does Not Move Without the Other'. She announces a new relation in which the identities of mother and daughter defy the binary polarisations and oppositions patriarchy demands and the separation between one woman and another. Irigaray speaks ambiguously as both mother and daughter. She does not write in the singular first person ('I'), nor address a second person ('you'), but speaks as an indistinguishable I/you: a 'we'. The 'we' here does not subsume or merge one identity with another but fuses them without residue or loss to either. They share both speech and pleasure, both textual and sexual rhythms. They can now take up a discursive and sexual space without need of men's mediation. This is a space of exchange without debt, without loss, without guilt, a space women can inhabit without giving up part of themselves.

Discourse and domination

To acknowledge the existence of the two sexes requires a major reorganisation of conceptual, linguistic and value systems. While it clearly also depends on antisexist revisions (for example, equal pay, abortion/contraception, etc.), it requires a thorough reworking of systems of meaning which ensure that, even if the two sexes behave in identical ways, their behaviour does not have the same meaning. Recognising feminine specificity implies seeing and developing other kinds of discourse, different forms of evaluation and new procedures for living in and reflecting on day-to-day life.

At stake for Irigaray are not simply words needed to name female specificity but, more seriously (for a thing does not need a name to be representable), new structures of knowledges, truths and scientificity which authorise and validate different discourses. Femininity cannot simply be added to existing discursive frameworks for there is no space for such an addition. Different ways of knowing, different kinds of discourse, new methods and aspirations for language and knowledges need to be explored if women are to overcome their restrictive containment in patriarchal representations:

> *When women want to escape from exploitation, they do not simply destroy a few 'prejudices'; they upset the whole set of dominant values — economic, social, moral, sexual. They challenge every theory, every thought, every existing language in that these are monopolised by men only. They question the* very foundation of our social and cultural order, *the organisation of which has been prescribed by the patriarchal system. (1977:68)*

Patriarchy does not prevent women from speaking; it refuses to listen when women do not speak 'universal', that is, as men. Women take up a place in the symbolic order only as variants of men. In Freud's understanding, women can take up a post-oedipal or symbolic position only in one of two ways: they can identify with men, acting and speaking as if there were no difference, in which case they suffer from what Freud calls the 'masculinity complex'; or they can accept their 'castration' and their 'inferiority' to men, and accept a symbolic position only through the mediation of men. Both positions are phallocentric. For Irigaray, women's autonomy implies women's right to speak, and listen, *as women*.

Contrary to popular misconceptions of her work, Irigaray does not aim to establish *a new language* for women but to utilise the existing language system to subvert the functioning of dominant representations and knowledges in their singular, universal claims to truth. She aims excessively to overburden existing forms of language and dominant discourses with their own ambiguities, the affirmations they unconsciously make, the materiality they refuse to acknowledge — in other words, the processes of their production (including the sexually coded positions of enunciation[16]). She affirms and makes explicit what lies dormant in these discourses, which, at the very least, must disavow the sexualised positions from which they are produced.

Rather than the singularity, monologism and univocity of masculine self-images, Irigaray advocates undoing their self-evidence. This is not because she believes that the feminine *is* plural, multiple, ambiguous, per se. As the terms repressed in order for their binary opposites to be validated, these terms occupy the position of passivity and dependence in the same way as femininity does in relation to masculinity. Not only do these terms serve as an historical *analogy* with women's subordination, they are instrumental in providing whatever associations culturally code femininity and masculinity:

> *Speak, all the same. It's our good fortune that your language isn't formed of a single thread, a single strand or pattern. It comes from everywhere at once. You touched me all over at the same time. In all senses. Why only one song, one speech, one text at a time? To seduce, to satisfy, to fill one of my 'holes'? With you, I don't have any. We are not lacks, voids, awaiting sustenance, plenitude, fulfillment from the other ... (1985b:209)*

Her texts not only demand but also enact the overflow of meaning, structure, argument, putting phallocentric oneness into question. To speak with a multiplicity of meanings precisely within those disciplines which require precision, clarity, a single line of argument, the 'translatability' of concepts independent of their materiality, formalisability, truth functions and so on, reveals what must be repressed and unspoken in phallocentric discourses:

that there is always a *different way of proceeding*, other kinds of knowledge possible, and no singular, uncontestable position un-approachable from other directions. If knowledges and discourses thus far valorised in our culture are isomorphic with male sexu-ality, her aim is to create the conditions necessary for discourses isomorphic with female pleasures and corporeality:

> *If we don't invent a language, if we don't find our body's language, it will have too few gestures to accompany our story. We shall tire of the same ones, and leave our desires unexpress-ed, unrealized. Asleep again, unsatisfied, we shall fall back upon the words of men — who, for their part, have 'known' for a long time. But not our body. Seduced, attracted, fascinated, ecstatic with our becoming, we shall remain paralyzed. Deprived of our movements. Rigid, whereas we are made for endless change. Without leaps or falls, and without repetition. (1985b:214)*

She challenges the apparent neutrality and universality of know-ledges, claiming that this 'universality' is possible only by ignoring the specificity of particular groups (women, homosexuals, children), and by disavowing its own masculinity. Irigaray raises the question of enunciation — of who speaks for whom, from what positions and with what interests. Philosophers, psychoanalysts, theorists, male 'experts' have long spoken of and for women. Women and femininity are the objects of their various (sometimes aggressive, sometimes chivalrous) speculations, a source of metaphors and images, a motivation for intellectual production denied access in their own terms to a speaking position, the position of the 'I', the position of theoretical production: 'A language which presents itself as universal, and which is in fact produced by men only, is this not what maintains the alienation and exploitation of women in and by society?' (1977:67).

The masculine domination of the right to speak on behalf of the feminine is an effect of its capacity to achieve a certain distance from its objects of analysis. The masculine is able to speak of and for women because it has emptied itself of any relation to the male body, thus creating a space of reflection, of specul(aris)ation in which it claims to look at itself and at femininity from outside. This presumed 'outsideness' is equated with objectivity.

This conceptual and self-reflective space is precisely what is required for the creation of *metalanguage* and *metatheory*, a space of hierarchised reflection. Metalanguage is the consequence of a distinction between discourses and discourses *about* discourses.

Metalanguage is language used to talk about language itself. This opposition presumes (and creates) a separation between a self-contained language (the object-language), and a parasitic language, dependent on the other for its content and object (metalanguage).

The distinction between these two levels of language functions to order, unify, judge and correct the ways that language is able to generate paradoxes, to position and use each term in its proper place. It is a tool for controlling and purifying language use. While metalanguage is able to analyse and reflect on its object-language, however, it is incapable of *self-reflection* without recourse to meta-metalanguage, which, in its turn is incapable of self-reflection *ad infinitum*.

Metalanguage imposes clear-cut boundaries and limits on the otherwise potentially disarrayed field of the object-language. It categorises the object-language as a self-contained, cohesive totality. Metalanguage effectively seals itself off from the impure contamination of the object-language's murky ambiguities, ambiguities which lead to logical *aporia*, paradoxes and contradictions.

This metalingual confinement of terms, procedures for restricting the meaning and hierarchising the forms of language, Irigaray suggests, is isomorphic with male sexuality, and alien to a femininity defined as other than the masculine:

> *a feminine language would undo the unique meaning, the proper meaning of words, of nouns: which still regulates all discourse. In order for there to be a proper meaning, there must indeed be a unity somewhere. But if feminine language cannot be brought back to any unity, it cannot be simply described or defined: there is no feminine meta-language. The masculine can partly look at itself, speculate about itself, represent itself and describe itself for what it is, whilst the feminine can try to speak to itself through a new language, but cannot describe itself from outside or in formal terms, except by identifying itself with the masculine, thus by losing itself. (1977:65)*

A discourse that considers language capable of logical formalisation, of 'translation' into unambiguous terms, wishes to limit the free play of terms in order that only one meaning is possible. This discourse disavows its own (discursive) materiality. Like oedipalised male sexuality, it is a language that represses the plural pleasures/meanings of the whole body/text, to invest them in a single meaning/organ/pleasure. This is a language reduced to the expression of pre-existing, non-linguistic 'ideas'. This is a language reduced to the role of a communicational tool, whose purpose is the transmission of ideas from one subject to another. It has become a language without pleasure or play, without *différance*. Discourses, especially truthful ones, are unable to admit their reliance on an active, inscribing language, one which produces rather than reflects 'reality' or 'ideas' — that is, a language which introduces an uncontrollable, arational principle into every discourse.

Textual practices like poetry, which aim to explore and play with the undecidability of language, are socially tolerable when they remain sharply divided from other modes of (true, scientific, serious) discourse. When poetry is separated from either prose on the one hand, and non-fiction or theory on the other, the self-image of phallocentric knowledges is preserved. It is only when the poetic text threatens to insert itself into the very heart of 'serious' theoretical writings, blurring the borders between poetry, fiction and knowledge, that discourses more amenable to the positive inscription of the female body may be established and explored. By raising the question of the poetic or repressed elements of philosophical and theoretical writings, Irigaray challenges phallocentric self-images of the natural divisions between texts; and at the same time, given that the divisions between them are phallocentric, she helps establish a space for alternative discourses and representations.

In demonstrating that there are other possibilities (of sexuality/ textuality or pleasure/production), Irigaray makes clear the violent appropriation by masculine representational and libidinal economies of a richly heterogenous field of possibilities. A language that is isomorphic with an autonomous, non-reductive femininity and pleasure would have to overcome the domination and universalisation of the masculine.

As a metaphor of the threatening, transgressive potential of a self-defined femininity, Irigaray evokes Lacan's account of the mirror phase. Her claim, in brief, is that Lacan's model of the genesis of the ego provides not a universal or human phenomenon, one preceding sexual difference; for her, the mirror reflects only an image placed in front of it: the (implicitly) masculine being. The specular relation is thus composed of man and his self-reflecting other, an image of himself that he takes to be his other, woman. This speculative mirror in which *his* world, his experiences, his position(s) are projected onto the other must be traversed in order to clear a space for women's self-representations, for women to become the subjects looking.

This may explain Irigaray's attraction to Alice, the character in

Lewis Carroll's *Through the Looking-Glass* and *Alice in Wonder-land*. She acts as metaphor for the woman who, like Irigaray (herself an A-Luce), steps beyond her role as the reflective other for man. She goes *through* the looking-glass, through, that is, the dichotomous structures of knowledge, the binary polarisations in which only man's primacy is reflected. On the other side is a land of wonder, a land that can be mapped, not by the flat mirror, but by the curved speculum:

> *That 'elsewhere' of feminine pleasure can be found only at the price of crossing back through the mirror that subtends all speculation. For this pleasure is not simply situated in a process of reflection or mimesis, nor on the one side of this process or the other: neither on the near side, the empirical realm that is opaque of all languages, nor on the far side, the self-sufficient infinite of the God of men. Instead, it refers all these categories and ruptures back to the necessities of the self-representation of phallic desire ... It is not a matter of interpreting in discourse ... the operation of discourses while remaining within the same type of utterance as the one that guarantees discursive coherence ... For to speak of or about woman may always boil down to or be understood as, a recuperation of the feminine within a logic that maintains it in repression, censorship and non-recognition.*
>
> *In other words, the issue is not one of elaborating a new theory of which woman would be the* subject *or the* object, *but to jam the theoretical machinery itself, of suspending its pretension to the production of a truth and a meaning that are excessively univocal. Which presumes that women do not aspire simply to be men's equals in knowledge ... (1985b:77–8)*

Irigaray refuses to speculate on what a feminine form of language would be (this involves speaking for other women, and thus engaging in a phallocentric politics of representation). Yet she can specify what it could or should *not* be: if it is to displace phallocentric domination, it can no longer function as the sole or singular representative of truth, a perspectiveless position, one meaning, hierarchical organisation, the normative privilege of the subject-predicate form, the syllogistic structure of arguments, the belief in the translatability of concepts — for these rely on the self-distance, denial of materiality and excess concordant with the privileging of male sexuality:

> *How then does one try to define this working of language which would leave a place for the female? Let us say that every*

*dichotomising — and at the same time redoubling — break in-
cluding the one between enunciation and utterance, has to be
disrupted. Nothing is ever to be posited that is not also reversed
and caught up again in the supplementarity of this reversal ...
Linear reading is no longer possible: that is, the retroactive
impact of the end of each word, utterance or sentence upon its
beginning must be taken into consideration in order to undo the
power of its teleological effect, including its deferred action.
(1985b:79–80)*

To speak as woman means to undo the reign of the 'proper' —
the proper name, property, propriety, self-proximity. It means to
evoke rather than designate, to overflow and exceed all boundaries
and oppositions. It involves speaking from a position in the middle
of the binaries (the so-called position of the 'excluded middle'),
affirming both poles while undoing their polarisation. To speak
with meanings that resonate, that are tactile and corporeal as well
as conceptual, that reverberate in their plurality and polyvocity.

This is congruent with and a necessary condition for women's
attainment of self-determined pleasures, a self-defined position, a
position from which to speak and write as women. Through the
creation of new pleasures, new representational systems, new
knowledges, women's identities may be constructed in different
ways which do not cast out or denigrate maternity or femininity.
In itself, this is not possible unless accompanied by major discursive upheavals:

*Between our lips, yours and mine, several voices, several ways of
speaking resound endlessly, back forth. One is never separable
from the other. I/you: we are always several at once. And how
could one dominate the other? impose her voice, her tone, her
meaning? One cannot be distinguished from the other; which
does not mean that they are indistinct ... (1985b:209)*

Hysteria and mimesis

If women are defined according to masculine interests, given no
place as active, self-defined subjects and no language to speak
their specificity, then how is change possible? If the alternatives
offered to women in psychical development are conformity with
patriarchal law (the position as castrated, passive object) or identification with masculinity and refusal to accept differences between the sexes (the 'masculinity complex'), it is difficult to see

what resources women might have at their disposal to articulate, let alone satisfy, their needs and interests, or to introduce positive changes to social and linguistic frameworks. Within patriarchal cultures and representational systems there is no space and few resources women may utilise in order to speak, desire and create *as women*. For this reason women must become familiar with the patriarchal discourses, knowledges and social practices which define and constrain them: these provide the only sources and tools against patriarchy. Only through its own techniques can patriarchy be challenged and displaced.

The impasse of patriarchy for female self-determination is described precisely by Freud in his analysis of feminine psychical development. When faced with the oedipal interdict prohibiting her corporeal relation with the mother, Freud suggests that the girl has three options: she can accept her castration ('normal femininity'); she can refuse her castration and consider herself phallic ('the masculinity complex'); or she can renounce her 'inferior' clitoral pleasures and refuse to convert her sexual organ and orientation to vaginal (paternal) heterosexuality ('frigidity').

Little has been said about this third possibility open to the girl. It deserves more attention insofar as it is the only position resistant to the patriarchal requirements of heterosexuality, even if it exacts its price from the woman herself. We need to examine this category more carefully to see what Freud means by the term. Frigidity, it should be noted, is not a refusal of sexual pleasure per se. It is the refusal of a specifically *genital* and orgasmic sexual pleasure. The so-called 'frigid woman' is precisely the woman whose pleasures do not fit neatly into the male-defined structure of sexual pleasure, a teleological structure directed towards an orgasmic goal. Irigaray's response to this designation is simple. She induces laughter, a laughter that reveals and is itself a pleasure other than or beyond the genital:

> *Many women believe they are 'frigid', and they are often told this is so. When a woman tells me that she is 'frigid', I laugh, and tell her I don't know what it means. She laughs too, which brings about a release, and above all a loss of guilt towards a 'frigidity' for which she feels responsible, and which means, first of all, that she has been moulded into models of male sexual 'techniques' which do not at all correspond to her sexuality—namely the teleology of the orgasm ... The teleological model is, to repeat, possible for a man—even if he thus loses pleasure—but not for a woman ... (1977:66)*

If frigidity is not the abandonment of sexuality altogether, it is an attempt to retain polymorphous pre-oedipal pleasures in spite of oedipal demands. It is an attempt to remain within the pre-oedipal maternal relation (as does the girl in the 'masculinity complex'), while at the same time recognising the patriarchal reality of women's (social) castration (as does the 'normal', that is, castrated woman). In fact, it is probably closest in form to hysteria, the feminine neurosis *par excellence*.

Like frigidity, hysteria is commonly misunderstood in its aetiology and significance. Freud persistently regarded it as a thwarted or morally inadmissable heterosexual desire, a desire or wish which, because of its 'impropriety', is unacceptable to the subject and thus repressed. He disregards the evidence he himself relates, most notably in the case of Dora, that hysteria is the *symptomatic acting out* of a proposition the hysteric cannot articulate.

Contrary to Freud, hysteria can be seen as the woman's rebellion against and rejection of the requirements of femininity (requirements which are humiliating for her insofar as they presume women's castration). It is a refusal rather than a repression of heterosexuality, and an attempt to return nostalgically to the pre-oedipal, homosexual desire for the mother. It differs from the masculinity complex insofar as the 'masculine' woman denies her castration through her *belief* that her clitoris will grow or that she is not really castrated, while the hysteric *displaces* her 'phallic' attribute onto another part of her body, which becomes the hysterogenic zone. Dora's throat, the paralysed limb, the unseeing eye become 'sexualised', that is, take on the meaning of the subject's sexual life. The hysteric refuses heterosexual passivity and the sexual compliance with social norms by transferring sexual intensity and meaning onto her symptoms.

Dora is both extraordinarily seductive, and at the same time 'frigid'. She appears to be genuinely attracted to Herr K., and she certainly does nothing to discourage his romantic gifts or his acts of courtship (he sent her flowers every day for nearly a year). In fact, in many senses, she seems to egg him on, actively to encourage his ardour. If, however, as Freud suggests in his retrospective footnotes, Dora in fact desires *Frau K.* rather than Herr K., her behaviour can be seen as a 'gift' of love to Frau K. For Frau K., she will distract Herr K. from his wife's affair with Dora's father.

Dora's hysterical symptoms can be seen as a refusal rather than the expression of desire. They emerge after Herr K. has put her in a compromising position (twice) where she is reduced to passive dependence on him—that is, where she demonstrates the attributes of 'normal femininity'. Her situation precludes an abreaction of the traumatic seduction—in the one case, her parents did not believe her (the scene by the lake), and in the other, she was literally trapped in Herr K.'s office. Instead of saying 'no' (and being understood as saying 'no'), she chokes, gags, finds it difficult to breathe. Her symptoms are the final phases of an (unconscious) strategy of *enticement*: she *uses* her femininity, her social image and expected position to encourage the men of the case (including Freud) in the expression of their desires for her; she provokes a kind of passion and jealousy. She urges them to demonstrate their attachments and then—at the last minute—she refuses their expectations. In a word, she engages in (unconscious) *prick-teasing*.

The hysteric 'articulates' a corporeal discourse; her symptoms 'speak' on her behalf. While hysterically induced symptoms commonly *imitate* organic disorders (Charcot had to separate the hysterics from tuberculosis victims because the hysterics would take on tuberculoid symptoms after a short time), relying on what Freud calls 'somatic compliance' of organically significant parts of the body (Dora's hysterical throat symptoms date from an organically caused catarrh she had during the time of her oedipus complex), they are always *excessive*. Hysterics *mime* the disorders of others (this is why they have commonly been described as 'malingerers'); yet they do so according to superficial or apparent connections, common cultural ideas instead of a scientific or medical understanding, of organic connections (it is for this reason that hysterical paralyses will often incapacitate muscles that should function in organic paralyses and leave mobile those which should not be operational organically speaking).

The hysteric thus attempts to 'cope' with the demands and expectations of a male-dominated culture which relies on women's renunciation of their relations to other women, and of their unmediated relations to their own bodies and pleasures, by summoning up an apparently incapacitating 'illness', which prevents her from giving satisfaction to men while satisfying herself in a compromise or symptomatic form. Hers is a mode of defiance of patriarchy, not the site of its frustration. In this sense, the hysteric is a proto-feminist, or at least an isolated individual who, if she had access to the experiences of other women, may locate the problem in cultural expectations of femininity rather than in femininity itself. The hysteric's defiance through excess, through *overcompliance*, is a parody of the expected.

This may, incidentally, provide an alternative to the more typical explanations of that modern expression of hysteria, anorexia nervosa. Anorexia is not the result of a diet that has gone out of control. That is, it is not the woman's overzealous attempt to *comply* with the cultural ideals of femininity. Rather, it is a defiant taking-to-extremes of these ideals. The anorexic seems to be saying: 'Alright, you want me to be slim, I'll be slim. I'll be so slim that you'll no longer find me attractive. This is what you want; but what you'll get is much more than you bargained for.' In other words, it is a not always successful attempt at self-determination.

Because it represents one of the few possible positions that women may occupy in rebelling against the confines of patriarchal definitions, hysteria figures as a central 'figure' in Irigaray's subversion of phallocentrism. The hysteric occupies the central point of her (specul(um)ative) subversion of idealist philosophy in *Speculum*.... However, Irigaray does not naively advocate hysteria as a strategy for *women in general*. Rather, in her own *rereading of philosophy*, Irigaray herself acts as the hysteric. Her strategies are mimetic, not of organic disorders, but of philosophical and psychoanalytic texts. She imitates/parodies women's hysterical positions in discourse. Rather than act as a mimic — the mimic reproduces behaviour marked by its *difference* from behaviour (this is what distinguishes the mimic from what he or she mimes), its excessiveness over it, Irigaray mimics the hysteric's mimicry. She mimes mime itself.

The central chapter and turning point in *Speculum*..., the point at which A-Luce traverses the (speculative) mirror, is called 'La Mystérique'. In it, Irigaray announces a resistant locus *within* patriarchal discourses which threatens male self-certainty:

> *It is in order to speak to woman, write to women, act as preacher and confessor to women, that man usually has gone to such excesses. That he accepted the need to take the detour through metaphors that can scarcely be called figures. That he has given up his knowledge in order to attend to women's madness. Falling — as Plato would say, no doubt — into the trap of mimicking them, of claiming to find jouissance as 'she' does. To the point when he can no longer find himself as 'subject' anymore, and goes where he has no wish to follow: to his loss in that a-typical, a-topical mysteria. (1985a:191–2)*

Irigaray herself is the hysteric insofar as she wants to make woman's body *speak*, be representable, articulate itself. Like the hysteric, her techniques and procedures are pre-eminently *seduc-*

tive. Her critical technique, her amorous flirtation with phallocentric texts is hysterical prick-teasing, phallo-deflation. It is the
only way that she is able to both inhabit and challenge phallocentrism without being entirely absorbed by her investments and
history in it. For this reason, her style is feminine in the extreme:
it is based on masquerade, semblance, mimesis, artifice and
seduction — all the characteristics of the feminine 'resolution' of
the oedipus complex:

> *this philosophical mastery ... cannot simply be approached
> head on, nor simply within the realm of the philosophical itself.
> Thus it was necessary to deploy other languages ... and even to
> accept the condition of silence, of aphasia as a symptom —
> historico-hysterical, hysterico-historical — so that something of
> the feminine as the limit of the philosophical might finally be
> heard. (1985b:149–50)*

Her strategy, then, is hysterical in that it relies on 'feminine
wiles': her 'tools' are 'nuptial': 'The tool is not a feminine attribute.
But woman may re-utilize its marks on her, in her. To put it
another way: the option left to me was to *have a fling with the
philosophers*, which is easier said than done' (1985b:150).

The hysteric is traumatically 'seduced' (raped?) by an unsolicited
attack by an other. The traumatic event lies dormant until is it re-
evoked through a similar event, an event which provokes the onset
of the hysterical symptom. The symptom is an act of (unconscious)
defiance. It is provoked, not directly by the repetition of a precipi-
tating event, although the symptoms only appear after a second
event, but in an earlier 'seduction' to which the child was passively
subjected. This earliest seduction is not simply a chance event but
is seen by the child as an anticipation of her position as a feminine
subject in patriarchal culture, an omen of what is to come. Her
symptom is a strategy to ward off the violations with which she is
expected to comply.

Irigaray's writings are self-consciously modelled on the hysteric's
symptomatic struggles to achieve autonomy. Like her, Irigaray is
attacked, violated by the imposition of phallocentric philosophies
and theoretical paradigms; like the hysteric, she is unable simply
to accept her predesignated role as passive, marginalised support
system for the One subject who counts — the male (husband-
knower). She refuses the position of 'philosopher's wife' insofar as
this silences woman and precludes her from knowledge except
through him, for it covers her with his projections, needs and
fantasies:

*'The philosopher's wife' ... is thus pledged to the service of the
'philosopher's' 'self' in all forms. And as far as the wedding
celebration is concerned, she is in danger of being no more than
the requisite mediator for the philosopher's celebrations with
himself, and with his fellows. (1985b:151–2)*

The hysteric's symptom is a response to her annihilation as
active subject, a resistance or refusal to confirm what is expected
of her. Not able to take up an active position by will alone (this
would mean, at most, acting like a man), she lives out and uses
her passivity in an active defiance of her social position. She
(psychically) mutilates herself in order to prevent her brutalisation
at the hands of others — hence the tragic self-defeat entailed by
hysterical resistance. Irigaray shares the hysteric's *excessive*
mimicry, the conversion of her passivity into activity by taking on,
in the most extreme forms, what is expected, but to such an
extreme degree that the end result is the opposite of compliance: it
unsettles the system by throwing back to it what it cannot accept
about its own operations.

Unlike the hysteric, however, Irigaray's strategy is self-
consciously undertaken and does not or need not reproduce the
ultimately self-destructive and self-defeating debilitation of hysteria. If Irigaray is similar to the hysteric in a number of respects,
she is also, in others, more like the analyst. Her procedure is not
the *acting out*, the *charade* of hysterical expression, where a
'script' is performed by the body; it is more like the analyst's ideal
facilitation of the hysterical discourse, giving speech to what has
remained unspoken and unabreacted in her psychical life. The
'cure' is possible only with social upheavals which grant women
autonomy as subjects. This may explain why hysterics are notori-
ously difficult to 'cure' while often being surprisingly compliant
(suggestible?) to the analyst's counter-transferences. Irigaray's
aim is to say what has up to now remained unspoken of women's
pleasures, experiences and perspectives. Her approach is positive
to the extent that the hysteric remains reactive, negative and
critical.

*Hysteria is all that she has left ... As a result of suspension,
within a suspension, of the economy of her primal instincts, she
will do 'as' she is asked. But this 'as' or 'as if' is not ludic, not
under her control, though sometimes it seems that way and is in
some measure, a foretaste of what the 'play' between the sexes
might be. But here the game is controlled ... by the Phallus's*

mastery of the sexual economy. And women will play it with the ground rules that the phallus is to be equated with the appropriation of the desire (for) origin. (1985a:71–2)

Irigaray's strategy is not to use the rules to win (the game is in any case rigged) but to disrupt the old game in order to initiate new ones, 'jamming the theoretical machinery' in order to enable new 'tools', inventions and knowledges to be possible.

5 Luce Irigaray and the ethics of alterity

I RIGARAY'S current work on sexual autonomy revolves around a surprising cluster of terms which could be loosely organised around a conception of the *divine*. She shares with Kristeva a concern for the ways in which religious discourse represents femininity and maternity. Yet unlike Kristeva, Irigaray is not interested in analysing the place of femininity within given patriarchal texts, for she is also committed to creating alternatives which go beyond the confines of their patriarchal predecessors to make a divine possible for women. Irigaray's work explores repressed or archaic concepts of the cosmic or celestial order; ways of reconceptualising received notions of space and time; a rereading of the Empedoclean and alchemical notions of the four elements, and a fascinating analysis of the repressed prehistory of our culture, of which Greek mythology gives us a glimmer: a prehistory and an ontology appropriate to the recognition of alterity, divinity and ethics. These three terms, while shared with a number of French theorists (for example, Foucault's interest in ethics, Kristeva's in religion and a generalised French preoccupation with alterity), are opened up to the question of sexual specificity in Irigaray's recent writings.

This cluster of terms is not usually associated with academic feminism but, if anything, with a more 'spiritually' minded feminism. 'Mystical' feminism (for want of a better description), however, tends to be strongly anti-theoretical, more interested in matriarchal religions, astrology, separatist lifestyles and naturalist conceptions of the two sexes than in interrogating philosophical paradigms. Thus Irigaray's interest in the masculinity of existing conceptions of ethics, alterity and divinity, and her goal of constructing models appropriate to women presents a rare coming together of political and academic concerns.

In this chapter I analyse four broad concerns; her interest in the

domain of ethics, which is related to Emmanuel Levinas' understanding of the *encounter with alterity*; second, her notion of the
ways in which sexual exchange, exchange between sexually different subjects, may be possible; third, her conception of God and
the divine; and fourth, the place of the elemental in her reformula-
tions of occidental ontology.[1]

The ethics of sexual difference

For Irigaray the question of sexual difference entails rethinking
the relations between the self and the other. The self has always
been presumed masculine: at best, it is sexually neutral, modelled
on what men consider are 'neutral' characteristics. This does not
mean that women are automatically or always equated with
otherness; rather, the other, whether male or female, is always
understood as a variation of the sameness of self. Irigaray wishes
to explore the conditions needed for and the space occupied by a
subject considered as female. What kind of alterity would a
feminine subject presume? This, for Irigaray, is the fundamental
question of ethics, a consequence of the self's necessary confrontation with the other. The other is a necessary condition of
subjectivity. The other makes possible the subject's relations to
others in a social world; ethics is the result of the need to negotiate
between one existence and another. Ethics is thus framed by and
in its turn frames the subject's confrontation with the other.

The otherness of the other can not be understood on the model
of the self: the other is irreducibly other, different, independent.
Yet ethics has hitherto recognised only one sort of subject, the
male, formulating its principles on the presumption of the singularity and primacy of this subject. In seeking an ethics based on
the recognition of alterity rather than modelled on the self-same,
one of Irigaray's more influential sources is the Judaic scholar,
phenomenologist and theorist of ethics Emmanuel Levinas.[2]

Levinas' work is located in the interstices of a number of
interests Irigaray also shares. His work analyses a repressed Judaic
tradition underlying Greek logocentric thought. He is one of the
few contemporary philosophers of secular ethics whose sources are
derived from rabbinic and Talmudic texts.[3] His aim, among other
things, is the establishment of an *antihumanist ethics*, an ethics
not in opposition to or replacing politics but in continuity with it.
This is an ethics which positions the human subject as product,
rather than ethical agent: ethics is *prior* to and provides the

grounds for metaphysics, ontology and epistemology. For Levinas ethics does not spring from human nature or from what can be known; rather what exists and what can be known are effects of the subject's radical dependence on and responsibility to the other.

Levinas' conception of alterity is central to Irigaray's understanding of relations between sexually different subjects. For him alterity cannot be represented in terms of any sameness of self. Thus it resists oppositional definitions and notions of complementarity. The other is distant and different from the subject, and the other has a perspective on the subject. Several elements distinguish Levinas' position from that of his humanist contemporaries, especially Sartre.

For Levinas alterity exhibits four major characteristics[4]: first, it is a form of *exteriority*, separate from and unpredicted by the subject. The other *astonishes* and fills the subject with wonder and surprise. Second, alterity is the site of *excess*, an unabsorbable, indigestible residue the subject is unable to assimilate to itself. Thus the other is a form of independence, resistant to the subject's aspirations and wishes. Third, alterity is an *infinite* category: by this Levinas means that it exceeds all boundaries, borders, constraints and limitations which the subject attempts to impose on it. Fourth, alterity is conceived by Levinas as an *activity*, in relation to which the subject is passively positioned. For Levinas it is the other who initiates actions, brings about encounters, makes approaches to and incites responses from the subject.

In short, the other calls, beckons, summons up the subject. The subject, for Levinas, is exposed to and opened up by the appeal of the other. The other opens (up) the subject to others; it opens (up) things, the world itself, to the subject. It enables the world to have meanings, to be open to other senses. The subject is chosen by the other, and is thus not the active agent of moral choice. By *facing* the subject, the other makes the subject responsible for actions, and even crimes, which are not his or her own. The other's behaviour is the subject's responsibility, even if it is beyond the subject's control. The other necessarily implicates the subject from the outside. In being chosen by the other, the subject is positioned as an 'identity', located as a being in space and time. The otherness of the other is, for Levinas, the precondition of the sameness of self. Thus the other necessarily poses the ethical question: the response to the other's appeal is the field of ethics.

Otherness is thus not conceived on the Hegelian model of mutual recognition of two equal self-conscious subjects; rather, the other is the irreversible and non-reciprocal material support of the subject. It is prior to the subject. Ethics is the domain of the response to the other's needs; it is a responsibility for the other's actions — even if those actions are inflicted on the subject.

Levinas' work is especially relevant to Irigaray's current preoccupations, given his refusal to conceive of either the subject or the other as disembodied beings. For him, they are corporeal subjects, sexual subjects, subjects capable of touching, seeing, engaging and negotiating with the other's materiality. Rarely is ethics conceived on the basis of incarnated subjects or corporeal specificity (this has generally, where it is considered at all, remained the province of politics or 'morality' rather than ethics). The Kantian categorical imperative, for example, only has relevance insofar as it is universalisable, that is, insofar as it can function independent of any particular corporeality, experience or subjective position. This may explain Levinas' fascination with the sexual encounter, the erotic meeting of two sexually different beings.

Rather than represent the sexual encounter as a form of corporeal caress, Levinas claims that the *face* signals the exposure of the subject to the alterity of the other. The face presents the other as a form of proximity or contact. It is simultaneously an open invitation to and an injunction on the subject: both a vulnerability to the exposure of the subject, destitute, poverty-striken and in need of protection; and an imperative, an assertion of the 'I' over the 'you'. It presents the first command:

> *The first word of the face is the 'Thou shalt not kill.' It is an order. There is a commandment in the appearance of the face, as if a master spoke to me. However, at the same time, the face of the Other is destitute; it is poor for whom I can do all and to whom I owe all. And me, whoever I may be, but as a 'first person', I am he who finds the resources to respond to the call. (Levinas, 1985:89)*

Contact between the subject and the other implies their *difference*, their radical outsideness to each other. This proximity is not the result of the caress, or direct touching, for instead of yielding a closeness or intimacy, the carnal caress signals an ever-elusive, receding impossibility of any direct grasp of alterity: 'In a caress, what is there is sought as though it were not there, as though the skin were a trace of its own withdrawal, a langour still seeking, like an absence which, however, could not be more there' (Levinas, 1981:90).

Proximity is a response to being summoned by the other's need:

In proximity, it is the absolutely other, the stranger, that I already have in my arms, already bear, according to the Biblical formula, 'in my breast as the nurse bears the nurseling'. He has no other place ... no country, not one inhabitant exposed to the cold and heat of the seasons. Reduced to the recourse of me, such is the neighbour's homelessness or strangeness. (Levinas, 1981:91)

Against a Sartrean concept of the sexual encounter as a sadomasochistic overcoming of one subject by the other[5], in Levinas' view the sexual encounter implies a recognition and acceptance of the other's alterity. Derived from Hegel's master–slave dialectic, in which each self-consciousness attempts to contain and control the autonomy of the other in a life and death struggle, Sartre implies a necessary power struggle between lovers, a kind of competition in which each strives to become the other's ideal. For Hegel, Absolute Knowledge unites 'the identity of the identical with the non-identical', the overcoming of all alterity in a universal inclusiveness. By contrast, for Levinas the corporeal caress entails the possibility of *sexual exchange* between the lovers who recognise their differences, limits and specificity. To encounter or face the other is to open oneself (up) to the other's needs, the other's claims, which are prior to the subject's own. In this sense, Levinas reverses the primacy that phenomenologists since Hegel have accorded to the subject over the other. For Levinas it is not the subject who is given but the other:

Proximity, therefore, is an anarchic relationship with a singularity without the mediation of any principle, any ideality ... it is an assimilation of me by another, a responsibility with regard to men we do not even know. The relation of proximity cannot be reduced to any modality of distance or geometrical contiguity, nor to the simple 'representation' of a neighbour; it is already an assignation — an obligation, anachronistically prior to any commitment. (Levinas, 1981:100–1)

Erotic alterity cannot presume two basically similar subjects, but necessarily involves a direct encounter with an altogether *different* other. Levinas theorises the erotic encounter not only in the abstract terms of a self and other relation, but also in the concrete relations between male and female. He captures at least some of the qualities of mutual respect and irreducible autonomy Irigaray also seeks.

The difference of sex is not the duality of two complementary terms. For two complementary terms presuppose a pre-existing whole. Now to say the sexual duality presupposes a whole is to posit in advance love as a fusion. The pathos consists, to the contrary, in an insurmountable duality of beings; it is a relationship with what forever slips away. The relationship does not ipso facto *neutralize alterity, but conserves it ... What matters to me in this notion of the feminine is not merely the unknowable but a mode of being which consists in slipping away from the light. In existence, the feminine is an event, different from that of spatial transcendence or expression which go towards the light, it is a flight before the light. The way of existing before the light. The way of existing of the feminine is hiding, or modesty. So this alterity of the feminine does not consist in the object's simple exteriority. Neither is it made of an opposition of wills. (Levinas, 1979d:78–9)*

The erotic encounter provides a privileged access to the other, who is bound by mystery and awe, and exists necessarily outside of its patriarchal containment by more or less explicit forms of sadomasochism:

It is only by showing in what way eros *differs from possession and power that we can acknowledge a communication in* eros. *It is neither a struggle nor a fusion, nor a knowledge. One must recognise its exceptional place among relations. It is the relationship with alterity, with mystery, that is, with the future, with what in the world where there is everything, is never there. (Levinas, 1985:81)*

To illustrate his notion of the ethical response the other summons in the subject, that is, the involuntary or imposed nature of ethical relations, Levinas cites two rather striking examples: the *hostage* and the *mother*. The hostage is held captive; yet, for Levinas, even in this apparently passive, victim-like position, the hostage is nevertheless accountable, not for what is done to him, but for what happens to the other: 'It is through the condition of being held hostage that there can be in the world pity, compassion, pardon and proximity ... The condition of being held hostage is not the extreme test of solidarity but the condition of all solidarity' (Levinas, 1985:117).

The other appeals to the subject in the form of an imperative. To acknowledge this imperative is to *put oneself in the other's place*. To answer the other's needs is to become responsible for the other's actions, even if those actions are, as in the case of the hostage, inflicted on the subject. Putting oneself in the other's place does not mean identifying with the other, but presupposes an act of *substitution*. The ethical response to the call of the other is the act of putting oneself in the other's place. (Incidentally, for Levinas this movement of substitution, in which terms substitute for each other without becoming identical, is the condition of signification itself. Thus even representation itself is preconditioned by ethics.) If the hostage represents an extreme form of the other's (ethical) hold over the subject, in day-to-day life this captivation by the other is represented in *maternity*.

For Levinas, as for Irigaray, maternity bears the material burden of the other's needs, nourishing the other from her own body. Maternity represents the unconditional response to the other's appeal. In a rare exception to the phallocentric reduction of women to subhuman or pre-ethical status, for Levinas maternity represents the paradigm of what it is to be an ethical subject: subjectivity is the openness or susceptibility to the other's call, a response to the other's existence. The mother gives herself up to the other's needs.

If Levinas' conception of the other's priority over the subject, and the establishment of the domain of ethics as a consequence of this confrontation with otherness, provide one of Irigaray's major themes in her project of an ethics of sexual difference, it is because Levinas is prepared to accept the *autonomy* of the other as an *a priori* principle. If ethics is constituted out of the confrontation with another who is fundamentally different, then the relations between the sexes constitute *the* ethical question. For Irigaray the sexes have hitherto been conceived only according the phallocentric singularity of the masculine subject. Ethics has only represented the subject's encounter with his own reflection and not with an autonomous, indeed, primary other. An ethics of sexual difference would have to rethink the encounter between the self-same subject and an irreducibly sexually different other, an exchange between two beings who must be presumed to be different.

The economy of sexual exchange

Irigaray confronted the question of exchange in an earlier paper, 'Women on the Market' (in 1985b), through a reading of Levi-Strauss' *The Elementary Structures of Kinship*, Marx's *Capital* and Saussure's *Course in General Linguistics*. Here she deconstructs the Lacanian (and Levi-Straussian) notion of the symbolic order, the order which founds and regulates symbolic exchange. She projects a marxist theory of commodity production onto Levi-Strauss' understanding of the patriarchal exchange of women — that is, the axis of class onto that of sex — reviewing the unspoken position of women in kinship and economic relations.

Marx and Levi-Strauss analyse exchange relations in which the *content* or *matter* of what is exchanged is less important than the meaning or information the object of exchange signifies. Ultimately, what is exchanged for both are *signs*. This allies Marx and Levi-Strauss to Saussure and Lacan, who are also interested in the functioning of the exchanges of meaning/matter: for Saussure this exchange is linguistic, and for Lacan it is the substitution of one object of desire for another. Irigaray exploits the commonness linking commodities (Marx), family names (Levi-Strauss), signs (Saussure) and desire (Lacan). Her claim is that it is the silent bodies of women, especially mothers, which provide the supports for these various exchange relations. This implies that while women are the conditions of symbolic exchange and thus of culture, they function as objects of exchange and are prevented from being participants or active agents within exchange. This means that the social order and the exchange relations which guarantee it are *hommosexual* (sic), relations between men alone. Women are merely the 'excuses', the 'goods' and mediating objects linking men to each other.

Each of these prevailing models of symbolic exchange — where 'sisters' are exchanged for 'wives', where commodities are exchanged for money, where one sign is exchanged for another and one desire (for the mother) for another — presumes the fundamental likeness or similarity of exchanging subjects, and a basic commensurability of exchanged objects: two orders within exchange, each homogeneous and based on identity, one the identity of subjects, the other the identity of objects. Irigaray points out that in these exchange systems there is always a *master term*, a key element which ensures this underlying identity. For Marx the 'general equivalent of exchange', the thing against which all commodities acquire their relative (exchange) value, is a commodity separated from all others (the gold standard, coined money); for Levi-Strauss (and Lacan) it is the Name-of-the-Father; and for Lacan each subject takes up his or her place only with reference to the master signifier, the phallus. Thus, for each, women are on the side of the excluded, the lack, the nameless or the valueless condition of value: 'Marx's analysis of commodities as the elementary form of capitalist wealth can thus be understood as an interpretation of the status of women in so-called patriarchal cultures' (Irigaray, 1985b:172).

In recognition of women's relegation to the status of commodity or object of exchange between men, Irigaray advocates two kinds of strategy: the first is articulated in 'Commodities Among Themselves' (1985b): here she defiantly approaches women's object-like status in exchange. Granted that women's roles as objects cement harmonious relations between men, she asks how women's autonomy and self-defined status as subjects would upset the *hommosexual economy*. She signals the potential force of insurrection in women's passivity: if women are rendered passive objects of male exchange, what would happen, she speculates, if women refuse their designated positions and instead assume an active role. How would the *hommosexual* economy react to women's autonomy?

Commodities can only enter into relationships under the watchful eyes of their 'guardians'. It is out of the question for them to go to 'market' on their own, enjoy their own worth among themselves, speak to each other, desire each other, free from the control of the seller-buyer-consumer subjects ...

But what if these 'commodities' refused to go to the 'market'? *What if they maintained 'another' kind of commerce, among themselves? (Irigaray, 1985b:196)*

In this paper Irigaray aims to upset this economy through womens refusal to play the game. Her strategy here, as elsewhere in her earlier works, is to defy women's phallocentric relegation to subordinate counterparts of men and to affirm the existence of two autonomous sexes. However, in her more recent works, she seems more interested, following Levinas, in renegotiating the exchange relation so that symbolic exchange between irreducibly different beings becomes possible and workable.

This is an extremely difficult project, for it involves rethinking the presumed relations of equivalence, reciprocity and measurement which have thus far governed exchange relations: questioning, that is, the criteria governing who the subjects, who or what the objects and what the measurements of value are. Exchange relations to date have posited a basic universality or sameness of the agents of exchange, thus guaranteeing the commensurability of exchanged objects. But if this presumed sameness, this measure of uniformity, is ruptured, in what ways can different objects of exchange have comparable value? If the phallocentrism of economic, social and sexual exchange relations is questioned, and replaced by systems cognisant of sexual difference, how would the exchange relation function? What can be produced from such exchanges between the sexes? In what ways can sexually different beings share and produce, give and take? Is giving/taking without loss possible?

In a closely related paper, 'Women, the Sacred and Money' (1986b), Irigaray develops a reading of René Girard's text *Violence and the Sacred* (1977). Girard founds religion and the realm of the sacred on the overcoming of man's inherent violence and his tendency to conflictual relations, which he believes is a consequence of mimetic desire. Desire, for him, is always an effect of rivalry with another. The object of desire, in other words, gains its value from being desired by another: 'The subject desires the object because the rival desires it ... We must understand that desire itself is essentially mimetic, directed toward an object desired by the model' (Girard, 1977:145–6).

For Girard the function of religion is to mediate social conflicts (ultimately sexual conflicts between male rivals). Sacrificial and religious rites, especially involving the socially sanctioned scape-goat onto whom the violence of rivalrous conflict is deflected, are the results of a social mediation and representation of the inherent violence of competitive desires, desires which are in conflict because they are the same:

All sacrificial rites are based on two substitutions. The first provides by generative violence, which substitutes a single victim for all the members of the community. The second, the only strictly ritualistic substitution, is that of a victim for the surro-gate victim. As we know, it is essential that the victim be drawn from outside the community. The surrogate victim, by contrast, is a member of the community. (Girard, 1977:269)

Irigaray questions Girard's correlation of mimetic rivalry be-tween two (male) desires with the foundation of sacred ritual. That the rivals are necessarily men, who enter potential exchange relations with the woman as the object of exchange, is apparently unnoticed by Girard himself.[6] Irigaray seems to use his text to disentangle men's rivalrous relations and sacrificial religions from the sacred considered more generally. She thus asks why the totemic animal is devoured, consumed and annihilated in the ritualistic practices of totemism? Why does the institution of social law and community harmony have to be enforced by acts of symbolic sacrifice, negativity and violence? Why must there be a scapegoat? What is the link between sacrificial religions and male violence? Why must the sacrificial *deed* supplement the religious *word*? In other words, what of the divine is unexpressed when religion is articulated in acts of sacrificial violence?

> *Why did speech fail? What was missing? Why kill, cut up and eat as a sign of the covenant? And isn't it possible to analyse why speech was so inadequate that such an act became necessary? Was it, for instance, because of a lack of harmony between words, acts and bodies? Are cultures sacrificial if they manage to unite acts, words, microcosmic and macrocosmic nature and the gods? In that case how are systems of exchange and sexual difference possible? (Irigaray, 1986b:7)*

Why, for example, does Freud found culture on the totemic devouring of the primal father's body? Why is culture for Freud founded on the renunciation or sacrifice of the mother? What kind of culture could exist in which the covenant with the divine is not sealed by loss, circumcision, castration, abstinence? Irigaray links sacrificial religions to the imposition of a particular cultural onto the cosmic order. In other words, relations to the divine require a sacrifice insofar as the body, space and time, the concrete specificity of the subject, must be regulated and governed by abstract, general law. Irigaray implies that the human/masculine is projected onto the natural and cosmic orders in religious discourses and practices:

> *I would attribute the following meaning to the eucharist: I am going to be sacrificed, I am giving you something other than my flesh (namely the fruits of the earth, which I have consecrated) to share out before the sacrifice so that my body can enter into glory and not, once dead, be eaten by you in my absence. (1986b:8)*

Irigaray analyses the conditions under which it may be possible for women to enter into relations of exchange as autonomous subjects. In order for this to occur, women (not to speak of men) must be represented in terms different from their traditional constriction into men's opposites, reflections, doubles or complements. The open recognition of two types of sexually specific being, occupying two kinds of position and points of view, entails, for Irigaray, a 'transvaluation' of existing values, a new conception of space, time, place, matter, the elements and, above all, the divine.

God

Irigaray's interest in and exploration of the divine must be distinguished from more traditional theological and mystical adherences. Her terms cannot be assimilated into a divinity or concept of God which is seen in phallocentric terms. Indeed, she seems to regard formulaic religious assurances of salvation and grace as forms of escapism and evasion of ethical responsibility. Our culture is presently, she believes, suffering from a malaise of repetition of the same under the guise of the different. These repetitions result in a stultifying cultural crisis, which involves, among other things:

> *the consumption society, the circularity of discourse, the more or less cancerous sicknesses of our epoch, the non-reliability of words, the end of philosophy, religious despair or regression to religiousness, scientistic or technical imperialism without consideration of the living subject, etc. (1984:13)*

In her understanding religion functions as an anachronistic leftover, tying the present and future to the past. However, given the impossibility of abandoning the order of the religious, it is possible to re-evaluate, revise, re-experience the divine in terms different from its traditional (Christocentric) representations:

> *The exclusion or suppression of the religious dimension seems to be impossible. It re-emerges in various and frequently degraded guises: sectarian, religiosity ... we do, however, need to rethink the religious question, particularly its scope, its categories and its utopias, all of which have been male for centuries and remain so. (1986b:6)*

A blind recourse to religious doctrine evades the implications of sexual difference. Irigaray is not advocating a return to the kinds of pious devotion that have hitherto marked women's submission to religious orthodoxy. She disdains the kinds of religiosity attributed to such female saints as Lacan's favourite, St Teresa, and the large list of devout women who, in protest at their social subordination, and in a manner similar to that of the modern-day hysteric, use patriarchal religion as a kind of expression of and compensation for their social powerlessness.[7] This simply repositions women within the strictures of men's forms of self-worship, guaranteed by a God built in their own image. It reinserts women into a passive and compliant position, against which many have struggled. Rather, Irigaray's interest in the concept of God and the divine needs to be contextualised by her analysis of the conditions necessary for the establishment of an autonomous identity for women.

The concept of God has been used by men to disavow their debt to femininity and maternity. Men conceive of a divine, omnipotent being, regarding themselves as formed in His image and thus partaking in His divine creativity. At the same time they effectively contain women in a sphere outside of the divine (women's relations to God are mediated by men) while continuing to rely on women's resources. Her attitude to the Catholic Church is particularly bitter:

> *when this minister of God only, of God the Father, pronounces the words of the eucharist: 'This is my body, this is my blood' according to the cannabalistic rite which is secularly ours, perhaps we could remind him that he would not be here if our body and our blood hadn't given him life ... And that it is us, women-mothers whom he thus gives to be eaten. (1981a:33)*

Irigaray does not, by contrast, advocate the creation of a women-centred religion, a kind of female self-worship which is a counterpart to masculine religious ideals. This is simply the reversal of received religions, and not a transformation to accommodate *two* sexes.

> *Far from thinking that we should continue the process of deification on the pattern of our ancestors and their totem animals, that we should make a regression back to the siren godesses, in particular against men gods, it seems to me that we certainly have to incite a return to the* cosmic, *but at the same time asking ourselves why we were stopped as we were becoming* divine. *(1986a:3)*

Feuerbach and the Essence of Christianity

Two rather atypical sources (at least within theology) seem to inform Irigaray's preoccupation with the divine, the cosmic and the celestial: Feuerbach's text *The Essence of Christianity* (1957), and Levinas' Judaic ethics, particularly *Quatre lectures talmudique* (1968).[8] They share little more in common than this: that for both Feuerbach and Levinas, God is a form of alterity affirming the human.

According to Irigaray, for Feuerbach 'it is not possible to affirm a genus or a human kind without a god and probably without a trinity' (1986b:11). To have a goal or purpose, to project into an unknown future is to have a religious attitude. God is the perfection, the ideal, end or goal of an infinite becoming. In this sense, for Irigaray it is not adequate simply to rely on received formulas of worship which affirm a male-defined God. The task for women is not to include themselves within a pre-existing image of God but to find a God for themselves:

> *How could our God be imagined. Or our god? Is there a quality pertaining to us which could reverse the order and put the predicate in subject position (as Feuerbach does for God and man in the analysis of the Essence of Christianity?) If there is not just one, how will we choose among them to conceive our perfect being ... All men (especially according to Feuerbach) and all women, except when they remain submitted to the logic of the essence of man, should imagine a God for themselves, an objective and subjective place or path for the possible assemblage of the self in space and time: a unity of instinct, heart and knowledge ... Only a God can save us and guard over us. The feeling or experience of a positive, objective and glorious existence for our subjectivity is necessary for us. Such as a God who helps and guides us in our becoming, who holds the measure of our limits — women — and our relation to the infinite, which inspires our endeavours. (1986a:9)*

For Feuerbach God is the perfection, extension and projection of 'man':

> *God, as an extramundane being, is however, nothing else than the nature of man withdrawn from the world and concentrated in itself, freed from all worldly ties and entanglements, transporting itself above the world and positing itself in this condition as a real objective being; or, nothing else than the consciousness of the power to abstract oneself from all that is external, and to live for and with oneself alone, under the form which this power takes in religion, namely, that of a being distinct, apart from man. (Feuerbach, 1957:66)*

God is the image and ideal of man. Feuerbach posits a duality of the divine specific to Christianity. The divine is not represented simply by God, but primarily by God the Father, God, the progenitor of God the Son. This singularity of God in itself is asocial, areligious in any communal sense. Thus, in opposing the solitary nature of the Judaic God, God is incarnated in the Son:

But from a solitary God the essential need of duality, of love, of community, of the real, completed self-consciousness, of the alter-ego is excluded. This want is therefore satisfied by religion thus: in the still solitude of the Divine Being is placed another, a second, different from God as to personality but identical with him in essence — God the Son, in distinction from God the Father. God the Father is I, God the Son is Thou. The I is understanding, the Thou love. But love with understanding and understanding with love is mind, and mind is the totality of man as such — the total man. (Feuerbach, 1957:67)

The Father and the Son thus embody *both* the totality of 'man', man as an individual who partakes of the divine, and also the community, through the relation between I and Thou or self and other. From the two who constitute the divine, Feuerbach derives the third component of the holy trinity. Paradoxically, he introduces the third person, not as the completion of a kind of holy family, not, that is, as the *mother*, a divine feminine principle, but as the love between the Father and the Son. He argues that this third person has been invested by received religion as a persona different from the first two, but in fact the Holy Ghost is nothing but the principle of the unity of Father and Son. Father and Son alone are necessary to represent what he calls the 'principle of multiplicity' (p. 68) from the posited solitariness of God.

Feuerbach challenges the Protestant excision of the mother as a holy principle, claiming that the 'veiling' as he calls it (p. 73) of the Mother of God is a fundamental denial of the humanity of the Son. But if the third person of the trinity is only the love between the Father and Son, on what grounds can Feuerbach justify the Catholic belief in the Mother of God?

Why did the Son betake himself to the bosom of the Mother? For what other reason than because the Son is the yearning after the Mother, because his womanly, tender heart found a corresponding expression only in a feminine body? It is true that the Son as a natural man, dwells only temporarily in the shrine of this body, but the impressions which he here receives are inextinguishable; the Mother is never out of the mind and heart of the Son ... If ... we perceive the love of God to us, that he gave us his only-begotten Son, i.e. that which was dearest to him, for our salvation, — can we perceive this love still better when we find in God the beating of the mother's heart. The highest and deepest love is the mother's love. The father consoles

154

himself for the loss of his son; he has a stoical principle within him. The mother, on the contrary, is inconsolable; she is the sorrowing element, that which cannot be indemnified — the true in love. (Feuerbach, 1957:72)

The Mother is thus necessary for the completion and perfect embodiment of the Son as well as the love which links the Father to the Son. No mere vessel for procreation, in Feuerbach's text she functions as the most perfect representative of the humanity, the compassion, suffering, sorrow and emotion of divinity.

Instead of seeing Irigaray as a 'born-again' Christo-feminist, her notion of God, or gods, and the divine is part of her general strategy of deconstructive textual reading of philosophical (not simply theological) texts. This is an attempt to replace a metaphysical, masculinist onto-theology, in which man defines, and is not in turn defined by, God, with the idea of sexual (and presumably cultural) specificity. Not a single, paternal God, whose unity and universality sweeps away a polytheistic pantheon, but sexually specific gods, gods who represent the extension and perfection, the infinite becoming, of sexually specific subjects.

From Feuerbach, then, she derives the notion of God as a limit and perfection point of human (read: male) self-completion; and the necessity of including *both* sexes within any notion of the divine. His holy trinity of Father–Son–Holy Ghost can be read, although he himself precludes this, as a metaphor of the human family, a structure which is necessarily and essentially dependent on the position and contributions of the mother, as much, if not more than the father. Alongside of this reading of Christian doctrine in her works is the strong influence of Levinas' Judaic conception of the divine.

Levinas and the Judaic

In Levinas' writings she finds an ethics and a concept of the divine which is developed in recognition of the end of metaphysics and the demise of onto-theology. Metaphysics has constricted ethics and confined it to the domain of being. What an appropriate action is has long depended on what exists. Greek ethics and its Christian 'translations' imply that the good must be known *before* it can be enacted. Knowledge, being, existence precede the good. By contrast, for Levinas the good, ethics, is prior to ontology, its unspoken condition:

There is more to being than being. The surplus of the Other's nonencompassable alterity—not the alterity of horizons—is the way ethics intrudes, disturbs, commands, being—from height and destitution. It is the demand made by the very face of the Other in a nakedness which pierces the face which can be objectified. (Cohen, in translator's introduction, Levinas, 1985:10)

The Judaic tradition provides a different notion of the divine from that produced in Greek or Christian theology. Levinas' sources are Talmudic and Chassidic, dating from medieval modes of interpretation, although his orientation to the fundamental *textuality* of God, that is, to the Torah as the book of creation, is based on much earlier traditions. The Judaic God is of course paternalistic. But He is characterised as a loving God as much as a law-giver.

God is not revealed. He does not manifest Himself directly or indirectly; He is not made present by an incarnation or through a corporeal representative. Rather, He speaks, He commands, He calls on the subject. The subject is called, summoned, rather than sees God revealed. The Jew does not choose faith; he is chosen, called on, commanded from the outside, beyond all will and consciousness. There is no disclosure, or *alethia*, no tangible presence of God; on the contrary, it is His absence, his invisibility that commands: 'As a transcendence, refusing objectification and dialogue, it signifies in an ethical way. It *signifies* in the sense in which one says to *mean an order*; it *orders*' (Levinas, 1987:171).

In opposition to onto-theology, in which presence ordains and sanctifies actions and truths, the Judaic tradition is founded on lack, on infinite interpretation and uncertainty, not truth. Levinas' God is represented in self-conscious opposition to the Christian concept. If the major differences—at least insofar as they are relevant to Irigaray's notion of the divine—between the Judaic and the Hellenic-Christian tradition could be summarised in brief points, the following may prove pertinent:

1 Where the Hellenic/Christian tradition seeks the *origin* of terms in a paternity which explains their essence, the Judaic continually undoes or rewrites the 'original', displacing paternity. For Levinas, paradoxically, it is God's absence which underpins faith; this is a God's whose face is invisible, who is never manifested in Light:

Nobody can really say I believe—or I do not believe for that matter—that God exists. The existence of God is not a question of an individual soul's uttering logical syllogisms. It cannot be proved. The existence of God, the Sein Gottes, is sacred history itself, the sacredness of man's relation to man through which God may pass. God's existence is the story of his revelation in biblical history. (Levinas, 1985:18)

2 In the Hellenic/Christian tradition the Son resumes the place of the Father, and is heir to his position. In the Hebraic tradition the Father is always already dispossessed, and thus the Son occupies a position only insofar as the Father's word speaks to him. The Son cannot displace the Father, for both are already displaced and homeless: each owes his survival to the alliance they establish together.

3 The Hellenic/Christian tradition enables a reconciliation of the human and the divine through granting the human 'free will', choice, to guide the subject's relation to the divine. The subject is thus responsible for his or her actions and adherences. By contrast, the Jew is chosen, passive. For Levinas it is the 'suffering of the just for a justice without triumph'.

4 The Greek *logos* refers to an organisation alien to its Hebrew 'equivalent', *davar*: *logos* is essentially mimetic, separating being from representation and linking them isomorphically. The propositional form of subject-copula-predicate is thus preferred, for then truth can be represented as an imitation of or correspondence with a proposition and the reality it represents. A sentence is true when the relations between its internal parts corresponds with the arrangements of things in reality. The logocentric Graeco-Christian tradition aspires to a mathematical notion of language; language is imperfect, deceptive, a rough approximation of reality.

By contrast, *davar* is indistinguishably both word and thing. The word *is* a thing, not the representation of a thing. The Torah, for example, is considered a map or plan of creation. It has a direct relation to, a contiguity with, the world: the mysteries of the text are the same as those of the world: 'To understand creation, one does not look to nature but to the Torah' (Handelman, 1982:130). Truth is not located in the relation between a proposition and reality; rather, it is the provisional status of all that is mysterious, enigmatic and surprising. A Hebraic 'truth' is a kind that *could always be otherwise*. If all 'things' (including language) are ontologically equal, reality has no privilege over representation.

Thus for Graeco-Christian thought only a literal language can represent true being (truth as presence); the rabbis, by contrast, believe that the Torah precedes speech and reality. The divine act of knowing cannot be represented in the form of the logical syllogism but is found only in a process of endless interpretation.

5 In the Greek and Christian traditions time is linear, successive, solar, based on regular, continuous mathematical progression. By contrast, Hebraic temporality is based on rhythms and lunar repetitions, a cyclical timelessness. The Christian spatialises where the Jew temporalises knowledge. For the Christian, knowledge is propositional, while for the Jew it is discursive.

6 Where the Hellenic and Christian traditions rely on visual and vision-centered metaphors (knowledge as an image, the object as exhibitionistic, the knower as voyeuristic, thought is *specula*tive, revelatory), confirming identity and singularity, presence and completeness, the Hebraic is largely *auditory*. God is not manifested, present or incarnated but functions as *voice*. God speaks. The eye can choose to see or to be blind by being shut to the light. But the ear is always 'open'. The imperative always reaches its destination. This is why the Hebraic forbids iconographic representation, similitude or correspondences between the image and the thing. The specular image is a paganistic literalisation of the primarily verbal metaphor. The divine image is invisible and unrepresentable for the Jew. Vision has no power to command, this is the power of the voice: 'Hearing is the way to perceive God ... Hearing is the knowledge — abolishing all distance — of knowing oneself encountered, of recognizing the claim of him who speaks' (Rudolf Bultman, quoted by J.F. Lyotard, 1977:402).

The Torah is itself a 'translation' of God's name, a name no mortal being can utter. This name is encrypted in the holy text, which differentially plays on it. Writing/scripture (in French, *écriture*) is a play on the permutations of God's name. Like poetry itself, God's name has no meaning but is the condition of all meaning. This emphasis on the divinity of language radically ruptures the idea of totality and identity. The Torah is itself composed of fragments: fragments of God's words, mixed with fragments of commentaries. Always incomplete, open-ended, opening up new interpretations rather than confirming old ones, interpreting interpretations *ad infinitum*. The Torah is thus the Book of books, the book of infinitely interpretable signs.[9]

Women's god(s)

Irigaray's God is not conceived in naturalistic, personal or judg-mental terms. God is not a totality, unity or origin. If anything, in her usage, it refers to the principle or ideal, a projection or perfection of the (sexed) subject—a kind of ego-ideal specific to the concrete subject. God is a mode of self-completion with no finality, no end point, an asymptotic tendency of becoming. God is the condition of the subject's certitude, of the finite subject's identity as a law-abiding being. It is the condition, for Irigaray, of having a *genre*. Here Irigaray plays on the full resonances of the term: it summarises men's domination of the personal and familial structures ('genre' as 'genus', 'family' or 'humankind'); knowledges ('genre' as 'kind', 'manner' or 'sort', the imposition of organising conceptual categories), and socio-cultural achievement ('genre' as 'aesthetic type', 'taste', 'style' or 'fashion'):

> *Man can exist because God helps him to define his* genre, *to situate himself as a finite being in relation to the infinite ... To set up a genre, a God is needed ... Man did not let himself be determined by another genre: feminine. His only God was to correspond to the human type which we know is not neutral as far as the difference of sex goes. (Irigaray, 1986a:3–4)*

God, then, is the term necessary to position or locate one's finite being in the context of other finitudes (sexual, social, terrestrial) and the infinite. God provides the genre, the context, milieu and horizon of the subject. For this reason, while she remains highly critical of patriarchal religions, Irigaray nevertheless refuses to abandon its language. God's place as ideal and horizon remains a political, ethical and aesthetic ideal:

> *If women lack a God they cannot communicate, or communicate among themselves. The infinite is needed, they need the infinite in order to* share *a little? Otherwise the division brings about fusion-confusion, division and tearing apart in them/her, be-tween them. If I can't relate to some sort of horizon for the realisation of my genre, I cannot share while protecting my becoming. (Irigaray, 1986a:4)*

Her notion of God is an inversion and displacement of its theological origins. God provides a metaphor for several concepts essential to her understanding of women's autonomous identity: first, it represents an idealised perfection, an actualisation of the potential to which women can aspire; second, as a mode of situating space and time (insofar as these coordinates are God-given); third, as horizon and context of identity; and fourth, as the supreme form of an alterity which institutes ethics: one can love the other only if one also loves oneself and (a) God. 'Gods are necessary and linked to the constitution of an identity and a community' (1986a:12).

> *There is nothing moral about the love of God. It shows a way. It is the engine of a more perfect becoming. It is the vector, the bowstring, the bow, the horizon extended between the furthest past and the furthest future, the most passive and the most active — permanent and always in tension. God holds no obligations over our needs, except to become. No task, no obligation burdens us except that one: become divine, become perfect, don't let any parts of us be amputated that could be expansive for us. (1986a:9)*

In her view God represents the possibility of a perfection, an ideal, goal and trajectory for the subject, but only on condition that this God is one's own. Thus far, however, God or the gods have represented male ideals, male self-representations and horizons. In adopting them as their own, women submit to their reduction to variables, props and supports for men's aspirations to divinity. For Irigaray women need to find or formulate a God of their own, a God in their image: no longer the mother of God, the vessel through which God is manifested, but a God who, with the masculine God, can together occupy a heaven, 'becoming gods together':

> *Woman lacks the possibility of becoming a God for herself and for the community. Perhaps for God. Certainly for the coming together for the universe, for which she is the generatrix through her feminine sex, according to certain traditions. To be faithful to her natural and political genre, and to make it divine, woman must accept it and accomplish it as a limit. And morphologically ...*
>
> *There is nothing to be desired about being the term of the other. This paralyses us in our becoming. Divinity and goddess for and of man — we are deprived of our goals and paths. It is indispensable for us to be God for us so that we can be divine for the other, and not an idol, fetish, images already proliferated and determined. (1986a:11)*

The angel as intermediary

Insofar as God represents the most celestial order and the human the most terrestrial, Irigaray seems fascinated with exploring the possibility of an intermediate between them, a middle ground between the bird and the fish, God and human, man and woman. This may explain her recent interest in the concept of the *angel*. The angel is a messenger of the divine who announces the coming of divine events. The angel traverses distinct identities and categories to foretell the union of differences, particularly the union of the sexes in marriage, conception and birth, announcing sexual productivity and exchange. The angel thus represents the divine union of the sexes, without, significantly having a sex of its own:

> *the angel tells of a journey between the envelope of God and the world, the micro and the macrocosm. They announce that this journey is accessible to the body of man. And especially to woman's body. They represent and speak of another incarnation, another* parousia *of the body. Irreducible to philosophy, theology, morality the angels appear as messengers of the ethics evolved by art — sculpture, painting or music — without which something other than the gesture which they represent cannot be said. (1984:22–3)*

Although angels signify the possibility of a bridge between the mortal and the immortal, the terrestrial and the divine, male and female, they are usually disembodied, sexually neuter, intangible, incorporeal. They move between one order and another while being identified with neither. They are thus able to act as ideals of a meeting or middle ground between the sexes. While the two sexes seek divine or angelic status, their marriage or union entails having/being a sex. In her ideal union of and exchange between the sexes, each seeks to become a corporealisation of the angelic, a sexualised, shimmering, always moving being. The *embodied* angel may be able to represent the possibility of a divine union, without residue or leftover. The angel thus represents the possibility of a *sexual ethics*:

> *A sexual or charnel ethics would require that the angel and the body be found together. A world to construct or reconstruct ... from the smallest to the greatest, from the most intimate to the most political, a genesis of love between the sexes would be still to come. A world to create or recreate in order that man and*

*woman can again or finally cohabit, meet and sometimes remain
in the same place. (1984:23)*

The divine is not simply the reward of earthly virtue—heaven
in its traditional sense. For Irigaray it is the field in which
creativity, fertility and production must be positioned. It is the
space for what is new, what remains unthought, the space for the
projection of possible futures. It is a becoming without *telos*, a
movement linked, above all, with love, self-love, love of the other
and of the Other.

Irigaray's project is the exploration of some of the necessary
conditions for constructing a *female divine*, a God, gods, a heaven,
a genre and social position which is feminine, and can represent
women's aspirations to an ethical order, as men's God has represented theirs. Forging access to the divine for women is the
condition of an identity and a self-determined position, as well as
for social transformations (of knowledges, discourses, ethics, social
organisation, sexual relations) transgressive of patriarchy.

*Only a God in the feminine can look after and hold for us this
margin of liberty and power which would allow us to grow
more, to affirm ourselves and to come to self-realisation for each
of us and in community. This is our other still to be realised,
beyond and above of life, powers, imagination, creation, our
possibility of a present and a future.*

*Isn't God the name and place which permits us the appear-
ance of a new epoch of history and which resists this event?
(1984:12–13)*

The Greek pantheon

Along with Christian conceptions of the holy trinity and a Judaic
conception of God as infinitely interpretable, Irigaray is also
strongly influenced by the image of the gods in Greek mythology.
Rather than concentrate as Freud does on the oedipal myth, in
which the son's role is crucial, she utilises the images of women,
particularly daughters, in Greek mythology. Among others, she
mentions Antigone, Clytemnestra, Ariadne, Athena, Korè and
Persephone. Her interest in them is partly a response to Freud's
neglect and partly a result of her search for a 'genealogy' and
archaic prehistory for women. These female figures do not represent a pre- or non-patriarchal narrative, but are the consequences
of an already functional patriarchal order. Nevertheless, they
represent an excess or superfluity that overflows their patriarchal

context. Irigaray does not simply discuss their mythic representation within Greek texts, but tends to analyse the ways in which
such figures function (as metaphors, references, points and images)
within more recent writings, particularly Nietzsche's.

When, for example, Freud postulates that culture is founded on
the patricide of the primal father and the totemic devouring of his
body, Irigaray insists that underlying this ancient murder is an
earlier, more archaic and unspeakable killing: a matricide. The
father's death is not the first cultural act; at best, it is the first
recognised or recorded act. For the father to occupy his dominant
position, in control of all the women and the rivalrous sons, his
position must *already* be a consequence of a 'murder' of a kind:
the severance of the umbilical link between mother and child. The
father's name and law must anchor themselves precisely in the
most intimate of all corporeal connections, metaphorically, the
navel, that locus/hole which ties the child umbilically to the
maternal body:

> *Isn't the mother already torn to pieces by Oedipus' hatred when
> she is cut up like this in stages [representing partial objects],
> each part of her body being invested and then disinvested in
> order to grow? And when speaking of the father's dismember-
> ment by the sons of the primitive horde, doesn't Freud forget, in
> complete disavowal and misrecognition, she who was torn be-
> tween sons and father, between sons? (1981a:19)*

Greek mythology articulates our shared cultural narratives. Yet,
given their rich ambiguity and openness to re-interpretation, they
are always capable of being read *otherwise*.

Athena, Persephone and Ariadne represent three of the 'masques'
Irigaray adopts as her own in her interrogation of Nietzsche
(1980:65) in order to 'seduce' him, to flirt in his own (poetic,
ambiguous) mode, to flatter, play his game, making clear
Nietzsche's own forms of containment of women.

Athena is born of no woman but is spawned from Zeus' head
after Zeus devours his pregnant wife. Athena is thus a motherless
daughter, a passionless woman, preserver of patriarchal law and
justice. Athena arbitrates conflicts, moderates passions. She is the
necessary mediator of the father's law, taking the place here of the
repressed, devoured mother. Irigaray sees the Athena figure as
part of the strategy of phallocentric containment of women in
men's image. Veiled from head to foot, the virgin figure conceals
her beauty, her corporeality and her femininity, revealing only her
face. This is her seductive power: veiling her corporeality, her

163

lack, her sex, she speaks words that are not her own (they are her father's), she brings harmony to those around her. She promises status but has none in her own right:

Femininity — an indispensable intermediary for the father in making his law prevail. The simulacrum which introduces the false into the true, effaces their difference, substituting for this difference an interval of pretense: the neutrality of femininity. Even God needs femininity in order to present himself as the only creator. In order to pass himself off for — what he is not ...

With the patriarchal order, femininity forms a system. Dissimulation of woman in the thought of the father. Where she is created fully-clothed and armed. Veiled, her beauty concealed. Nothing visible except her face. Therefore, not woman. ... Femininity understands how to seduce, knows how to attract and captivate with the folds of her garments — a dissimulation which multiplies, multiplies her. She calculates her effects, times her blows ... (1983c:99)

Athena dissimulates femininity, particularly the feminine productivity of maternity and women's sexuality; she recuperates and harnesses the mother's/woman's passion, repositioning it in the service of the father. Athena represents, for Irigaray, the father's projection and idealisation of woman. Product of nothing but his jealously protected creativity, speaking no words other than his, she represents that sexless, indifferent (for she is neither different nor the same) incarnation of his own image:

Adorned, femininity — manifestation of the father's idea of feminine power. Appropriating the mother's power, swallowing it up, introjecting it, he engenders, produces this daughter who (only) gives herself for that which she is not: a simulacrum assumed by the God to help him in his work, to establish his empire. An empire of pretense which claims to do without the body, an empire of death. (1983c:102)

Athena epitomises a femininity formed in man's image; she mediates his relations to the natural, to productivity and fecundity. In this sense she represents not only the veiled (and hence alluring) woman; she also represents science and knowledge. In her reading of/with Nietzsche in *Amante Marine*, Irigaray refers to his acknowledgement of the hatred the scientist feels in confronting nature, a hatred against which he protects himself through the abstract rules, laws, 'veils' (see Nietzsche, 1974:59): 'Their dream: to cover the natural with veils. To climb always higher, to remove themselves even further, to abandon themselves to the certainty which, from the hazardous summits, they no longer even discern as an evasion—but as their plains, their plans' (Irigaray, 1983c:108).

If Athena represents order, harmony, subordination of the feminine to the masculine, she also, through Nietzsche's use of her as metaphor, represents scientific and philosophical knowledge. Athena functions, then, as an emblem of women's general position as men's image, mirror or fantasy; as a particular 'kind' of woman, one who 'collaborates' and acts as a mouthpiece for masculine values; and as men's representations of nature and the cosmos, veiled and adorned to prevent too intimate a contact and too ensnaring an engagement.

Counterposed to Athena in *Amante Marine* is Persephone, who represents the relations between the celestial and the terrestrial, the underworld and the heavens, a continuing theme in Irigaray's texts. Persephone is the infernal goddess, queen of the underworld. She begins as an object of exchange between men. As *Korè*, virgin, she is stolen from her mother by her father and taken to the Hades: 'The *Korè* is given by the heavenly god to the infernal god, who only takes possession of her in ravishing her. Stolen, violated, veiled (*volée, violée, voilée*), a second time' (1983c:112).

Carried off to Hades, she weeps, unseen, beneath the earth. Her mother, Demeter, the mother of the earth, can hear her but does not know where to find her. She is taken from her mother-nature and placed in death's region—yet not dead, not entirely suffocated. Demeter mourns her lost daughter and refuses to produce 'nature' in her absence. Persephone remains with her husband thus only one season a year, in winter. Here she is a frozen being (ice/mirror = *glace*), removed from herself, in suspended animation. She ascends to the surface to spend spring and summer with her mother, during which time her mother, the earth, can be fruitful. Split between her husband and her mother, she represents a divided femininity only partially captured by patriarchy. The strength of the maternal bond, her mother's strength, can exact compromises with death, with the abyss, so that she can, unlike Athena, remain her mother's daughter as well as her husband's wife. In a sense she is pure dissimulation. Never visible, only veiled, she never acts or lives alone: she is divided between two worlds, two loves, two places. Yet she exceeds her designated position(s) and roles. She remains a paradoxical being, inhabiting mutually exclusive domains:

*Bathing and illuminating everything without becoming visible.
A tactile substratum, dedicated to forgetfulness, when the eye
and the ear alone wish to marry.*

*Her affirmation already takes place this side of or beyond
appearance, without a veil. She diffuses herself, like a harmony
which sub-tends, envelops and subtly 'fills' every spectacle,
prior to the caesura of forms and according to a movement other
than scansion into syncopes. A continuum to which even the veil
will lend the material support of its fabric ...*

*Harmony, in itself, in her, ceaselessly recrosses the limit from
the outside to the inside of the one. It/she always brings
together at least two. Not two unities, but a two which passes
from the interior to the exterior, from the exterior to the interior
of the ones, and without a break. Immediate mediation which
never represents itself, never exposes itself as such. Not that
it/she is covered by a veil, not even of appearance. When
appearance manifests itself, she can still draw enough to mark
out the folds, seams, and looseness of these coverings and
dissimulations (1983c:116)*

Ariadne is the third major mythical figure whose voice Irigaray
adopts in her interrogation of Nietzsche. She is Zarathustra's ideal
woman.[10] Ariadne, who is the daughter of King Minos, falls in
love with Theseus. She provides him a sword with which to slay
the Minotaur, and some thread by which to find his way out of the
labyrinth. When he succeeds, Theseus takes Ariadne as his companion to the island of Naxos, where he abandons her while she
sleeps. On waking to find herself deserted, Ariadne weeps with
grief. In pity, Venus promises her an immortal love to replace the
mortal one she lost. As Ariadne laments, Bacchus, on whose island
she is left, consoles and marries her. As a wedding present he
presents her with a golden crown encrusted with jewels, and when
she dies Bacchus throws the crown into the sky, whereupon the
gems are turned into a cosmic constellation.

Irigaray questions Nietzsche's attempt to contain Ariadne as an
answer to *his* mysteries and his questions, enclosing her, as it
were, in his own labyrinthine self-reflections. In *Ecce Homo*
Nietzsche asks, 'who besides me knows what Ariadne is? She's a
riddle, an answer to ... solar solitude' (1969:308). A riddle, *for
him*, not a being in her own right. Speaking in Ariadne's voice,
Irigaray rejects his 'icy marriage' which would deny her autonomy,
positioning himself within the very labyrinth, the eternal return,
that he attempted to impose on her. In her strategy of asserting

two sexual symmetries where normally there is only one, Irigaray suggests that each sex could have been the labyrinth for the other, both the maze (mirror-maze?) and the way out, if only Nietzsche, the man, would let go of his 'disguises' and 'go on a fling' (Irigaray, 1980:80) with her as amorous partner.

> *Beneath all these/her borrowings and artifices, this other still sub-sists. Beyond all these/her forms of life or death, still living. And as she is dis-tant—and in 'herself'—she threatens all values with instability. In her they can always collapse: truth, appearances, will, power, eternal return. Miming them more or less adequately, this other remains un(equ)ivocally. Who serves the master inasmuch as she hinders none of his impulses, espouses all of his standards. Faithful to him in all her infidelities she protects his 'ambience'—permitting him to withdraw and to return—diverge between him and herself—according to the demands of his power. (Irigaray, 1983c:118)*

Although she takes on his forms, his values, like the hysteric she mimes a femininity which is men's mirror-image. And like the hysteric she always exceeds what is expected. Ariadne, Persephone and even Athena always figure *more than* their patriarchal containment:

> *So she who is always mobile renders him the possibility of movement in remaining, for him, the persistence of his being. Truth or appearance, according to his desire of the moment, his appetite of the instant. Truth and appearance and reality, power ... she is—by virtue of her inexhaustible aptitude for mimicry—the living support of all the staging/production of the world. Variously veiled according to the epochs of history. (1983c:118)*

Athena is a 'mode of representation of ourselves for man's desire'. She speaks for and represents men's interests, but only at the expense of her own sexual pleasures and identity as a woman. Contained in men's worlds, Persephone nevertheless acknowledges and desires precisely what Athena has had to renounce in order to exist as her father's daughter—her link with the mother. Ariadne speaks from the watery, fluid realm of the oceans, confronting Nietzsche's landscape of earthly heights and plains. She speaks as multiple and fluid, a fluidity Irigaray has already posed as feminine in 'The Mechanics of Fluids':

> *I chose to examine Nietzsche in terms of water because it is the*

place of the strongest interpellation, it is the element of which he is the most afraid. In Zarathustra, we hear his fear of the deluge. Water is what disturbs rigidity of both frozen forms and mirrors. It is a place which I wouldn't call opposite but different, in relation to the sun. (1981a:43)

To understand Irigaray's particular use of the imagery of water to challenge Nietzsche and to represent female gods of antiquity, more attention now needs to be devoted to her understanding of the four elements.

The elemental

Starting with *Amante Marine*, Irigaray has been concerned to explore a mode of women's materiality and corporeality which has been unable to find adequate representation in phallocentric paradigms. This search for a materialism outside of traditional definitions is necessary for her project of establishing an identity for women cognisant of women's corporeal specificity. If, up to now, materiality has been identified through vision, women can only be *seen* as lacking and castrated. Irigaray thus turns to models and theoretical systems outside of or repressed within mainstream philosophical and religious discourses. In her use of the metaphor of the four elements, she relies on the work of the pre-Socratic philosophers (particularly Empedocles) and the traditions of medieval alchemy which posit all things and all change according to the interactions and transmutations of the four elements, earth, air, fire and water.

Like his predecessor, Parmenides, Empedocles was a materialist. However, unlike Parmenides, for whom all change is illusory, change is for Empedocles the fundamental principle of being. Becoming is the essence of being. Matter is the arrangement of four types of building blocks or substances, unchangeable particles. Through their mingling they form all concrete objects. The four elements are characterised by him as gods: Nestis is water, Zeus is fire, Hera is air and Hades is earth (see Kirk, Raven and Schofield, 1983:286).

The elementary particles form alliances with others to create material objects through a process which Empedocles describes as love or attraction; correlatively, material things can be broken down into their components through strife or hate:

at one time they grew to be one alone of the many, at another again, they grew apart to be many of the one—fire and water

*and earth and the immense height of air, and cursed Strife
apart from them, equal in every direction, and Love among
them, equal in length and breadth. Her must you contemplate
with your mind, and not sit with eyes dazed; she it is who is
thought innate even in mortal limbs because of her they think
friendly thoughts and accomplish harmonious deeds, calling her
Joy by name and Aphrodite. She is perceived by no mortal man
as she circles among them ... (quoted in Kirk, Raven and
Schofield, 1983:290–1)*

The unity of things is a consequence of the plurality and
harmony of their elements. Love is the mingling of the different
elements, the harmonious coming together and productivity of
simple or elementary particles. The coming together and breaking
apart of their relations is an infinite process, with no beginning or
end. We have here the earliest anticipation of Nietzsche's conception of the eternal return or 'cosmic life-cycle'. Each of the
elements must be equal, in its difference, to the others, and Love
and Strife, though opposed principles, taken together are the
equivalent and counterbalance of all the elements.

Empedocles' representation of the four elements thus provides a
startling yet apposite metaphor of the meeting of different substances, a perilous meeting which, through Love, can bring productivity and unexpected creation, and through Strife can break
down apparent unities and stable forms of co-existence. It is thus a
rich metaphor for contemplating the possibilities of autonomy and
interaction between the two sexes.

This may help explain why Irigaray has undertaken a tetralogy
of texts each written according to one of the four elements, in her
exploration of an ethics of sexual passion. In *Amante Marine*
Irigaray analyses of Nietzsche from the point of view of water,
playing the role, as the title suggests, of the seafaring lover, not
because Nietzsche's texts themselves abound in water metaphors
but precisely because it seems to be the element left obscured and
unrepresented in his works. He continually resorts to land-based
metaphors, metaphors associated with the earth, air and fire. But
it is water, the most 'amniotic' of elements, the most primordial
and 'feminine', that he seems to resist most actively, as if in fear of
drowning. *Amante Marine* is a text saturated with fluidity:

*[Amante Marine] is an attempt to mark a difference, hence the
choice of a marine element which evokes the amniotic fluids
which thwart the eternal return. One knows of the desire
Nietzsche had to be a mother, and how much he suffered from*

*not being able to be one. The marine element is therefore both
the amniotic fluids, the deepest marine element which can't
simply be an appearance and to which Nietzsche will never
return, which escapes him forever, and it is also, it seems to me,
something which represents feminine* jouissance *quite well, including in a movement of the sea, of going and returning, of
continuous flux which seems to me to be quite close to my*
jouissance *as a woman, and completely foreign to what an
economy of erection and detumescence represents. My movement,
let us say of feminine* jouissance *is more maritime than scaling
or descending a mountain. (Irigaray, 1981a:48–9)*

Passions élémentaires (1982) is the second text in her proposed
quartet. In it she explores and enacts what she describes as the
'dividing up of the earth', a pre-biblical analysis of desire which is
also a song to erotic love. Male and female subjects within this text
rediscover the elements out of which they and the world itself are
composed, playing in a relation of 'harmonic discord', 'in which
opposites unite in an intense mêlée' (1982:125). Love, the strongest, the most powerful of the passions is the creative encounter of
opposites rather than their annihilation. Each sex must see the
other as autonomous, independent, capable of giving and taking,
capable of sustaining two sexual symmetries:

*Love is either the mode of becoming which appropriates the
other to itself by consuming it, introjecting it into the self until it
the self disappears. Or love is the movement of becoming that
allows the one and the other to grow. For such love to exist,
each one must keep its body autonomous. One must not be the
source of the other, nor the other or the one. Two lives must
embrace and fecundate each other with no preconceived goal or
end for either. (1982:32–3)*

In *This Sex ...* (1985b) Irigaray is concerned, among other
things, with the possibility of exchange between radically different
subjects, who, like the four elements, are capable of interacting
and combining together to form 'things'. There are no fixed
boundaries between them; rather, all bodies, heavenly or celestial,
terrestrial and corporeal have permeable relations capable of being
reconceived and acted out in different terms, confounding a binary
logic that divides the inside from the outside, the near from the far
and the masculine from the feminine:

Before the separation of the sky from the earth, the continents

from the sea, the dark from the light. A mingling of rock, fire,
water, ether. Where violence is still wed to softness. The heroic
body spilling over with tenderness. Its arms still those of an
original innocence. Which confounds all decisive distinctions
and returns all divisions to their original nuptials. (1985b:125)

L'oubli de l'air (1983b) is the third text; it is an exploration of
Heidegger's works from the point of view of air, the breath,
transcendence, ascension. The fourth and final text is planned but
not yet written or published, although Irigaray has already provided hints about what its contents may include (in 'Women on
the Market' [1985b]). It was to have been on Marx, from the point
of view of fire:

There is a Marx text, which hasn't been done and which I still
don't know whether I will do, which would have been in terms
of fire. It would have been on this aspect of fire in Marx. In
order to specify what could be called the technological or
technocratic use of fire, say in industry and also what fire would
be in terms of desire. (1981a:44)

The striking use Irigaray makes of the four elements in her
deconstructive analyses of philosophical texts cannot be seen as an
ontological commitment, designed to replace the more modern
concepts of elementary particles proposed by physics; rather, it is
strategic. It reveals what is at stake in other ontologies, and
demonstrates, using the archaic language of our own culture's
prehistory, the possibility of alternatives. If, as she argues in 'The
Mechanics of Fluids' (1985b), scientific, biological, chemical,
evolutionary and physics models are implicated in phallocentrism,
it is necessary to depart from these paradigms while recognising
their role in forming the contemporary horizons of knowledge.

In utilising the language of ancient alchemy, she reverts to a
proto-historical world-view, one preceding the imposition of
reasoned science in Ancient Greece. She uses a logic of interactive
forces or combinatory 'particles', the 'atoms' of all matter in the
universe. Taken together, they indicate a logic, not of being, but of
perpetual *becoming*, a world in continuous flux and change. Earth,
air, fire and water are the primal ingredients of subjectivity as well
as material objects, and their particular modes of combination
indicate what are called the 'passions' of the subject as well as the
subject's relation to the natural world. Irigaray justifies this usage
by claiming:

I wanted to go back to this natural material which makes up our bodies, in which our lives and environment are grounded: the flesh of our passions ...

The passions are to do with fire and ice, light and night, water and submersion, earth and the discovery or loss of ground, respiration in its most profound and most secretly vital sense. (1986a:1)

An elementary language has the advantage of providing a corporeal model of sexual difference using a vocabulary repressed or latent within our own cultural (pre-)history, to describe the powerful relations and productivity of love and exchange between the sexes.

The marine, celestial, volcanic and organic aspects of sexual identity, those fish-like, bird-like or snake-like components which construct our corporeal existence, provide images and metaphors by which different, non-hierarchical relations between the sexes may be represented. The elementary symbolises an unrepresented or latent materiality within phallocentric knowledges, conditioning but unacknowledged by them. Irigaray makes clear the foundations of phallocentric discourses in the disavowal of their own processes of production. Like all processes of material creativity, the production of texts involves a reciprocal interaction between material elements: 'Our so-called human theories and our most banal discourses are moving away from these things, progressing through and with a language which forgets the matter it designates and through which it speaks' (1986a:1).

The elemental thus provides Irigaray with a language in which to represent a materiality respectful of the different modes of existence of two sexes. Its function is tactical: the language of the elements both precedes and exceeds that of scientific discourses and truths, revealing the ways in which being and becoming have been cut off from their intellectual origins and their processes of production. It is no more 'truthful', more scientific or inclusive than the languages of the traditional sciences. Indeed, it is just as arbitrary. This seems one of her major goals: by means of an arbitrary schema of physical existence to reveal the historical arbitrariness of received and dominant representations of corporeal and material existence. Yet, in themselves, without a reformulation of the cosmological order and without a reorganisation of notions of space and time, this elementary language remains of historical and not of current political and ethical import. These metaphors of Irigaray's, in other words, need to be recast into a different representation of space–time, and ultimately, of God.

Space, time and the cosmos

Irigaray connects the problematic of space and time directly to the concept of God, seeing that they are categories ordained by and properties associated with God. Space, time and their 'contents' — persons, things, nature — are amenable to philosophical scrutiny only insofar as the elemental is divided into, named and constituted as distinct categories by God's primordial acts of division (this is true whether one adheres to the position proposed in *Genesis* or to the mythology of Ancient Greece). And in the relations between the way space and the way time are conceived, Irigaray discerns the underlying association with the male/female opposition: time is the projection of a (masculine, divine) subject's interior, while space is represented as the exteriorisation of a (feminine) subject:

> *Gods, God, first creates space. And time is there, almost in the service of space. The first day, the first days, the Gods, God, make a world by separation of the elements. Then this world will be peopled, and a rhythm founded between the occupants of the world. God would be time itself which is unsparingly given or exteriorised in his act in space, in places.*
>
> *Philosophy is going to secure the genealogy of the task of Gods, God. Time will become the interiority of the subject himself (this problematic is developed by I. Kant in* The Critique of Pure Reason*). This subject, the master of time, becomes the axis of the management of the world, with its beyond the instant and eternity: God. He effects the passage between space and time.*
>
> *Is this inverted in sexual difference? Where the feminine is lived as space, but often with the connotations of the abyss of the night (God being the light/space?), the masculine as time. (1984:15)*

In Kant's conception, space and time are *a priori* categories the subject must impose on the world to perceive it. They create a unified manifold. Even if our measurements of space and time are arbitrary or conventional, that we conceive of things necessarily located in space and time, and that we conceive of space–time as an inextricable complex are *a priori* principles of the mind. For Irigaray this means that the ways space is conceived are ultimately dependent on the quantifiability of time. Projecting the temporal one-after-another relation outside of the subject marks space as a measurable field, extended from the most minute point to infinity. In short, woman has been represented as the space or place by and

173

in which man can find a position and locate himself. As the corporeal horizon of his existence, the mother cannot be seen as occupying a place of her own. She *is* space, place or 'home' and consequently *has* none herself.

> *The maternal-feminine remains the place separated from 'her' place, deprived of 'his' place. She is or becomes the place of the other who can't separate himself from her. Threatening therefore —without knowing it or wanting it to be so—with what she lacks: a place of 'her own' [also, 'a* proper *space, 'un lieu "propre"'']. It would be necessary for her to re-envelope herself with herself, and at least twice: as she who is woman and as she who is mother, which implies modifying the whole space-time economy. (1984:18)*

If woman has no place of her own, either as woman or as mother, she is readily assimilated to the status of thing, for things likewise do not have their own places, only those deemed useful for men. Irigaray sees women's secondary narcissism, represented in a passion for jewellery, makeup, clothing, as an attempt to give themselves a place, an envelope, a covering instead of their own self-defined space. Women, especially mothers, are considered the dwelling, home or haven from which man comes, his nostalgic place of origin. But this is a place the man must leave in order to create his own. In exchange for losing any possibility of her own space (she must be a subject, with an interior and a temporality for this to be possible) the mother or, rather, her substitute, the (sexually available or marriageable) woman, exchanges her possibilities of a place for his place, his home:

> *In exchange—which is not one—paying for a house for her, sticking her inside it, imposing a limit on her, the opposite of the unlimited site where he unwittingly places her. He envelopes her in walls whereas he envelopes himself in her flesh, and envelopes his things with it. The nature of these envelopes is not the same: invisibly alive, but barely perceptible in their limits, on the one hand; visibly limiting, sheltering but risking being imprisoning and murderous, if the threshold is not open, on the other hand. (1984:18–19)*

It is only if the two sexes each have a place/space (and a time) of their own that, paradoxically, they can encounter each other as subjects and share the same space and time, a here and now. This cannot occur simply by positioning both sexes within a space–time framework which has been formulated according to male experience (both personal and scientific), for this is to deny women their space and time and to link them only to men's. For the possibility of an encounter, a meeting, in passion and wonder between the two sexes, for each to face the other, each must both have and be a space, both for itself and for the other. Once again, Irigaray asserts two sexual symmetries where tradition has posited only one.

She uses some of the metaphors developed in physics in making explicit the need for women to define themselves as subjects, and thus as beings subjectively and objectively located in space–time. Traditionally, men and women have been represented as the positive and negative poles of the atom, the proton and the electron respectively. The problem with such a model of the two sexes is that each 'particle' or sex remains in a given position, with no possibility of exchange or interaction. Rather than this phallocentric plus and minus, Irigaray advocates a recognition of the subject *qua* divided atom, that is, as composed of both poles, atomic particles capable of forming molecular relations, which involve genuine exchange and productivity:

> *In the terms of contemporary physics, it could be said that she remains on the side of the electron, with all that this implies for her, for man and for their encounter. If there is not a double desire, the + and the − poles are spread between the two sexes in place of the establishment of a chiasma or a double loop where each can go towards the other and return to him/herself.*
>
> *Without these + and − in both, always the same one attracts, the other remains in movement but without its 'own' place. What is missing is the double pole of attraction and subsistence, which excludes disintegration or rejection, attraction and decomposition in the place of that separation which emphasises the encounter, the encounters, and permits speech, the promise, the alliance. (1984:16–17)*

Each sex, then, has a 'double polarity', a symmetry of plus and minus in its own terms. This position of Irigaray's must not be too readily equated with the kind of bisexuality affirmed by Kristeva, where each sex is both masculine and feminine. Kristeva leaves unresolved the question of whether the two sexes would thus be fundamentally the same, each split, divided, disunified, but the same in their internal divisions. In Irigaray's model, by contrast, each sex may have a negative and positive pole, or masculine and feminine attributes, but they must mean different things. The plus or minus, the masculine or feminine cannot be universalised independent of sex but must be always sexually specific. What women consider to be plus or minus, or masculine or feminine, cannot be the same as for men. In other words, there are always (at least) two sexual symmetries.

What then is necessary for the formulation of a space–time framework suitable for women? What are the conditions under which each sex can have its 'identity' (of whatever sort), its corporeality, its place without giving up access to the other? If each sex is recognised as autonomous, what reorganisations of space, time, ontology, transcendence, ethics, are needed to accommodate them? What kinds of encounter are possible?

The sexual encounter

What if each sex were autonomous and had its own perspectives on the world, on itself and on others? What if each sex were self-defined, and thus able to exist as both subject and object with its own place(s) in the world? How would they meet? On what grounds and with what effects would their encounter be possible? What kinds of exchanges, productions and transformations would be effected by their meeting?

If the two sexes have something in common, up to now, this has been represented only in men's terms, as sameness, opposition or complementarity to the male norm. But what if the masculine no longer provided the model by which women are judged and measured? What if, instead of one symmetry, there were (at least) two? These questions provide the general domain of Irigaray's most recent researches. Her work is now largely directed to analysing the conditions necessary for a meeting of the two sexes, and theorising the exchanges that may be possible between them. She focuses both on what kinds of social but also on what kinds of interpersonal changes this would imply.

What would constitute an ethics of sexual difference? Such an ethics requires the recognition and acceptance of the irreducible alterity of each to the other, an acceptance of the externality and indeed priority of the other for the subject. Such an ethics would also need to take into account the effects or products of any meeting of the two sexes. Irigaray asks what the passions appropriate to such an ethics would be. She resorts to Descartes' text *The Passions of the Soul* in order to use his notion of *wonder* (*l'admiration*). Wonder, she claims, is a non-oppositional term, a term that is always singular insofar as it refers to the surprise of a first encounter. Thus in place of the hostility and contempt held for women's alterity in a patriarchal culture, Irigaray reverts to this first of all 'passions': 'When the first encounter with some object surprises us and we judge it to be new, or very different from what we supposed that it ought to be, that causes us to wonder and be surprised' (Descartes, 1953 'The Passions of the Soul' in *Philosophical Works of Descartes*, 1970, 53, I:358).

When an object exceeds our expectations, particularly with its self-contained, unpredicted autonomy, this causes surprise and wonder. It is encountered for the first time, without preconceptions or a definite goal or purpose. It strikes us as new or unfamiliar; the subject is awe-struck with its originality. It is, for example, common to feel wonder in viewing the stars or even a work of great prodigiousness or even a 'wonder' at the universe. What would happen if the two sexes experienced this wonder (or its Spinozist correlate, *joy*) in the recognition of the sexual difference of the other?

> *What the other is, who the other is, I never know. But the other who is forever unknowable to me is the other who is sexually different from me. This astonishment, marvelling, wonder in the face of the unknowable should return to its place: that of sexual difference. The passions have been either repressed, stifled, reduced or reserved for God. Sometimes a space of wonder is reserved for the art object. But never is it situated nor dwells in this place: between man and woman. In this place, attraction, avidity, possession, consumption, disgust, etc. emerge. Not this wonder which looks at what it looks at forever, always for the first time, and which never seizes the other as its object. To whom this object remains unable to be taken (in), unable to be possessed, irreducible. (Irigaray, 1984:20)*

When two sexually different beings encounter each other, in acceptance and respect of their own and their partner's specificities, their meeting will be marked with astonishment, wonder. When two autonomous sexes meet, each marvels at and is surprised by the other's difference. This wonder is based on the recognition that 'the two sexes are unable to be substituted, one for the other, in the status of their difference' (1984:20). Each is awed by the other's irreducible specificity. Only then can each give to and take what the other has to offer.

> *Wonder keeps the two sexes non-interchangeable regarding the status of their difference. It maintains between them a free and attracting space, a possibility of separation and union ...*
> *There would never be an overstepping of the interval. There*

would never be an accomplishment of consummation. This accomplishment being a deception. One sex is not entirely consumable by the other. There is always a remainder. (1984:20)

An encounter between the two sexes must thus leave something of a remainder of each untapped by the other, a residue that is irreducible to their relation. This untapped reservoir is what guarantees the radical alterity of each to the other, and yet explains their attractions and the fruitfulness of their encounter. Neither seen as identities, opposites nor complements (for these phallocentric forms leave no resistant leftover for the female), the two sexes occupy their own spaces, create their own ideals. The meeting of two sexually different beings is generative, fertile, productive:

man and woman is a most mysterious and creative couple. This isn't to say that other couples may not have a lot in them, but that man and woman is the most mysterious and creative ... You can love the difference, but only if you're able to love those who are the same as yourself. (1983d:199–200)

The fecundity or productivity of sexually different partners has generally been understood only in terms of their 'product', the child. As Irigaray sees it, the remainder left over by the procreative couple, that unconsumable residue within each sex, has commonly been reserved 'for *God*. Sometimes a portion was incarnated in the *child'* (1984:21). Beyond procreation and divine creation, however, is a whole world of material production which can now be rethought. The encounter with a radical alterity is capable of generating an entirely different relationship between subjects, between the subject and the world, and, Irigaray claims, between the subject and God:

It is true that for the work of sexual difference to take place, there must be a revolution in thought, and in ethics. Everything must be re-interpreted concerning the relations between the subject and discourse, the subject and the world, the subject and the cosmic, the micro- and the macrocosm. (1984:14)

Summary

Irigaray's 'elemental' texts are extremely difficult, dense and sometimes obscure. It is thus no easy task to present a brief compression of her ideas. Nevertheless, given the rambling and apparently disconnected nature of her ideas concerning the divine, the elements and an ethics appropriate to the meeting of sexually different subjects, it is necessary to make explicit the underlying integration or connections between these various concepts, for they all form part of her commitment to making clear the conditions necessary for the social and psychical acceptance of sexual difference.

As I see it, Irigaray's wide-ranging interests spring from her notion that there is not simply one set of interests, values and perspectives at work in culture, which have been described as 'human', 'universal', or 'cultural' in a neutral sense; rather, there are always at least two, one of which (the masculine) has taken it upon itself to represent the other (the feminine). The feminine has thus far functioned in muted, suppressed or unheard ways, obscured by the domination and pseudo-representation of the masculine. In order for the feminine, for women, to be able to speak and be heard as autonomous beings, a series of wide-ranging upheavals is necessary, for it is not adequate simply to affirm women's value and worth in a culture that leaves no space for value and worth other than the masculine.

For women to be accorded autonomy as women, the entire social fabric requires major reorganisation: only *half* the possibilities, the alternatives, world-views, interests (at best) gain social expression or recognition. Half of heaven, half the earth, half of creativity and history is yet to be developed. The problem is how to create a space, a consciousness, a concrete means, by which these possibilities may be explored. When women occupy such a space, for the first time in our history, only then can exchanges and encounters between the sexes produce a world that reflects both sexes.

For this to occur women must not only be seen as autonomous sexual beings and carnal subjects, subjects as well as objects of desire; most particularly, the cultural debt to women's maternity must be openly acknowledged. The debt of materiality, life, existence, that both men and women owe to the mother *cannot* be paid back, it cannot be reciprocated. But in exchange for this life which comes from the mother's body, the child/father/culture must acknowledge that, beyond her maternal roles, the mother is also a woman, a subject, with a life, sex and desires of her own. The mother cannot be entirely consumed in/by maternity. The excess or remainder left over is her specificity as a woman. The child clearly cannot suffer under the yoke of an all-consuming debt, obligated and being thus tied to the mother forever; on the contrary, when the mother is also recognised and accepted as a woman, the child will be free of the engulfment/suffocation or fear of abandonment so many children experience today.

In order to stop being merely the supports or underside of the social order, in order to have their own identities as women, women must develop an horizon, a framework appropriate to them. This means, among other things, having a history, a genealogy, a recognised and validated past within which to locate themselves. In the first instance this means acknowledging the socially effaced link between daughter and mother, daughter and grandmother and so on. It also means an awareness of the roles or possible roles women have played throughout the history and mythologies of cultures, roles that are commonly unrecorded and unseen within historical record. This may explain Irigaray's fascination with Greek mythology, which forms a kind of repressed precondition for the establishment of our culture's images and self-representations. The role of women within Greek mythology, as in psychoanalytic theory, is paradoxical: within mythology women are both subordinated to patriarchal representation, yet their representations also exceed the tolerable limits of patriarchal order.

Claiming a heritage, a past and a genealogy is a condition for women's identities as women in the present. But a past alone is not enough. To be able to live the present as one's own, it is also necessary to have some conception of the future. This future need not be predictable, a plan or projection of step-by-step progression. Rather, a trajectory, a broad direction, a *mode of becoming* is necessary. A being situated only in the reflection of the past and the immediacy of the present has no autonomy but is inert and fixed. It is in this connection that I see Irigaray's work on the divine. The divine is the projection of self-chosen ideals, paths of development to a chosen 'perfection'. God or the gods are not simply external beings, watching, judging the subject. God is, for Irigaray, the ideal or perfected self-representation of a desiring subject. At the same time as representing a future path, a kind of temporal horizon for women's existence, God is also a name for an infinite space, a space which, in other terminology, is the *cosmos*. In order for woman to find/make an identity for herself, she must situate herself (and be situated by others) within a natural or terrestrial order as well as a cosmic or celestial order. The natural and stellar provide the broadest context for subjects. Of course, the subject does not exist as a natural part of this cosmos, for the image one has of the cosmos itself is a function of one's social and representational order. Within the constraints of meaning provided by available representational systems, however, the subject needs some conception of the cosmos, and of her place as subject and object within it.

If God represents the possibility of a location in space and time, the concept also represents the supreme example of the subject's necessary subjection to alterity. If, on the one hand, God represents the supreme perfection of one's own self-image, on the other hand the concept also represents the most powerful and commanding of others. In this sense God stands for the other sex: God represents the possibility of an (ideal) relation to a radically different other.

The subjection to and celebration of a God of one's choosing, a God in the image of one's self and one's representation of the other, signals the possibility of a (mutual) relation with the other. Women have long known what it is like to be subjected to the other. For men to be conceived as the other and for women to conceive of themselves as subjects requires a major shift in our conceptions of theory, of psychical relations and the sacred. Women have suffered a subjection to the *one*. For them to be subjected to an *other* is to take up a position as subjects. Men must, in turn, learn to take on the positions of object-for-women (if they expect to be able to have relations with women as women); and, more particularly, to accept women's self-contained and irreducible alterity. When each sex acknowledges the radical otherness of the other, then mutually rewarding exchanges between them become possible.

Where God and the divine represent what Irigaray has called a 'sensible transcendental', a transcendental yet material ideal, the terminology of the four elements provides her with a series of powerful metaphors to represent materiality, corporeality and the harmonious and disharmonious relations between the corporeal and its material (social/representational/natural) environment. They also provide her with a series of terms by which the co-mingling of inherently different elements/particles/bodies can occur. As fundamental constituents of all being, earth, air, fire and water attest to the relatedness of all matter, from the cosmos to the individual. The elements provide a way in which bodies can be discussed, not as natural or preordained, but as culturally represented. They provide a primary language of the *passions*, of sensations, perceptions, passivity as well as the subject's potential for activity.

As opposed to reason, especially a reason defined by the exclusion of the passions, the passions are the repressed conditions of philosophical, scientific and speculative theory. The passions, usually associated with femininity and passivity, are repositioned by Irigaray as central to the establishment of an ethics of alterity, an ethics sensitive to women's specificity and the possibilities of mutual exchange with men. As well, she uses them to re-theorise fundamental questions of ontology and epistemology. As metaphors of a repressed femininity within philosophical thought, the passions can function to deconstruct and render problematic a reason defined only according to phallic masculinity.

To challenge the prevailing methods, norms and values of philosophical systems, as Irigaray aims to, means, for her, a cultivated seductiveness, the traditional device available to women in patriarchy. As she acknowledges, she flirts with the philosophers, playing with them, seducing them, not in order to gain sexual conquests, but to reveal what each must leave unsaid. She speaks thus obliquely to them, miming their words, but in order to claim some others, other forms, other knowledges and ways of speaking, as her own. To claim, in other words, a position within philosophy as a woman, as a being other than the rational, phallic, knowing subject. She does not wish to dismantle philosophy, dislodge its concepts (like reason, knowing, being and so on) but to enable other kinds of philosophy to be spoken.

This project is part of her overall aim of establishing an exchange between the sexes. Not only can the sexes exchange bodily fluids, sexual passions, desire, producing a child as a consequence; perhaps more interestingly, they can exchange points of view, positions, words, knowledges, making a different kind of production possible. This exchange is not to be understood on the model of the symbolic gift but more as a bringing together of different elements. Its model is not the appropriation of what the other has to offer but rather, interlocution, a reciprocal and reversible relation between addressee and addressor, where neither position is reducible to or occupied by the other. Within this communicational relation, however, neither addressee nor addressor has primacy or control over the dialogue, for this is the product only of their mutual interaction. Each must recognise the specific place the other occupies, be attentitive to what the other says, yet receive it only from his or her own position. Neither can subsume the other, neither is master of the dialogue circulating between them.

Such an interchange, in which *the saying* has as much value as what is said, constitutes an ethics as well as an ontology and epistemology. It is ethical insofar as it involves, for each subject in the relation, the recognition and valuation of the other as other; it is ontological insofar as it is based on the existence of two fundamentally different beings; and it is epistemological insofar as it implies two irreducibly different positions and ways of knowing. It may constitute a new mode of politics and poetics as well, for if each sex is to be accorded its place within discourse, it cannot remain as it has; new kinds of speech, new ways of using language, new kinds of meaning may be generated by this fertile exchange.

Michèle Le Doeuff and the philosophical imaginary

ICHÈLE Le Doeuff's work seems to share little in common
with the work of Kristeva or Irigaray. Her major interests
do not directly focus on the textuality of texts (as Kristeva
does), nor on the position of women or femininity within representational systems (as Irigaray does). More clearly and less ambiguously than either, Le Doeuff's work is located within the discipline of philosophy. Yet there is nevertheless considerable overlap
between the work of all three, even if the connections are oblique
and indirect. Like Kristeva and Irigaray, Le Doeuff is committed
to a largely deconstructive project: revealing the elisions, blindspots, loci of the *unsayable* within texts. To this extent she is
strongly influenced by a Derridean unravelling of the processes of
the production of knowledges and historically privileged discourses.
Perhaps her major difference from them is her refusal to adhere to
a psychoanalytic framework. Clearly she is not ignorant of Freudian
and Lacanian psychoanalysis: her texts contain many references
which reveal a thorough and detailed familiarity with psychoanalytic theory; yet her writing is not internal to the analytic
framework, and psychoanalysis is merely one of many reference
points in her investigations of the 'philosophical imaginary'.

Le Doeuff is influenced in her work by a number of disparate
thinkers, whose works are relevant also to Kristeva and Irigaray,
but who are less evident there. Given the location of her framework
in the detailed textual elaborations of seventeenth- and eighteenth-
century texts in the history of philosophy, and her strong interest
in the history and philosophy of scientific discovery and epistemology, it is not surprising that Gaston Bachelard provides many
concepts and key questions which she explores. While she could be
seen to be undertaking a Derridean deconstruction of these key
texts at the birth of modern philosophy, it is also not surprising
that Michel Foucault's work figures strongly. Foucault not only

surveys a similar period of time in at least some of his texts[1], but also provides a number of methodological insights connecting the production of knowledges (including philosophy) to social, historical and institutional relations, bringing together the production, evaluation and use of knowledges with the operations of power relations. Along with Bachelard, Derrida and Foucault, Le Doeuff seems to be influenced (in what ways we will explore further) by the work of French feminists, Irigaray in particular.

For the purposes of this chapter, I will concentrate on her major text, a collection of papers titled *Recherches sur L'Imaginaire philosophique* (1980a), and a number of papers directly related to the project she announces in this book, and leave aside her more technical papers on the history of philosophy and scientific discovery, including her researches on the work of Francis Bacon, which comprise her most recent writings. Given that the corpus of her work is considerably smaller than the prolific writings of Kristeva and Irigaray, it will be possible to concentrate on a detailed textual analysis of her understanding of the philosophical imaginary and its relation to feminist theory in greater detail than has been possible in the earlier chapters.

L'Imaginaire ... is a collection of disparate articles, written over a seven-year period and linked together in the most marginal and indirect of ways through Le Doeuff's notion of the philosophical 'imaginary'. The 'imaginary' is not used by her in Lacan's sense — that is, to indicate the dimension or order of interpersonal and narcissistic identifications between an ego and its 'other'; rather, it is a loose term hovering between rhetoric (in which case it seems to refer to imagery), philosophy (where it refers to the image, in opposition to the 'pure' content of the philosophical *concept*) and psychoanalysis (here, not in its specific Lacanian sense but more closely related to Freud's notion of the repressed or the unsayable, a kind of textual unconscious). Le Doeuff herself never defines or clearly specifies the term, seeing it more as a point of convergence for her disparate researches than as a fixed entity or readily definable term. The various chapters of *L'Imaginaire* ... have in common the analysis of particular modes of 'thinking-in-images' within philosophical discourses, where they 'properly' have no place.

The imaginary of philosophy

It is her argument that there is not just an imaginary registered in philosophy — a set of images which the discipline cannot admit is

185

central to its functioning—but that there is a specifically *philo-sophical* imaginary, an imaginary constructed by and necessary for philosophy as such: 'Philosophical discourse inscribes itself—labels itself as philosophical—by means of a deviation from the mythic, the fable, the poetic and all that is image-making' (Le Doeuff, 1980a:9).

Philosophical discourses readily admit to the uses of images, myths, fables:

> *statues that breathe the scent of roses, comedies, tragedies, architects, foundations, dwellings, doors and windows, sand, navigators, various musical instruments, islands, clocks, horses, donkeys and even a lion, representatives of all crafts and trades, scenes of storm, forest and trees, in short a whole pictorial world capable of brightening up even the most cut-and-dry 'History of Philosophy' (1980a:10),*

but it regards these as mere embellishments, devices for enlivening texts, heuristic techniques or mere illustrations which could readily be excised without loss to the fundamental *concepts* they represent:

> *If anyone attempted to write a history of philosophical imagery, would this history ever be recognised as a history of philosophy, by the same right as the history of concepts, procedures, systems? ... The images that appear in theoretical texts are normally conceived as being outside the work, so that an interest in them is considered as philosophy only from a strictly anecdotal viewpoint (1980a:10)*

Le Doeuff's project, as she states it in her introductory essay to the book, is to consider the necessary, indeed, constitutive role of these images, this imaginary within the very discipline in which they are considered alien or extrinsic. Her point seems to be that in philosophical systems, where rigour, precision, objectivity and 'plain speaking' are considered desirable attributes, and metaphor, allusion or 'style' unnecessary or decorative embellishments, the discipline is unable to rid itself of its dependence on images. These images, observable in all philosophical discourses, are both necessary and ineradicable: they are both 'the *legitimising* figuration of the practices and hopes of philosophers ... [and] at the same time, a figuration of dangers, obsessions, negative forces ...' (1980a:177).

Le Deouff formulates a working hypothesis which guides her researches in the book, an hypothesis expressed in two forms, one a weak and the other a strong version:

A restricted version: the interpretation of image-sequences in philosophical texts (taken in its widest sense) goes together with the eliciting of lines of stress in a work. Or again, imagery is connected to the difficulties, the sensitive points of any work.

An extended version: the meaning conveyed by images works both for and against the system that uses them. For, in that they provide the basis for what a system cannot justify, yet is necessary for it to function. Against, for more or less the same reason: their significance is incompatible with the possibilities of the system. (1980a:11–12)

Philosophy establishes its value and validity by distinguishing itself from other kinds of discourse, which may be labelled poetic, visionary, literary, fabulous. Yet it must surreptitiously reintroduce these discourses — even in fragmentary form, as figures or tropes — in order to be able to express what it is unable to say in other terms. Philosophy, in other words, must rely on precisely what it needs to exclude in order to posit its identity and particularity. These images indicate points of great sensitivity, neuralgic loci which cannot be readily overcome without major transformations in philosophy's own self-representations. These images are not foreign to or outside of philosophy but are its necessary underside, its unacknowledged supports. This lack of philosophical know-ledge, this inability to reflect on its own modes of inclusion and exclusion critically, constitute what Le Doeuff calls the 'internal scandal' or the 'shameful face' of philosophy; philosophy is a discipline which parades as rational and self-knowing or self-reflective, while at the same time it remains unable to accept its necessary dependence on what is conceived as being outside its domain.

In order to justify or rationalise its dependence on these images, particular philosophies project this need onto various external 'others'. It is not philosophy, then, that requires these images, but rather, a non- or proto-philosophical *other*. The strategy is to attribute these images to a need of those outside the discipline or learning their trade within it, a kind of device for communication beyond the interests of the 'real' practitioners of the discipline:

the imaginary we see in theoretical texts is dependent on the theoretical enterprise itself (on its difficulties), that stricto sensu *is at work in these texts, and that is specific to their production ... relate to the position of the learned few, with all the lures this position has put forth in order to sustain itself; it is consequently related to one of the misunderstandings that are constitutive of philosophy: when the learned few think up the theory of the imaginary, it is always 'the Other' that is in question — it's the people who live on legends, as if this undifferentiated entity called the people (like the other one baptised as folklore) had an independent existence outside the field of representation where a caste projects its own existence in opposition to this massive category. (1980a:14–15)*

For Le Doeuff this strategy involves the projection of the 'internal scandal' of philosophy either, as she describes it, 'upstream', as precondition, or 'downstream', as effect. 'Upstream', these images are justified with reference to a 'primitive', archaic or infantile soul in the philosopher: 'the paradigms of this sort of projection are the child (insofar as we have been children, before becoming men), nursery tales, the crowd (irrational by nature), old wives' tales, folklore etc.' (1980a:15–16); 'downstream', there is a pedagogic or heuristic need, a need to touch the 'common person', the non-philosopher, to provide a bridge between a philosophically learned subject and one ignorant of philosophical techniques: 'a sort of leftover from somewhere else, a double meant for the uncultured mind of the reader, which could be spared us, if only philosophers talked exclusively to other philosophers' (1980a:16). In this case the presumption is that, as a pedagogical device, the image-in-words is simply a form of translation or transposition of philosophy into lay terms, a technique for teaching the ignorant which can be superceded or bypassed when the technical language of philosophy has been mastered by the fledgling philosopher — a kind of device for teaching 'baby-philosophy'. Thus the image is shorthand for communicating what could be otherwise rigorously and non-imagistically theorised in technical language *but* for the needs of the non-philosopher for the non-philosophical elements within philosophy.

This projection of its own scandal onto externalised others is an effect of philosophy's incapacity to accept its limitations, particularly its dependence on language, and its necessarily incomplete or lacking character, its inability to cover the whole field of (possible) knowledges. Philosophical self-reflection, in other words, abrogates the right to (sole) self-critical understanding. Its capacity to constitute itself as a metaphilosophy depends on its ability to accept this thinking-in-images as only an aberration capable of elimination: 'This metadiscourse regularly touches upon the non-philosophical character of thought-in-images. This attempt at exclusion, however, fails regularly and 'as a matter of fact Socrates does speak of loaded donkeys, blacksmiths, shoemakers and tanners' [Plato, *The Symposium* 221e] (1980a:15).

The function of these thoughts-in-images is to·cover over the neuralgic, weak points within discourses, those points where they are unable to say 'directly' and non-metaphorically what they 'really mean'. At the same time they signal to the learned philosophical community that these passages are not worthy of close inspection and can be readily ignored as trivial or unimportant.

It is in administering its own legitimacy, in establishing its own value, that philosophy is led to define and describe its own myths, to rely on spatial or narrative distribution, to make play in its discourses with stories of pierced barrels, islands surrounded by all sorts of dangers, of chains to be broken or forged. (1980a:15, fn 4)

This very process of philosophical self-legitimation is already an imaginary construct since it is not possible for a discourse to validate its *own* foundations: the discourse cannot reach outside itself to explain its own grounds or conditions of possibility without overstepping its range of competence. As Le Doeuff argues, this attempted self-justification is one of the major themes of the history of philosophy. Philosophy has taken the right, not merely to set the limits on what is properly theoretical and what is not for itself, but also for all other discourses as well. This indicates what Le Doeuff understands as the *corporate* character of the discipline, its attempted domination of an 'intellectual economy' in a monopoly or cartel-like form: the discipline uses, without adequately acknowledging it, the image to mediate between a philosophical addressor and a non-philosophical addressee. As a pedagogical device, it gives entry into the corporate practice for the novice or uninitiated outsider; and as an immediately recognisable token, a transparent 'password', it is a sign to the philosophical expert that this is an area of the text that can be ignored or left unjudged.

This bifurcated understanding of the image — as password and token — enables it to function as a key, if unspoken, form of self-justification. Metaphors and images are not simply contingent or superfluous excesses of philosophy, used merely to bring out more clearly what the text means for the uninitiated:

on the one hand, it points to the same direction as the inner coherence of the system, the major themes of which it reproduces down to the last detail. On the other hand, it also gives a place to all that the critical work tends to eliminate, or failed to

*account for; it balances all the cuts required by the theory.
(1980a:28)*

The image indicates a place within texts where the text, or rather, its author, cannot own up to what is being postulated and where, at the same time, it is necessary to make such claims in order for the text to function as such. The image, as Le Doeuff implies, does not belong here but the text cannot work without it.

The image thus pinpoints a locus within the text where the text must exceed itself and the methods on which it relies. It marks a place, not rationally or with philosophical validation, but with desire, excess. This place is that region in the text where 'subjectivity is structured according to the mark of the guild' (1980a:30):

Barthes attributes to the whole of language the paradoxical status of making subjectivity institutional. It is roughly in these terms that I now conceive of the philosophical imaginary: it is something that is completely philosophical insofar as it is dictated by the needs of the theoretical enterprise. This justifies an intellectual analysis, a reading that absorbs the imaginary into the theoretical problems of the system. But at the same time, it re-echoes on the emotional level, and by the same token, it makes this affectivity particular ... texts that operate through images are loaded with inner value-systems, affects and desires. (1980a:29)

The philosophical imaginary thus functions on (at least) two different levels, serving two distinct purposes: on the one hand it functions on an intellectual level, marking those places in texts which cannot be said directly and in a 'pure' philosophical language, places where the philosophical system, in sensing its own weakness or incapacity, must find another way of presenting its speculations. This is a site of conceptual excess, a dishonestly covered place within the text, where the philosophical system may flounder on its own presuppositions. On the other hand it functions on a specular and psychical level, marking those places in texts where philosophical subjects (senders as well as receivers) must inscribe themselves. These places are marked by their 'affects and desires', their needs for recognition and location within the field of philosophical inquiry. In this sense it marks the place where the subject is produced and constituted in the text as a philosophically legitimised subject. These images indicate regions where the subject's love and libidinal identifications are attracted.

This does not mean that philosophy is reducible to the subject's psychical needs or desires, or that the philosophical text is amenable to a kind of 'psychoanalysis' to reveal what concrete or personal desires lurk there; rather; it indicates that the desire for reason, for truth, for philosophical objectivity, are intimately bound up with the structures of self-delimitation that philosophy must exercise in its relation to other discourses and knowledges. Philosophy and the dream are thus not two utterly different discourses, nor two sides of a single discourse: they are two discourses related through a dialectical tension which is both productive (of philosophy's determinate characteristics and forms) and destructive (of the history and trajectory of philosophy's borrowings from other discourses and discursive methods), like the dream itself:

> *Philosophical work is not automatically the extension of phantasy or vice-versa ... The notion of a dialectical link between dream-formation and theoretical work can only lead, for me, to a study of the peculiarities of a social minority, its points of contact with other forms of thought, other discourses. It also takes into account the tension that exists between what we would like to believe, what it is necessary to think and that about which it is possible to be logical. There is no enclosure of discourse, given that discourse is already a compromise, an arrangement between what we can legitimately say, what we would like to put forward, and what we are forced to recognise. (1980a:30)*

This quotation brings out a third function or purpose in Le Doeuff's understanding of the philosophical imaginary — its necessary link to a 'social minority', that is, its given relation to a sociological ensemble. Indeed, if her work can be characterised as philosophical in its orientation, it must also be recognised that the other parameter guiding her various researches is sociological and political. Each of Le Doeuff's analyses of philosophical texts and the various images they presume is also linked to the operation of prevailing, historically determined institutions, institutions which condition and provide a (usually unrecognised) context for particular philosophies and their popularity (or lack of it) at that time.

Significant in this context is the relation she posits between the philosophical activity and two particular kinds of sociological relations. The first is the relation between the production (and reception) of philosophy and the apprenticeships the would-be philosopher must undergo in institutionalised instruction preparatory to philosophy itself — the techniques and procedures of the gymnasium, the college and the university (including examinations, assessment, curriculum, relations of tutelage and discipleship). She elaborates this in some detail in her first paper published in English, 'Women and Philosophy' (1977), in outlining the forms of repressive tolerance and exclusion the discipline exercises on women, but she also makes clear that the various debates over educational and pedagogical practices circulating in the seventeenth century have a direct relation to the pervasive fascination that writers, especially political philosophers, have in theorising the utopian society (or conversely, the state of nature).

The second powerful source of influence which sociological relations exercise over the production of philosophical texts relates less to the institutional constraints on access to knowledge and knowledge production in education and more to the external linkages between philosophy and popular opinions, socio-economic transformations and social movements. The effective functioning of the philosophical imaginary must rely, at least to some extent, on conventions, traditions, commonplace beliefs, which do not need to be articulated in detail in order to be grasped. For example, common phallocentric assumptions about masculinity and femininity feed into and sustain Pierre Roussel's more technical 'chiasmic' speculations on women's moral and sexual peculiarities (see Le Doeuff, 1981/2). Roussel's recognised position as a medical practitioner, and the weight and value placed on medical expertise in the eighteenth century, enabled him to produce a text which is only in the most marginal of ways connected to medicine, being a self-avowedly moral and philosophical tract on women and femininity.

If, then, the operations of a specifically philosophical imaginary are made possible by the internal demands of the philosophical enterprise, the psychical needs of its practitioners and readers, and the sociological contexts (both localised and generalised) within which it is located, a fourth set of interconnections is also necessary to explain philosophy's need to utilise those literary resources Le Doeuff describes under the category of the image. These may be generally described as historical, in the sense that, once again, the domain of the historical is divided into one specific to the philosophical discipline, in the one case, and, in the other, into a more generalised dimension of historical movements and transformations.

Here, Le Doeuff is more precise than in her characterisation of the sociological dimension. In the first case, that of historical or temporal relations within the philosophical domain, she is explicit in claiming that the operation of the imaginary requires precise historical location in order to reveal both what a particular text owes to its own (pre-)history and what it initiates or anticipates, that is, what a future culture or philosophy will need to sustain itself from texts which predate it. In the one case the philosophical imaginary utilises, revives and renders technical, images and fables that have been created or used earlier. In the other the imaginary is essentially innovative, enabling the 'emergence of the not yet thought' (1980a:83)

> *The images of philosophy are regularly taken from precedent texts, which means that the study of those images would point out a history of the literate motifs of the fable-genre ... [W]e need to keep in mind not only the precedents of the usage of these motifs by other philosophers but also to find a definite source, that is to say, an image that, at the very level of the signifier will be close to the object of our analysis. (1980a:18–19)*

The precise history of various images and myths, the borrowings from one text or another, are not merely contingent events in the production of contemporary knowledges; rather, the location of one text historically relative to another from which it borrows its images is an index of what must remain hidden in the contemporary text, and of what is at stake in utilising an already familiar image in a different context. Not exactly a philosophical 'con', nevertheless the ways in which philosophical images are picked up and traced from other texts enables what is constructive in this borrowing to be overlooked. In her preface to *L'Imaginaire ...* Le Doeuff cites two examples, Kant's reworking of Bacon's metaphor of the 'island of truth' and Descartes' metaphor of the house, derived, she claims, from the Gospel according to Matthew (7.15):

> *One can imagine a number of functions for this kind of reactivation: to mask a lack or transgression, to reactualise an anterior blind spot encapsulated in the image (where an image is classical, one no longer notices the way it serves to palliate an impossible situation); to reiterate a wish or desire concerning philosophy; to attempt to validate an enterprise by putting it under the 'patronage' of an accredited authority ... (1980a:124)*

Le Doeuff argues that Descartes' use of the images of the garden and building cover over a major displacement, hiding a new intellectual manoeuvre under all-too-familiar metaphors. In

Matthew the building and horticultural metaphors function through analogy and opposition: the building erected on strong foundations versus that erected on weak foundations; the labour producing healthy fruit versus that producing bad fruit. However, when Descartes borrows them he transforms them without adequate acknowledgement so that, where their familiarity can be presumed, a subtle yet crucial transformation is effected. In the *Discourse on Method* (1970) (part IV) Descartes shifts the building metaphor from one based on foundations or grounds (incidentally, this metaphor is still a powerful one today, and is used in this sense by Althusser as well as contemporary epistemologists to refer to the production of social relations grounded on an economic base and the production of knowledges located on secure foundations, respectively,) to one related to the notion of *lodgings* or accommodation. He alters the orientation of the metaphor where it is used to highlight the foundations, solidity and permanence of construction, to one where the habitable nature of the building is in question. While Descartes himself has used the notion of principled foundations to theorise his epistemological project, in his ethical writings it is no longer the solidity and workmanship of the building that is at issue but its provision of shelter, its ability to be lived in that is now relevant. This surreptitious shift has the effect of rendering his ethical speculations compatible with his epistemological enquiries, when in fact his ethics seems to be in stark conflict with his desire for epistemic certainty. Similarly, the tree metaphor dates from the Stoics, and their use of the method known as Porphyry's tree, in which knowledges are based on a common trunk and roots but divided or branched when it comes to particular, concrete knowledges. Ethics is presented as if it is one branch of knowledge among others, yet at the same time Descartes believes that it presupposes a knowledge of the other branches, and is thus a consequence of their convergence, making it more like the trunk than the branches. This displacement, suggests Le Doeuff, is a consequence of the fact that ethics in Descartes' sense is not possible within the terms of his epistemological system. It is an anachronism, a nostalgia for an earlier philosophical schema, in which ethics takes its place alongside ontology and epistemology.

These evasions on Descartes' part are possible because he refers to and at the same time changes the historically locatable images on which his *Discourse* depends. Only by charting the historical transformations and altered contexts of these metaphors is Le Doeuff able to locate the kinds of change Descartes initiates and the theoretical leaps he makes without adequate justification. In this sense, at least, the historical dimensions of image production are essential to understanding in the assessment of texts.

In the case of Kant, whom she briefly discusses in the preface, Le Doeuff locates Kant's metaphor of the Northern island of truth in *The Critique of Pure Reason* to Bacon's *Temporis Partus Maximus*. Kant counterposes the Northern island, habitable only through hard labour, with the Southern island of the 'golden age', an easy-going, pleasurable island prolific in food (truth) that is readily obtainable by its inhabitants. To quote Kant,

> *We have now not only traversed the whole domain of the pure understanding, and carefully examined each part of it, but we have also measured its extent, and we have assigned to every-thing in it its proper place. This domain, however, is an island, and enclosed by nature itself within limits that can never be changed. It is the country of truth (a very attractive name) but surrounded by a wide and stormy ocean, the true home of illusion, where many a fog bank and ice that soon melts away tempts us to believe in new lands ... Before we venture ourselves on this sea, in order to explore it on every side and find out whether anything may be hoped for there, it will be useful to glance once more at the map of that country which we are about to leave, and to ask ourselves first, whether we might be content with what it contains, nay, whether we must-not be content with it, supposing that there is no solid ground anywhere else on which we could settle; secondly, by what titles we possess even that domain, and may consider ourselves safe against all hostile claims. (Kant, 1973:book II, 205–6)*

Derived from two pages in Bacon's text, Kant's island relies on Bacon's image of the seafaring explorers who leave their island home only to find themselves nowhere, explorers who risk getting lost in their attempts to find a better, or easier, land. Bacon's image occurs as part of his goal of instituting the natural sciences as a part of accepted knowledge. For Bacon philosophy had a crucial role to play in this 'instauration', given that the sciences were not yet established as such and only philosophy could play the role of justification of science. However, by the time of Kant's *Critique* ... , Kant relied on already established sciences and thus, claims Le Doeuff, a philosophical mode of justification is no longer appropriate, given the sciences' manifest capacity to justify themselves in terms of their achievements. Kant's use of the metaphor, in other words, no longer justifies the use of philosophy in the establishment of knowledges but, on the contrary, acts as a mode of self-justification for the specifically Kantian project of an auto-critique of philosophy by (Critical, that is, Kantian) philosophy. Kant's dilemma is this: how to persuade the island's inhabitants to remain there instead of exploring the unknown seas and risking everything for the unactualised possibility of a better island on which to live. How to persuade, given that the seas represent the unknown (unknowable):

> *Without his critique, 'it is inevitable' that the understanding will run ahead to meet with the greatest sorrows. It is so cold on the sea of illusion, and the sea is so rough ... Whereas with the help of Kantian philosophy the understanding will be able to stay on this island, whose charms, by the way, we know nothing about, except that this is the one place where we can hold our ground ... (Le Doeuff, 1980a:21)*

For Bacon philosophy *could* function to 'secure the grounds' which science would one day come to occupy. But for Kant it is now Critical philosophy which can secure the proper domain of the understanding. Kant refuses to acknowledge the vast difference between the Baconian project and his own conception of the role of philosophy. Kant's island becomes a desirable place to live only because the Critical philosophy can ensure us that the universe is otherwise uninhabitable — only, that is, on dogmatic grounds. It becomes desirable by default, the least painful alternative. Le Doeuff describes Kant's methods here as 'terrorist': 'we avoid the pain of the icy fog-banks, but at the price of renouncing all dreams of discovery, the attraction of new lands, and giving up almost all hope' (1980a:21).

At stake for Kant in this particular emblem is, first, a mode of self-justification for the Kantian project which ironically finds its own critical self-justification impossible to make in other terms; second, a covering over of its own 'weak spot', its inability to justify remaining within the confines of a reason that is unable to extend itself beyond its already known domain; thus, third, an elision of the differences between Bacon's entirely contrary project (in which philosophy does indeed anticipate a domain outside its own limits — that of scientific discovery) and Kant's — that is, a recuperation of the Baconian strategy, as if it were able to be exactly transposed onto Kant's own project; fourth, what Le Doeuff considers is the 'hegemonic and governmental function of philosophy in relation to other forms of knowledge, the idea that, without metaphysics, the most essential part of particular kinds of knowledge would remain eternally inactive, or potential' (1980a:21); and fifth, the delegation to Critical philosophy of a hegemonic position, not merely in the sphere of knowledge itself, but in the utilisation and reorientation of science and knowledge towards human happiness.

In sum, the philosophical imaginary is the locus for the articulation of philosophy's strategies of self-definition, and the site of justification of its modes of constraint, its forms of inclusions and exclusions of other kinds of discourse deemed non-philosophical. It reveals the strategies particular philosophies use to evade their sources and to deny their own none-too-pure histories of debt, their similarities with and influences on other (philosophical and non-philosophical) texts. Here Le Doeuff does not focus exactly on a philosophical *unconscious* but more on its 'bad faith', its disavowals and denials. While the imaginary signals a series of manoeuvres philosophy needs but is unable to theorise or admit to, her most convincing work is where she analyses the detailed, particular sites of the imaginary in concrete texts.

Utopias

The most sustained and detailed analysis of the imaginary of philosophy is probably Le Doeuff's readings of Thomas More's *Utopia*, which she discusses in several papers.[2] Her most sustained analysis of this text, in *L'Imaginaire*, presents as thorough a discussion of the imaginary as is found in any of her writings, and reveals clearly the power invested in philosophical discourses.

'La rêverie dans "Utopia"' is the first and for me the most convincing detailed textual analysis in *L'Imaginaire*. It is significant that although *Utopia* is classified as a text concerned with political philosophy, indeed, one of the first modern political texts, its 'politics' is not to be too readily understood as either a critique of the political institutions of contemporary Britain nor as a blueprint or a map of an ideal political organisation, although it is commonly interpreted as such. Le Doeuff proposes to read More's text not as a coherent work within an established genre of political theory, but as a kind of 'dream'. This is not to suggest that it has *no* political import but, rather, that the kind of politics for which it is relevant is not that about which it overtly theorises. In reading the text, or at least Book II of *Utopia*, Le Doeuff suggests that:

> *it is also a dream, and, as such, a thought in the service of desire, desire which is in no way a political passion. Here the*

197

private man is speaking, an individual is soliloquising, as soon as the characters of the book are back in the garden and the servants have been strongly advised to keep intruders away. It is an after-dinner dream, an 'afternoon discourse' in a closed garden. (1980a:35)

In Book II Utopia is not so much analysed by Le Doeuff in its political structure as described in terms of its posited geography and social structure. For Le Doeuff this is a clue to its imaginary function. From More's description of the island as shaped like a crescent moon, Le Doeuff argues that the island is both an island and at the same time a metaphor for the theatre (indeed, a French translation describes it as an 'amphitheatre'): the crescent shape is analogous to the seating in the theatre, and the sea, which, when surrounded by the crescent-like land mass, is like a theatrical stage. Because it is surrounded on three sides, the sea is less like an ocean and more like a tranquil lake, a reflective pool, reminiscent of Narcissus' mirror. Utopia is thus both an inhabited and protective land, guarded from any outside threats by its protective and self-sealing geography, and at the same a theatrical stage which, instead of staging performances for a paying audience, reflects the roles and movements only to its actors. Like the island itself, it admits no outsiders. This theatre–island image, an image which conjures up associations of insular self-containment and opposition to exteriority, Le Doeuff argues, is but a material projection of a kind of philosophical debate amongst the learned inhabitants of this perfect commonwealth:

This is a summary. The Utopians divided bodily pleasures into two kinds. First, pleasure comes from without ... when an object acts on the senses. Second, internal pleasure, the enjoyment of a quiet and tranquil state of the body in undisturbed good health, an ease unrelated to any external pleasure ... Some claimed that a steadfast and quiet good health should not be rated as a pleasure, since it does not cause present and distinct enjoyment to be perceived ... (1980a:38)

This debate mirrors in minute form the geography of the island and the image of the theatre. Once again there is a distinction between a self-contained, 'autarchical' existence, and one bound up with outsiders, a distinction, as Le Doeuff astutely notes, also represented in Freud's distinction between primary or infantile narcissism and secondary narcissism. Primary narcissism is a pre-object relation of the (proto-)subject to its own body, a self-contained pleasure, while secondary (or 'feminine') narcissism is a kind of self-love always mediated by another.

The question the utopian asks is: can one be aware of the quiet self-contentment that has no external object or marker? This question is the correlate of what, for More, is the crucial political question: can an island ruled in the best possible way (one, that is, which enjoys optimal health) be aware of its state?

> *To this question, which is never explicitly raised the imaginary geography gives a positive answer: the island is aware of its internal harmony because the island is a theatre, the stage of which is a lake, and reflected in this lake, it perceives its stage. It has a mirror (*lacus stagnans*) in its belly (*alvum*). (1980a:39)*

The dream underlying More's *Utopia* is the dream of a self-sufficiency untrammelled by any external exigencies. But underlying this dream is a nagging doubt: does the perfect existence, rule by the most benevolent of governments, lead to a kind of stupor in its inhabitants? Does perennial well-being lead to lethargy, indifference and an unstimulated complaisance? This political question is the social or macroscopic counterpart of the question of the health of the body and the body's self-sufficient pleasures.

More himself seems to prefer the claim that there can be a self-sufficient, internally induced pleasure, just as there can be a consciousness of the perfect political organisation. He affirms that the health and 'quiet' well-being of the body is the precondition of pleasure from external things, and that internally regulated political and social harmony is the condition of fruitful and productive cultural exchange. But is More performing something of a sleight-of-hand in his use of the theatrical metaphor and the correlation between the microscopic individual and the macroscopic island?

The theatrical metaphor, for one thing, is very peculiar. In his usage there is no audience, no ostentation, no show, with the actors acting both their parts and that of the audience (More's hostility to ostentation, costumes and showiness is evident in his attitude to the unwelcome Anemolian ambassadors who shamelessly display themselves):

> *The position of philosophy towards the theatre is always ambiguous; accepting on the one hand and rejecting on the other. Thomas More uses the theatrical model to think something (political perfection can be perceived); but what he borrows from is immediately denied, and the theatrical pattern is rejected through the condemnation of exhibitionism. This*

means that the theatre is diverted from its own [propre] mean-ing, to become a metaphor; it is accepted as a model only after it has been crossed out and rectified. (1980a:39–40)

This correspondence between the individual's and the island community's well-being is evasive in precisely the ways Le Doeuff has characterised the philosophical imaginary. The link between the theatre and narcissism can only serve as proof of secondary narcissism, and not, as More hopes, primary or internal pleasures: and the imaginary geography of the island, the same. The analogy breaks down insofar as the island may be capable of economic autonomy, providing for its inhabitants' needs; but the individual can in no way attain this kind of self-sufficiency. The health and well-being of the individual is only possible on condition that external objects, for example, food, drink, shelter—all external objects—are available.

Moreover, the search for a socio-political structure capable of generating pleasure and well-being for all of its citizens cannot, on such a model of autonomous, internal self-containment, generate a *political* theory:

If More's work is a dream, if it is centred around such a conception of happiness, then it is certainly not a political work. Happiness is not found in the relation to the world but in relation to itself. Then the world by which one is surrounded does not matter. If the subject is self-sufficient and blind to everything, why should he care about politics? (1980a:41)

Thus, the image signals a blindspot, a point of tension or even contradiction in More's writings, a point which is over-invested, in which More says more than he means, and exceeds what, in his system, it is possible to say. This reading of the imagery of Book II, Le Doeuff claims, nevertheless *is* political (though not based on an analysis of socio-political structures) insofar as this image is implicitly linked to the political work undertaken in Book I, where More analyses the injustice of British social institutions, especially those which generate poverty and starvation: 'It is not from the world that I derive my pleasure but the world can deprive me of the enjoyment of myself: it is in this way that we pass from More's dream to his political criticism, that is to say, from Book II to Book I' (1980a:42).

Le Doeuff claims that the inconsistencies between Book I, a clearly political text, and Book II can be located less in the imaginary geography of the island than in the notion of pleasure and well-being which More presumes yet obscures. If social life upsets the tranquillity and inner contentment, the health of the individual, at the same time it provides something better — stimulation, relations with others, happiness of a different type: 'If he had had another conception of pleasure, perhaps More would have had another conception of politics' (1980a:42).

In a later paper, published in English as 'Utopias: Scholarly' (1982a), Le Doeuff places the very enterprise of projected perfect societies — utopias — more clearly outside the context of political philosophy proper, and in the institutional and sociological context of the 'school', the educational apparatus. Taking up Bachelard's claim in *The Formation of the Scholarly Mind* that utopias are scholarly or scholastic, Le Doeuff claims that the conception of a utopian society, rather than reflect the ideal social and economic organisation for culture, is a design of society 'by and for the School' (1982a:441).

In analysing More's *Utopia* alongside other utopian texts, Bacon's unfinished *The New Atlantis* and Campanella's *The City of the Sun*, Le Doeuff is led to the following hypothesis: 'the major concern of a utopia is to focus thought on the conditions of possibility for optimal or maximal public (or state controlled) education' (1982a:446). This, she claims, is the overriding concern of all three utopians, and, indeed, of the revival of interest by philosophers, such as Kant, in utopian thought.

Whatever differences exist between their conceptions of the perfect society (More's *Utopia*, for example, abolishes private property, while Bacon's *New Atlantis* is openly mercantile), all three posit institutions and structures of learning as essential requirements of the good society. Their differences are certainly striking: More's conception involves an egalitarian economic structure in which all the members of society participate in all the necessary tasks of that society on a rotational basis. In Bacon's conception, society is centered on the advancement of learning and the production of new scientific knowledge, knowledge which would enrich the nation as a whole. Campanella's ideal involves the State regulation of births and reproduction, where the latter is distinguished from amorous and pleasurable sexual attachments. But whether culture is conceived as largely agrarian, mercantile or eugenic, each in his own way advocates a social organisation which will maximise the knowledge of each individual and, conversely, an educational framework which will maximise the ordered and regulated harmonious nature of society.

For More education is distributed equally to all individuals.

Given the productivity of the island's population, where only four hours work per day is necessary for subsistence, the considerable free time the Utopians have at their disposal may be, and usually is, devoted to learning and discussion. However, while all have access to knowledge and are encouraged to partake of it, there are those, naturally gifted with superior intelligence, who may be granted a 'perpetual licence from labour to learning' (1982a:453), establishing a kind of learned elite.

For Bacon, by contrast, learning and knowledge is represented by the emblem of the 'House of Salomon', 'the most beautiful creation of Bensalem and the fundamental pillar of that society' (1982a:454). Here, knowledge is not so much diffused to the greatest number as concentrated in educational hierarchies in a pyramidal, fundamentally elitist form. While for Campanella, on securing the appropriate forms of reproductive relation between its citizens, Solarian culture must guarantee the development of skills in the arts, sciences and a proficiency in teaching itself.

Political and social relations in each of these utopias is directed towards explicitly pedagogical goals. In this sense they are not really idealised or perfect social orders, fantasies or dreams of an impossible nature; rather, all three serve to initiate programs of socio-cultural reform, anticipating and thus serving to justify major educational upheavals which follow shortly afterwards. Le Doeuff links the emergence of learned societies — particularly the Collège de France, the Royal Society and the Academies of Science and State-controlled scientific and educational centres — to the programmatic speculations of these texts (1982a:460–1). Further, she claims that each functions at the same time to annul a fundamentally religious mode of social organisation and to replace it with a Renaissance humanism. Each, in other words, ensures the passage of a secular, indeed, State-regulated, humanism:

> *All three contain a more or less discreet rejection of martial values as a distancing from the ascetic values of Christian mysticism, even if these values are set aside with all possible respect. Chivalric heroism and religious mortifications are courteously dismissed so that room can be made for the glorification of that culture which renders more human. (1982a:461)*

But if these projected utopias anticipate the advent of secular humanism and help sever the ties of a feudal culture to divine ordination, they also do more than this. Above all, Le Doeuff wants to suggest, they produce an image of society that positions the school as central to society and, more alarmingly, posits a society for the school, 'the hope of scholars to annex the whole of society to their own ends, or, what amounts to the same thing, the incapacity to recognize these ends as their own, or private' (1982a:462). In other words they construct a society in the image and for the purposes of the educator, instead of, as they profess, creating an image of education for the public, that is, for social good.

Le Doeuff's overriding interest in utopias, however, is not merely historical, not merely rooted in a now-dead past and an out-of-date educational program. Her polemical interest in pedagogy is located in beliefs pervasive here and now, within educational institutions, and contemporary philosophy and political theory. She steers a course in between two poles or extremes: one which merely links the political to the educational in a wholesale manner, thus claiming that education is a form of social control and human alienation in which knowledge is identified with power (for example, in the case of the so-called 'New Philosophers'); and another, the opposite pole, which seeks to detach political functioning and, indeed, political philosophy from education (for example, in Rousseau's careful attempts to delineate the disjunction between politics and pedagogy by theorising each in isolation from the other — *The Social Contract* (1975) providing his account of politics, and *Émile* (1972) his views on education, as if they were separate discourses with little or no overlap). Both the conflation of power and knowledge, and their stark separation confirm for her the present, if unrecognised, influence of utopianism even today.

Women and philosophy

It may be appropriate at this point to ask what Le Doeuff's rather specialised researches into the philosophical imaginary have to do with women or feminism. In what ways do her readings of texts written in the seventeenth and eighteenth century by men with little or no explicit reference to women have to do with contemporary French feminisms? In what ways are her readings those of a feminist? What do they have to offer those concerned with the transformations of women's social, cultural and representational positions within our society? If, as has been indicated, Le Doeuff's researches are largely concerned with the deconstruction of philosophical paradigms and pretensions, and with philosophy's use of imagery as a form of evasion, what in her work is of specific relevance to other women? Or, put in other terms, what marks her work as that of a feminist?

Thus far I have refrained from introducing her more overtly feminist conjectures in order to make clear what her philosophical interests are; indicating what she means by the 'philosophical imaginary' is most easily facilitated by discussing those papers uncomplicated by other concerns. Yet none of her work is altogether free of feminist implications. Indeed, she suggests that one of the privileged figures of the imaginary in philosophy is precisely the feminine, although she qualifies this by claiming that there is not a universal representation (1980a:10), as some feminists assume, but historically determinate ones. Her interest in the imaginary was facilitated, she claims, by her interest in women:

> *It is certainly not coincidental that I came to formulate these ideas more clearly through my work on women and/in philosophy. The icon of the feminine in philosophical texts is not a universal representation. Obviously, it is formulated alongside some rather common phallocentric prejudices (which can be found in opinions, daily behaviour, and social practices that go well beyond the sphere of the learned few), but its specificity, i.e. its strangeness, became evident to me — no doubt because of my personal and sociological itinerary made me live elsewhere — in places in society where another image of the feminine is put forward and imposed so that women can identify themselves with it. (1980a:12–13).*

How her commitments to feminism infiltrate and make possible her researches on the imaginary can be made clearer through an investigation of her three papers most directly concerned with women, 'Women and Philosophy' (1977; also to be found in *L'Imaginaire* as 'Cheveux longs, idées courtes'), 'Pierre Roussel's Chiasmas' (1981/2, also published in *L'Imaginaire*), and her analysis of Simone de Beauvoir's relation to existential philosophy in 'Operative Reasoning' (1979).

In 'Women and Philosophy' Le Doeuff presents a comprehensive survey of the complex relations philosophy, as institution and as discourse, posits between itself, women and femininity. In opposition to the common feminist presumption, she argues that women have rarely been actively excluded from philosophy in the crude ways usually supposed. For her the problem is not really that of how to include women in this particularly hallowed space but to rethink the ways in which philosophy has participated in women's oppression. She thus discusses the historical role that femininity and conceptions of the feminine have played in philosophy's attempts at self-definition and delimitation. But she is not exclusively concerned with the conception of 'femininity'; of equal significance to her research is the role which actual, historically specific women have played in the creation of philosophy's identity. In this sense her scope is broader than those of other French feminists and yet also overlaps with their work. Her commitment to examining the empirical, concrete place of women seems underdeveloped in the work of Kristeva and Irigaray, and thus acts as a counterbalance to their more speculative, discursive and conceptual concerns.

While it is certainly true that history records the work of remarkably few women in the annals of philosophy — those before the nineteenth century can be counted on one hand — Le Doeuff points out that women have in fact had access to philosophical activity since its inception: Diotima is referred to by Plato (in the *Symposium*), and Diogenes Laertius refers us to Hyppatia with some reverence. Similarly, Heloise, Christine de Pisan, Elisabeth (Descartes' otherwise unnamed correspondent) and Queen Christina of Sweden (for whom, it is rumoured, Descartes gave his life[3]) have all left documents of various kinds as testimony of their philosophical proficiency. Nor, Le Doeuff stresses, has this implied that those rare women who have entered the discipline are thereby seen as any less feminine, in spite of Kant's protestations to the contrary.[4] The kinds of constraint the discipline has imposed on women are more subtle — and effective — as deterrence. She implies that a kind of repressive tolerance exists: women are not directly barred from philosophy because they are all the more effectively constrained by their limited and highly particularised roles within it — as amorous acolytes, as 'amateurs' and as faithful handmaidens: '[There is ...] a more subtle relation with the prohibition, a relation which can be described as permissive, as long as it is understood that permissiveness is a cunning form of prohibition, opposed to everything that comes under the heading transgression or subversion' (1977:3).

In other words women's contributions have not been prohibited as much as limited to a singular mode: in the main this has occurred by preventing women access to the *institutions* surrounding philosophy — the institutions of learning in the first place, of paid employment in the second, and of the public circulation and assessment of their work in the third. Consequently, those women who have, at least until recently, contributed to philosophy have done so through an 'erotico-theoretical transference' (1977:3) relation, that is, through a personal and usually passionate relation to a particular philosopher, a love object. Hyppatia's relation to Crates, Heloise's relation to Abelard, Elisabeth's to Descartes — and, one may add, de Beauvoir's relation to Sartre — are not, in a sense, unique love relations. Indeed, as Plato so astutely recog- nised, the love of philosophy is perhaps best fostered through an amorous attachment to a philosopher-mentor. In this sense most men, too, gain a love for the discipline through a transferential relation to a particular philosopher — either a beloved teacher, a noble role model or a phychically invested attraction to a dead writer. The difference between this 'normal' erotic attachment and women's restricting transferences resides in two things (Le Doeuff details only one): in the case of women this erotic attachment is frequently reciprocal and genitally consummated — based, that is, on a real and mutual rather than a fantasised and projected love; and, above all, in the case of women there seems to be no mediation, no third party, to ensure that the woman, like the pre-oedipal child, can detach from the particular figure of the beloved to identify with the institution and general discipline of philosophy.

For Plato the love of the disciple for the master, while erotic in the first instance, needs sublimation if the disciple is to acquire a love of philosophy itself. By contrast, for these women dotted throughout the history of philosophy, because they are literally excluded from access to the school, their relations to the philo-sophical master and/or protector defines not simply a first step but the limits of their relations to the discipline:

> *The reason why men (both now and in the past) can go beyond the initial transference, and why the love component of their transference is sublimated or inflected from the very beginning, so that it can return to the theoretical, is that the institutional framework in which the relationship is played out provides the third factor which is always necessary for the breaking of the personal relationship; the women amateurs, however, have been bound to the dual relationship because the dual relationship does not produce the dynamics that enable one to leave it ... Their relationship to the philosophical is limited, from outside the theoretical sphere, by the relationship from which they could not possibly detach themselves. (1977:4)*

Le Doeuff suggests that this relation confines women to the work of a particular philosopher but does not give them access to the philosophical field, which positions and limits the work of any particular philosopher in a broader context. Moreover, she suggests, this means that women develop an overly reverential relation to the work of the master, seeing in it the 'perfect system', an answer to all (philosophical) problems. This lack of mediation implies that she cannot accept what Le Doeuff sees as philosophy's *constitutive lack*:

> *A woman has the philosophy of her tutor-lover: but then she is no longer within the philosophical enterprise, to the extent that she avoids (is forbidden) a certain relationship to the lack, the particular lack from which, in my opinion, philosophy stems, a radical lack which the Other cannot fill. (1977:4)*

What Le Doeuff understands by the lack from which philosophy develops is not made clear by her, although it is a comment she also makes elsewhere. Nevertheless, her claim that an amorous and invested relation to a particular philosophy, which prevents women from a more generalised access to and familiarity with the discipline, can hardly be contested. The philosophy which women produce as a result of this kind of confinement is itself constrained into two forms: that of amateur (adoring disciple) or professional 'vestal', whose role is to comment faithfully on the work of a great man, altering nothing, adding nothing of her own, producing nothing new. This is in stark contrast with the commentary role of great men: indeed, there is hardly a philosopher within the history of the discipline who does not introduce his own contributions to the area through a commentary on his predecessors or colleagues. However, what marks this kind of commentary as productive or creative, as philosophy proper, is the capacity to depart from the text on which commentaries are based, to go further or in a new direction.

Women's confinement as amateurs is now in the process of rectification. The twentieth century has, and will, produce professional women, women trained within the school who gain their livelihood from it. However, the risk here is that women may then have to conform to other (sometimes unstated) institutional constraints, which Meaghan Morris in her paper on Le Doeuff has described as 'the danger of inducing a lethal conformity to purely academic norms of philosophical practice' (Morris, 1981/82:75). For those others, who write 'commemorative history', who are locked into what Le Doeuff describes as the 'phantasmogoria of the commentary', the situation is more difficult to rectify, and the consequences are women's loss of a voice and perspective recognised as their own. Thus, the opening of the institution to women's professional entry, and the recognition that commentary is never purely reflective and always entails a productivity, are necessary counterweights to the repressive tolerance hitherto containing women in the discipline. But they are not enough. The discipline itself must undergo radical upheavals to be conceived in different terms in order to accommodate women's contributions adequately.

What, then, is at stake for philosophy in the limited space it accords to women? Why has it defined and positioned women and femininity as a lack or incapacity, even as a danger to itself? Is it simply that philosophy fears its image and social value will diminish if it grants ready—even equal—access to women (like medicine and engineering in the USSR)? That is, is it simply a matter of establishing its credentials as an elitist enterprise, one suitable only for the best and most rigorous of (male) minds? Or is there something particular to the discipline which finds women and femininity dangerous or threatening?

Le Doeuff suggests that the very nature of the discipline relies on a containment of women's activities. This occurs for several reasons. In the first place, the erotic transference between disciple and master is particularly apt in the context of philosophy:

> *The theoretical devotion of a woman is very comforting for someone experiencing his own lack ... How can it not be gratifying to be seen as a completeness when one is caught in incompletion and disappointment. We still smile at the court of women who flocked round Bergson, but we systematically forget to wonder whether this court was not in fact satisfying (or inspired by) Bergson's own desire. (1977:4)*

For the male philosopher the admiring devotion of an attentive, especially a gifted woman serves to assuage the anguish of his personal confrontation with the lack constitutive of philosophy. But, beyond the personal or psychological needs of the philosopher, the discipline itself has a vested interest in the kinds of space it grants women: women are correlated with the very elements against which philosophy defines itself, with precisely those properties and attributes the discipline cannot admit of itself on pain of acknowledging its own lacks and incompleteness:

> *The incapacity of philosophical speculation, the fragility of all metaphysical constructions, the lack, the anguish, that torment every 'world system' are not radically unknown to the philosopher. The reference to women (or to any other subject 'un-*

fitted' for philosophy) allows this powerlessness to be overlooked, for there it is projected, in a radicalised form, onto a subject who is even situated on this side of the search for speculative truths. Or again, the fact that there is someone incapable of philosophising is comforting because it shows that philosophy is capable of something. (1977:6)

It seems that, for Le Doeuff, women do not simply satisfy philosophy's need to relativise its own *ontological* lack; they further serve to compensate for its demise as the 'queen of the sciences', that is, for its *historical* lack. That philosophy *is indeed* 'capable of something' only philosophers themselves believe (today, many believe this only cynically in any case). The funding of philosophy departments, their influence on the sciences, their practical utility in an increasing corporation-oriented monopoly form of capitalism has been increasingly less clear with the rise of the modern capitalist State. That philosophy is *worth something*, that it has some (social and intellectual if not economic) value is guaranteed by the *exclusivity* of its practices. Its status as 'high', 'refined' and 'pure' knowledge can only be sullied with the entry of increasing numbers of women (and unwanted others — blacks, migrants, the working class, etc.).

But perhaps most interestingly and 'philosophically', the correlation of women and femininity with what remains undefinable by or repressed within the network of privileged concepts and values in philosophy enables its most valued presumptions, criteria of assessment and constructed systems to go unquestioned. Femininity is aligned with that through which, in being expelled, repressed or overcome, philosophy is able to give itself an identity. In negating femininity and its correlates, philosophy thereby dialectically defines itself. Underlying the discipline's exclusion of other discourses — Le Doeuff lists 'rhetoric, the seductive discourse, inconclusive syllogism, occultism, ... analogical reasoning and arguments from authority' (1977:7) — is an unacknowledged process of self-constitution: 'the man/woman difference is summoned to symbolise the general opposition between defined/undefined, that is to say validated/excluded, an opposition of which the logos/mythos couple represents one form' (1977:7).

We have here, then, a feminist justification for Le Doeuff's explorations of the philosophical imaginary: the imaginary — *mythos* — is that which is internal to the discourse's functioning but which the discourse must cover over or expel. Whether these images are explicitly related to the feminine is thus irrelevant.

These images are at base expressions of a kind of femininity intolerable to the 'masculinity' of philosophy. In this sense, whether Le Doeuff theorises about islands, clocks, tables, she is also if indirectly discussing the terms *internally* hostile to philosophy, terms whose attributes are feminine:

> *Thus shadow is within the very field of light and* woman is an internal enemy. *For, in defining itself through negation, the philosophical creates its other, it engenders an opposition which, from now on, will play the role of the hostile principle, the more hostile because there is no question of dispensing with it.* Femininity as an internal enemy? *Or rather the feminine, a support-signifier of something that, having been engendered by philosophy whilst being rejected by it, operates within it as an indispensable deadweight which cannot be dialectically surpassed.* (1977:7, my emphasis)

In recognising the various ruses and strategies by which philosophy contains women, it is no longer possible simply to advocate the entry of greater (or even equal) numbers of women. To do so would be to position women as philosophical subjects in the same way men have been positioned — through a collective fantasy of what the discipline is and must be. The 'solution' to the maleness of philosophy is *both* opening itself up to women's contributions; but also to its own manoeuvres and tactics, and thus to a transformation of them. Philosophy must accept its own constitutive lacks, those lacks, which, as I understand it, imply the impossibility of a universal explanatory system, a knowledge that answers all questions, a knowledge that sees itself as complete. Le Doeuff sees this challenge to philosophy's hegemonic mode allied with the one initiated by Marx:

> *This struggle was begun by historical materialism, insofar as this is a rationalism which renounces the idea of the omnipotence of knowledge. From here on, one can trace a new form of philosophy, as a fellow-traveller of conflicts which arise outside its realm and which, similarly, will be resolved (if at all) outside it, not by means based on its power. Which is nevertheless to announce not the extinction of the philosophical enterprise, but rather a change which is quite difficult to think through.* (1977:8)

While it is not possible to dispense with philosophy altogether, nor to renounce all modes of reason as 'male-dominated' (for indeed the very categories feminists themselves use in defining and struggling for women's rights and needs are philosophical), nevertheless, the kinds of philosophy thus far produced, philosophies allied with anti-feminism, must take on limits that are no longer self-defined, that recognise others who have been hitherto excluded, and are able to let themselves also be defined by them. This would be an open-ended philosophy, neither a 'hegemonic reason' nor a 'revolt of unreason' (1977:8) but a philosophy willing to admit its partiality: 'I would say that the future of a philosophy that is no longer anti-feminist is being performed somewhere in the direction of Brechtian drama, which ... produces unfinished plays which always have a missing act and are consequently left wide open to history' (1977:8).

This would be a kind of philosophy which, like Pascal's *Pensées*, is able to accept its limitations, its shortcomings and its open-endness: 'Here is a form of writing which does not claim to reconstruct and explain everything, which slides along the verge of the unthought and develops only by grafting itself onto another speech and is willing to be its tributary' (1977:9).

Le Doeuff envisages a philosophy which can acknowledge its limits, not overstep its own boundaries or pose as a universal or singular perspective: in this sense her work closely accords with Irigaray's critique of phallocentric knowledges. Instead of proclaiming itself the one (and only) form of knowledge, philosophy, on such an understanding, is one among other forms of knowledge, existing alongside of, in opposition to or in agreement with them. It is no longer able to present itself as an hierarchical superior, capable of judging but unwilling to be judged by other points of view. On the other hand, and in this sense her position seems in sharp contrast to Irigaray, Le Doeuff seems to advocate a mode of philosophical rationality somehow unimplicated in the ways philosophy functions as phallocentric, a kind of 'pure' or neutral reason which could be retained in a philosophy compatible with feminism. Her plea is for a serious analysis of and challenge to the *irrational* elements of philosophy; she does not present an outright attack on reason itself:

I have never had anything against philosophical rationality. As for its irrationality, that's a different matter. To be more precise, it seems to me that is not a function of some strictly 'masculine' form of 'rationality', but philosophy often produces a misogynist style of imagination, by trying to be more than it actually is, trying to make rationalisation operate to an extent beyond what it is actually capable of. (1980a:134)

In her introduction to the 'Women and Philosophy' paper Le Doeuff explicitly contrasts her work with Irigaray's critique of the masculinity of reason, as presented in *Speculum*. Her claim is that if philosophy's 'speculative machinery' has demonstrated a certain historical alignment with the privilege of masculinity, this is not a universal characteristic: it is a judgment made possible only in what she calls a 'hermeneutic age', an age of the 'essence of order and not of history' (1980a:133). In other words although philosophy's history can be read in terms of a 'repetition of the same', this is not necessarily the most productive or appropriate way it can be read. In preference, Le Doeuff opts for a meticulous reading of the specificity or singularity of philosophical texts, one faithful to its particularities rather than its broad similarities to all other philosophical discourses.

Her position is thus neither an attempt to reveal and rewrite the masculinity of notions of the feminine in philosophy (as Irigaray's is) nor an attempt to develop a counter-philosophy for women, one that breaks dramatically with the male-dominated history of philosophy. The first project, for her, entails an affirmation and acceptance of a masculine rationality, against which it positions itself as a disruption; while the second project entails a blind acceptance of philosophical assumptions and terms, indeed the philosophical project itself, now purified and returned to its (feminine) strength.

One is left with a suspicion that, rather than render Irigaray's insights in her critique of philosophical phallocentrism historically and textually specific, as her comments may imply, Le Doeuff is instead acting as feminine preserver and commemorative historian of masculine wisdom. She is not a commentator who preserves a neutral, positionless representation of key philosophical texts; yet nevertheless, there is a certain reverence and respect, a propriety in her patient, meticulous, restricted readings, almost as if she were to claim that if philosophy is misogynist, this can be confined to those imaginary elements she has been concerned to reveal. Meaghan Morris expresses a similar uneasiness:

one may ask to what extent L'Imaginaire Philosophique (while introducing philosophical discourse to feminist questions) is at the same time merely engaged in a salvage operation to rescue philosophy from the more damaging charges of feminist critics in France — and if so, for what reasons. (Morris, 1981/82:77)

De Beauvoir and Sartre: Feminism and philosophy

In 'Women and Philosophy' Le Doeuff considers the relation
between de Beauvoir and Sartre as typical of the amorous–
theoretical attachment of the female disciple to the male master.
Le Doeuff is firm here in suggesting that, even as the author of
The Second Sex, de Beauvoir seemed unaware of her relative and
restricted feminine position in relation to Sartre's primary position:
'Simone de Beauvoir was confined to the feminine condition, that
is to say accepted a ready-made philosophy, or that, in accepting
existentialism as a constituted doctrine, she was excluded from the
philosophical enterprise . . .' (Le Doeuff, 1977:8).

However, in her more sustained analysis, 'Operative Philosophy'
(1979), Le Doeuff seems more concerned with rereading de
Beauvoir's use of existentialism than in criticising it. She seems to
use the 'case study' of de Beauvoir's use of Sartre's explicitly
misogynist text, *Being and Nothingness* (1977), in her feminist
writings to challenge Irigaray's contention that philosophy must be
disrupted in its phallocentric and masculine functioning. Le
Doeuff's claim, although it is merely mentioned instead of elaborated, is that, far from disrupting male philosophy, de Beauvoir
works within it and nevertheless uses it to produce feminist
insights:

> *in what respect, if any, is the choice of this or that philosophical
> reference-point a decisive factor in feminist studies? Over the
> last few years we have witnessed a certain philosophist inflation
> in the domain of theoretical productions. Thus, Luce Irigaray's
> books insist on the idea that, since it is philosophical discourse
> that lays down the law for all other discourses, the discourse of
> philosophy is the one that has first of all to be overthrown and
> disrupted. At one stroke, the main enemy comes to be idealist
> logic and the metaphysical logos. Simone de Beauvoir's book
> leaves me with the contrary impression, since, within a prob-
> lematic as metaphysical as any, she is still able to reach
> conclusions about which the least one can say is that they have
> dynamised women's movements in Europe and America for over
> thirty years. (1979:48)*

In opposition to those modern readers of de Beauvoir who wish
to separate her adherence to Sartrean existentialism from her
feminism, it is Le Doeuff's claim that Sartrean philosophy is used
by de Beauvoir as an 'operative viewpoint' for exposing the
character of women's oppression' (1979:48). One cannot dissociate

de Beauvoir's feminism from her existentialism, and thus if one accepts Irigaray's claims about the 'main enemy' being the metaphysical *logos*, it would be impossible to understand how de Beauvoir could generate a feminist position from an anti-feminist text.

It is Le Doeuff's claim that Sartrean existentialism is incapable of explaining either women's or any other form of oppression, given its heavy stress on the responsibility and free choice of the individual. This is a freedom which cannot be constrained in any way by any form of external force. If 'even the man in chains is free' then there can be no form of oppression so great as to limit the freedom of any individual. Indeed, it is a form of 'bad faith' for the individual to accept pregiven or external constraints as a mitigating factor or limitation of free choice. Not only is existentialism unable to explain, or even acknowledge, oppression, it is far from neutral in its account of individuality. The traditional patriarchal designations of masculine and feminine seem to mark Sartre's work even more strongly than most, for he relies on its imagery in his understanding of knowledge ('To see is to deflower', 'knowledge is at once a penetration and a superficial caress', quotes Le Doeuff [1979:50]), and his understanding of being or ontology itself (this is particularly striking in his evocation of the horror of the 'slimy', the in itself which threatens to engulf the sovereignty of the for-itself: the 'viscosity' of slime, of enveloping matter is 'comparable to the flattening out of the overripe breasts of a woman lying on her back' [Sartre, quoted by Le Doeuff, 1979:51]). That de Beauvoir could develop from this anti-feminist *oeuvre* the first sustained and systematic philosophical treatment of feminist issues is something of, in Le Doeuff's words, a *tour de force*.

What manoeuvres or strategies does de Beauvoir utilise in order to convert Sartre's misogyny into the foundations or framework of a feminist philosophy? Could her feminist insights have been expressed without the need for existentialist principles? Is her work a development of existentialism or does it constitute a break with it? These are crucial issues if Le Doeuff is justified in her critique of Irigaray and others.

For Le Doeuff, de Beauvoir's most significant transformation of existentialism consists in taking the completeness of existentialism as a *Weltanschauung*, a world-view, and changing it into a limited perspective or point of view (of the kind Le Doeuff advocates in 'Women and Philosophy'). By using it as a perspective on a determinate set of issues and experiences, those derived from women's experiences of oppression within patriarchy, de Beauvoir transposes Sartrean ontology into a methodology.

Her second transformation consists in recognising that external constraints can and are forms of social control, in accord with Sartre; not by remaining external but by being internalised and accepted as part of one's self-definition. It is only in this sense, and in contradiction of Sartre's view, that woman can be defined as the 'Other'. Seen from the other side, it could equally be said that the subject requires its self-affirmation in an exteriority, one which is actively denied to women within patriarchy. This admission of exteriority as a relevant factor in understanding consciousness is a considerable modification of the early Sartre, and a key step in analysing oppression as a form of externality impinging on the consciousness, and consequently on the freedom, of subjects.

Balanced against these two transformations are what Le Doeuff believes are the conditions provided by existentialism itself, conditions which enable de Beauvoir's feminist insights to be thought. In the first case Le Doeuff claims that only a philosophy which makes oppression groundless, as does existentialism, enables one to resist oppression as a matter of course:

> *This situation [women's oppression] itself still remains to be explained. This requirement, which assumes that the feminine condition is not a matter of course, could be posed by Simone de Beauvoir in its fully radical form only thanks to the ethic of authenticity which enabled her to sufficiently distance herself from the lot of women to be able to describe it as a shocking contingency, a strangeness, something non-natural to be trans- formed as rapidly as possible. (1979:53)*

Existentialism rules out the effects of both nature or being/ essence in its account of transcendence and freedom. The subject has no fixed essence and is in no way governed by nature. It is because existentialism rules out every form of constraint, because it entails that oppression, like freedom and identity, must be reinvented at each moment, over and over, de Beauvoir must devote so much detail and analysis to explaining the minute, interlocked everyday forms of women's subjugation — the strongest and 'most feminist' element of her work: 'the very impossibility of accounting for the enfeoffment of women serves only the better to expose the aberrant character of this subjection' (1979:55).

In the second place the existential problematic is able to engender feminist insights through its adherence to an individual- istic and fundamentally liberal mode of politics. In other words it is because de Beauvoir herself does not identify with the position of women (her notions of the female body and its constitutive limitation on women's freedom, together with her denunciation of maternity are testimony of her distance from what she sees as the feminine condition) that she is able to step back from it in order to see how women (*other* women, that is) are trapped within their femininity and refused access to the transcendence available to men. This distance enables de Beauvoir to regard women as the Other, without a recognition that woman can only be the Other *for men*; for *women, it is man who is the Other*. Nevertheless, any affirmation of women as subjects in a reciprocal, exchange relation to man, in which man may take women as object and other in relation to himself as woman takes man, risks ignoring the real, tangible history and pervasive presence of women's oppression by simply homologising women into a sameness with men. That de Beauvoir can adequately describe the socio-psychological position accorded to women within patriarchy is a function of her ready acceptance of the sovereignty of a single type of subject, with whom she identifies.

Thus, for Le Doeuff in contrast to Irigaray the masculinity of philosophical frameworks is not necessarily the major problem to be overcome in feminist analyses of philosophical texts. She claims that her position does not entail either indifference to the specificities of determinate philosophical positions nor a kind of reversed feminism in which the worst, most misogynist theories produce the best kinds of feminist analyses:

> *Should one then draw the conclusion of indifferentism (small matter whether you appeal to one philosophical position or another, once your practical aspirations are clearly defined; these aspirations will suffice to remodel your initial perspective), or that of the logic of 'worse is better'—the inaptitude of such and such a philosophy for the requirements of a theory of women's oppression serving as a kind of springboard for de-banalising that oppression? Either way would be to close the issue a little too rapidly. (1979:55)*

The feminine in philosophy

If the relation between de Beauvoir and Sartre enables one to assess the containment of women, empirical women, within the institution of philosophy, a number of other papers in Le Doeuff's writings examine the ways in which women and femininity are discursively positioned and represented in philosophical texts and paradigms. It is in this context that her paper 'Pierre Roussel's Chiasmas' (1981/2) needs to be positioned. Moreover, although her researches in the history of philosophy are frequently only indirectly related to the question of women and femininity, nevertheless, in her readings of Bacon's *The New Atlantis* and her commentary on Shakespeare's long poem *Venus and Adonis*, subjectivity, masculinity and femininity are never far from her concerns.

Her current interest in elaborating and commenting on the philosophies of the Renaissance (especially Francis Bacon and the theorists of utopia—More, Campanella et al.) is a feminist one in at least two senses. First, she is concerned to analyse and problematise conceptions of femininity and masculinity which are usually implicitly coded on Renaissance epistemologies and ontologies in order to bring out the sexual dynamic underlying their various dualisms. That, for example, nature is regarded as feminine, as something to be mastered and overcome by a reason conceived in masculine and sexual terms, is crucial not only in understanding these philosophies in their own terms but also in seeing their residues and effects in current forms of philosophy (this is particularly relevant insofar as the secular humanist problematic, so powerful in philosophy today, was born in Renaissance humanism, which also initiated modern concepts of scientificity and reason). Second, she also regards this kind of research into the history of ideas, especially scientific ideas, as crucial for women to undertake, given that women are rarely attracted to the philosophy of science, in order to prevent women's marginalisation in philosophy. In other words her current interest in the history of knowledges furthers her commitment to understanding philosophy as both discourse and as professional, institutionalised practice.

Le Doeuff is concerned to overcome the problem of women's marginalisation within knowledges. Women working within the humanities and social sciences have managed to eke out a position for themselves within their various disciplines: these disciplines have, through the sheer weight of feminist research, been forced to accept some recognition of the contributions of women and femininity to their fields of intellectual endeavour. However, the common response to such a recognition is the granting of a new area, women's studies, or a new approach, a feminist approach *within* mainstream knowledges, which leaves the basic, misogynist values of the discipline untouched. Women in such areas have been accorded a limited, restricted and marginal place, a 'women's place', which, in effect, has enabled these disciplines to ignore women's critiques of and contributions to the field—at best adding feminism to their agenda but leaving basic frameworks intact and insulated from feminist challenges. This anxiety regarding women's marginalisation within knowledges also underlies Le Doeuff's objections to Irigaray's and Cixous' and others' attempts to generate a 'feminine language', a language appropriate to the articulation of femininity and female corporeality. Her objection is strategic: such a goal risks being categorised as a form of feminist fiction, and consequently being ignored or categorised as merely experimental (or even utopian!). Dissolving the borders between philosophy and literature, in her understanding, risks ignoring the very specific history and strategies philosophy has used to provide its own forms of self-definition—although it is also true that, through its history, the dividing line between philosophy and literature or philosophy and science has been blurred or ignored. The specificity of philosophy—its unique history and the particularity of its methods and concepts (even if these are sometimes 'borrowed' by other disciplines)—is not the same as the strategies devised in other disciplines, for each takes its own concrete forms and thus each must be challenged in its own terms and on its own terrain.

Le Doeuff questions the strategies philosophy develops for protecting itself against the unwanted incursions of feminists in a short paper. 'Quelle modernité philosophique?' (1982c), where she explores the response of a number of male philosophers in terms of intellectual imperialism: while it is perfectly legitimate within philosophy for men to theorise about other men and women (and, one might add, it may today be accepted that women have the right to theorise about women), it seems intolerable to many philosophers that women now seize the right to speculate about men and the masculinitity of philosophy. When women speculate about men, they are commonly described as 'castrating':

> *when men covet territory said to belong to women (Nietzsche, or rather Nietzsche interpreted by Derrida; Comte, or Comte read by Scubla, etc.) they are absolutely right to do so for all sorts of reasons, but when women covet territory said to belong to these men, it is terribly reprehensive.*
>
> *Henceforth it is a question of a political discourse, and we could even forget that the protagonists are 'men' and 'women'. Subject A legitimately covets the territory of B, but B should not covet the territory of A, and it is A who gives an account of this:*

the structure is quite simply imperialist, because annexing the territory of another is always good, but you must not get annexed yourself. (1982c:22)

It is thus a political gesture on Le Doeuff's part to take on precisely the 'most masculine' of grounds within the history of philosophy — those occupied by epistemology and the philosophy of science — not as an imperialist strategy but as a form of counter-imperialism. This may explain some of her fascination with Bacon and the advent of the scientific project of knowing the world. Bacon's epistemology is not simply a philosophical justification for and precursor of scientific method; it is also an attempted imperialism which justifies itself by imagining nature as a woman to be conquered:

The raison d'être of the metaphor which is to assume such importance is this: to say that nature is a woman is to posit, in an imaginary fashion, that there is one active pole and only one, the human spirit. Because it is 'obvious' that the feminine implies subordination and submission ...

Finally, this metaphor has the secondary appreciable advantage of putting forward the image of a purely masculine scientific republic confronted by a global society characterised by an equality of the sexes ... one can advance the hypothesis that any discourse which insists upon the 'masculine' character of this or that theoretical construction is looking to posit the existence of a theoretical space which is superior to the profane confusion of the world of the city. (1983:148–9)

For the purposes of this chapter, it is worthwhile examining her analysis of the various phallocentric strategies and presumptions functioning in Pierre Roussel's text *Système physique et morale de la femme*, first published in 1777, for it serves as representative of both Le Doeuff's general approach to the question of the imaginary, and her particular relation to the analysis of scientific texts. At the same time it makes clear the feminist motivations underlying her detailed researches on texts in the history of ideas and of science.

A chiasma is a rhetorical device which, through denial and displacement, manages to shift the object of discussion onto everything but itself. It is a 'denial of a quality "x" to an object or place which common sense holds it to actually possess, with the compensating attribution of that same quality to everything but that object or place' (1981/2:40). In Roussel's text the chiasma functions so that sexual difference is seen to infuse every element of women's bodies and psychological-moral behaviour, *except* that which overly designates them as women. Where sexuality distinguishes the bones, muscles, nerves, blood vessels and tissues of the female body, making them softer, subtler, more labile, more rounded and more mobile than men's—indeed, 'there is no one who cannot distinguish *at the first glance* tell the difference between a woman's collarbone and the same bone in a man' (Roussel, quoted by Le Doeuff, 1981/2:43)—nevertheless, what is not capable of such ready sexual classification is the pubis, usually, to common sense, the most visible and direct confirmation of sexual identity: 'it is now recognised that these bones are no more mobile in women than in men (Roussel in Le Doeuff, 1981/2:45). This chiasma functions on the one hand to deny sexual differences in genital and childbirth functions (a typical function of phallocentric discourses, insofar as they cannot acknowledge the independent existence of two sexes but only one sex and its negation), and, on the other hand, it serves to insure that sexual difference (read: inequality) infiltrates all regions of woman's existence, including her moral, social and intellectual functions. To represent the pervasive influence of her sexuality on the rest of the female body, Roussel evokes the common analogy, much beloved in the seventeenth century of the hunchback: woman, like the hunchback, has her femininity inscribed in every organ and every movement of her body: 'A hunchback is hunchbacked from head to foot. The smallest particular defect has its general influence on the whole' (Diderot, quoted in Le Doeuff, 1981/2:42). Like the hunchback, in the case of the woman the whole of her body represents a 'system of necessarily connected deformities' (*ibid.*)

From Roussel's standpoint this entails that women's bodies, and all the social and behavioural consequences resulting from them, require a special study, for they cannot be generalised from the male, that is, from 'human' anatomy. It is significant, as Le Doeuff notes, that the corresponding book written by Roussel on the physical and moral system of man does not present an image of man parallel to that of woman. There, man is not masculine in every organ and in every behaviour. His sexuality is not suffused through the whole of his body but located genitally. And the non-genitalised, non-masculine image of the rest of the body can be thus easily represented as 'human': 'Roussel holds forth here on the stomach, the kidneys, suprarenal glands and skin without a single mention of any possible influence of sex ... there is no parity of the sexes as to the consequences of sex' (1981/2:42).

Roussel's chiasmic displacement of genital sexual specificity onto a generalised bodily form results in a second chiasmic operation—that which serves as a self-justification for Roussel's project of providing an analysis of social and moral relations of women. Here, the chiasma functions to displace Roussel's legitimated field of knowledge, in which he is as it were 'officially' qualified to speak—medicine, physiology, anatomy—onto one where he has no legitimated expertise: morality, psychology, sociology. He does everything to explain away the physiology of the female anatomy in order to give himself more space to map women's anatomical outlines onto their moral and social existence. In the book Roussel disqualifies the relevance of purely anatomical research, and instead grounds moral behaviour in women's unique physiology.

This chiasma functions only because the first has taken place: if women's sex is not simply genital and reproductive, if it is located in the whole of the female body, then sex is capable of determining what the body does and how it behaves. Medicine extends itself to morality and psychology. This manoeuvre relies on arguments or claims that what has hitherto been regarded as sexually specific or functionally reproductive—genital specificity—is really an effect of social causes. Roussel supposes that women's menstrual periods are 'far from being a natural institution, the menstrual flow is a factitious need contracted in the social state' (Roussel in Le Doeuff, 1981/2:45):

> *if women are timid, soft, hopeless at mathematics, disastrous in politics—this comes from nature; but if they have periodic haemorrhages—this is an acquired habit, due in the last instance to a psycho-historical cause! And whereas Roussel has attributed every possible other feminine quality to a genital cause, he is at pains to show that periods have nothing to do with procreation or fertility. (1981/1:45)*

Here Roussel displaces sex from its genital and reproductive location to sexualise the whole of the body, but as regards genital specificity there is no acknowledgement of the physiology or nature of female genitality. Women are rendered pansexual and marked everywhere by sex; yet without genital specificity, a 'female eunuch' (see 1981/2:49). If the pubis and menstruation do not anatomically distinguish women from men, the implication is that women are best defined by attributing to them the *lack* of a penis. A sexual lack that infiltrates all the body's activities.

In serving as a displacement from medicine — in which Roussel can be authorised to speak — to moral philosophy and psychology — in which he cannot — Roussel's text also makes clear the strategies eighteenth-century philosophy has at its disposal. Le Doeuff claims that in the context of its dwindling influence in grounding dogma and oppression, philosophy had to give way to other discourses, among them science and religion. It served more as a 'laboratory of ideas', a site of experimentation with arguments and rehearsal of claims rather than as an authority or imperative force. Roussel is able to ground his philosophical, moral and psychological pronouncements on the authority of medicine and its capacity to legitimise other discourses: 'thus physiological pseudo-knowledge proved to be a more effective and reliable tool than philosophical thought' (1981/2:50).

What is at stake in Le Doeuff's detailed explorations of this rather obscure physiologist of the eighteenth century? Why devote such a detailed reading to an author whose influence on us today is very slight? As far as Le Doeuff is concerned, there are several ways in which Roussel's project is relevant to current intellectual issues. First, his work has historical interest insofar as it gives us a remarkable literalisation of the philosophical image of women proliferated in many texts, including Rousseau's. *The Social Contract* is not anachronistic, given the pervasiveness of liberal ideologies in the present. Thus, although Roussel's text is dated in its moral and physiological terminology, it nevertheless articulates an image of women — and of nature and physiology — that supports and provides legitimation for various philosophical positions, including those of contemporary liberal humanism.

Second, Roussel's recourse to physiology, and the particular presumptions he brings to scientific and pseudo-scientific issues on the matter of sexual difference, are still common today. Analysing in some detail how his conclusions are drawn and arguments developed gives us some insight into current scientific justifications of sex-role divisions, such as those proliferating under the category of socio-biology today. Le Doeuff refers to a recent text, *Le fait feminin*, which is presumably similar to those biological and physiological texts justifying women's social subordination and containment within the private sphere on naturalistic or biologistic grounds.

Third, Roussel enables Le Doeuff to illustrate the ways in which knowledge produced within a specific sphere interacts with more generalised social knowledges and everyday belief systems: 'he transforms a *lettered* imagination (that which belongs to the general culture of the educated) into a *learned* imaginary' (1981/2:41). His text illustrates the ways in which philosophy (and science) draw on popular opinion to produce their various images; and also, how a popular culture draws on and is able to utilise a scholarly, philosophical text in the refinement of popular and learned ideologies.

Fourth, his text prefigures and renders explicit a number of strategies developed elsewhere, most notably in psychoanalysis, which affect our current understanding of women's sexuality. Le Doeuff refers explicitly to the Lacanians, who, she claims,

> *content themselves with possessing a partial competence, a specialised knowledge, a particular technique of cure. But it is no secret that they lay claim instead to a general competence, that, in other words they behave as though analytical theory possessed global explanatory value and jurisdiction over a whole range of problems — metaphysical (happiness, death), ethical, aesthetic, linguistic, epistemological ... (1981/2:56)*

Fifth, Roussel's writings reveal the ways in which women's bodies and specificities serve to underpin and found knowledges. His work is representative not merely of the use of phallocentric models of female sexuality but also of the ways in which male speculation about the 'enigma' of femininity serve as a condition and guarantee of (male) discourses and knowledges. The physiology of the female body in Roussel's text serves to justify the ethical, moral and psychological matters about which he reflects; without the chiasmic image of the woman as both pervaded by sexuality in every fibre and as peculiarly sexless, his other speculations, including those on male physiological and moral development, would not be possible.

'Pierre Roussel's Chiasmas' acts as a hinge, bringing together, indeed balancing, Le Doeuff's interest in the philosophical imaginary as an issue in the history of ideas, and her commitment to presenting feminist research, research on and by women. Her analysis brings with it the meticulous reading of strategic philosophical texts within the history of philosophy, and their self-evasions, their occupation of omnipotent or universal vantage points and their points of minimal justification with a detailed analysis of the reduction of women to men's speculative, and subordinated, objects, a phallocentric and imperialist reduction which precludes critical self-reflection or reciprocal interaction with other points of view or vantage points. In this sense it acts as a worthy representative of the kinds of research she has undertaken in *L'Imaginaire*, which all hover on the borders of an internal analysis and critique of philosophical systems on the one side, and a detailed understanding of the mechanisms and procedures whereby these apparently neutral, objective systems actively co-operate in the oppression of women, on the other.

Summary

Le Doeuff's various researches centre around three central themes that are evoked in more or less detail and with greater or less emphasis in all her work. They involve an analysis of central themes, texts and images in the history of ideas, especially in post-Renaissance epistemology and philosophy of science; an analysis of the roles women, femininity and the feminine have played in the constitution and construction of philosophy as a discipline; and the repressed or unspoken operative premises and presumptions functioning within philosophy which enable the discipline to justify itself and to extend its scope beyond its legitimated areas of expertise. These three themes are not entirely unrelated — the genealogy or history of modern knowledges enables one to locate more readily the ways in which prevailing techniques and procedures today gain their validation. For example, Le Doeuff is interested not only in the history of validated or confirmed knowledges but also in the history and genealogy of systematic *mis*-readings of key texts. Thus, in the paper 'En rouge dans la marge' (1980a), Le Doeuff interrogates the conditions under which mis-readings of texts are possible. She asks how the Cartesian concept of ethics, formulated in part III of the *Discourse on Method*, has been misrepresented and mistranslated so readily. Descartes' phrase 'une morale par provision' has been rephrased by a number of commentators as 'morale provisoire', a provisional morality, rather than a moral by provision. This apparently minor slippage represents the difference between a temporary or short-term morality, a first step to be rescinded when this morality is further developed, and a morality in its minimal sense, not to be rescinded but completed — a difference between a moral code which is to be replaced by a complete and reconstituted moral system; and a morality whose details need to be filled in. For Le Doeuff the interesting question is not simply which interpretation is the correct one, which one has textual justification, but how this kind of misreading is possible, and precisely when it becomes 'institutionalised' and 'authorised'. Her claim is that Descartes' text is amenable to a double or ambiguous reading; it is not simply a mistake on the part of a naive reader, nor is it clearly justified by Descartes' own writings. Rather, his text fosters this misreading. Thus, it is not a matter of providing a more meticulous or accurate reading which will clear up the problem: instead, it is a question of tracing those textual resonances which facilitate such a duplicit and ambiguous position. And, in the second place, Le Doeuff is interested in locating the socio-historical reasons for the acceptance and proliferation of this misreading. Why, for example, was there a sudden interest in a provisional Cartesian morality at the end of the nineteenth century when it is clear that, before this time, commentators on Descartes' work had either ignored his contributions to ethics or had presented a more or less 'accurate' account of it? Why does this particular (mis-)reading occur around 1880?

There is no single answer to this historical question: a number of factors come together at the end of the nineteenth century, among them: the emergence of a new philosophical 'style' which attempted to expand fragments and partial accounts into sÿ .emat-atic positions; an early 'sociological' interest in moral systems; Comte's opposition of the provisional to the definitive; but, above all, major educational changes to the French school syllabus in which moral instruction was proposed as an essential ingredient in primary-school education. The pedagogues' debate constituted an implicit attack on the ways in which philosophy claims to found morality, to justify or underpin it rationally. Would such moral instruction supplant philosophy in the curriculum, or could it serve as a point of entry into the study of philosophy? Philosophy's status as guarantor of other knowledges and social and educational practices are at stake in this misreading of Descartes' text. A provisional (as opposed to definitive) morality would require the justification and support of philosophy, where a more definitive morality may remain (relatively) autonomous from philosophy.

Thus, issues other than purely philosophical ones help to determine what kinds of readings of texts are available and what effects these readings have. Philosophy no longer acts as an adjudicator between moral disputants; rather, it is now one of the combatants with no hierarchical privilege over non-philosophical adversaries.

This meticulously detailed reading of texts and their location within a socio-historical and pedagogical institutional context reveals a series of strategies developed by the discipline to justify itself, to evade certain commitments which cannot be easily articulated and to rationalise its incursion into other fields. Le Doeuff's research is motivated by a political concern, a concern for the ways in which philosophy acquires, or denies its acquisition of, authority, legitimacy and relevance relative to other knowledges and other social practices. In this sense while her work is sympathetic to and compatible with feminist theoretical concerns, it is only indirectly feminist in its interests and approach.

Given that her objects of analysis include conceptions of the ideal society, the ways in which philosophical texts are produced and interpreted, the function of the voice in philosophy, the development of Galileo's law of falling bodies (in which time, rather than space, needed to be quantified—a counter-intuitive step in the seventeenth century), notions of the subject in Shakespearean poetry and drama, Francis Bacon's formulation of a program for the establishment of science and so on, it is not always easy to see how these objects are specifically relevant to feminist interests. At best, these various papers remain very marginally connected to feminist theoretical issues, even if they occupy the centre of philosophy's most invested concerns and self-representations.

However, in this chapter I have argued that these are indeed valid and relevant concerns for a feminist, such as Le Doeuff, working within a single discipline such as philosophy. The positions opened to feminists in their reappraisal of conventional frameworks of knowledge are limited: on the one hand feminists are able to present critiques of mainstream positions, in which case they must themselves occupy the terrain of the mainstream and adopt many of its procedures and criteria of evaluation; on the other hand feminists may be able to devise new topics, new issues, new methods, in which case they risk being marginalised and rendered irrelevant (or ignored by the mainstream), or positioned as incomprehensible and of no value in mainstream terms. The first position involves the very real risk of absorption into and cooption by the very mainstream one wishes to challenge; the second risks having no effect on mainstream traditions.

Le Doeuff undertakes neither of these projects. Nor does she undertake the project of either researching women writers/theorists/activists or the place of the feminine and women within masculine texts. She does not write specifically *for* women, nor *as* a woman. In what sense, then, could her writing be considered feminist? Besides two or three texts specifically addressing women and the position of the feminine, why may her work be of interest to feminist theorists?

Her understanding of the philosophical imaginary is crucial in linking Le Doeuff's patient, careful textual analyses to her more openly expressed feminist concerns in 'Women and Philosophy': her fascination with the various discursive, pictorial and literary figures within philosophy—the 'imaginary'—with those images which both reveal and conceal philosophy's conditions of production and self-justification, is linked to her concern to find a space for women in philosophy which does not, as she says, 'talk pidgin to please the colonialists' (1977:7). To find a space for women to write and teach philosophy means, above all, transforming philosophy.

There are many kinds of transformation philosophy may undergo: it may add women and women's issues to the agenda of appropriate, acceptable philosophical topics; it may screen its sexist pronouncements to eliminate all unjustified, 'unreasonable' codings of femininity in negative terms; and it may devise new, different procedures for investigation, ones more amenable to women's interests and uses (for example, substituting relativist for absolutist epistemologies or subjectivist for objectivist ontologies). But until it is prepared to renounce the possibility of its completion, perfection, absolute right of assessment of other positions —that is, while it sees itself as a progressively perfectable system —philosophy will not be able to accommodate women and open itself to what they have to offer. Only when philosophy is capable of seeing itself as one institutional practice and set of discourses, in the context of others which have an equal right to exist, only when it is seen as a set of discourses with a history in other disciplines and discourses and not as a form of mastery of the world, or of concepts, can it be open to what women have to offer. As Meaghan Morris claims in her comprehensive overview and assessment of Le Doeuff's project:

The difficulties in identifying each and every moment of Michèle Le Doeuff's work as 'feminist' and the writing's refusal of feminine display could lead a feminist reading to minimise the interest of L'Imaginaire Philosophique—*on the grounds, perhaps, that a woman writing philosophy only writes that 'women can write it too'* ... *the classic position of* pre- *(that is* non-*)feminism in theory. But there are other possibilities. Le Doeuff's practice as a woman writing philosophy is one which precludes the ventriloquy of the dutiful daughter, since it demands a different articulation of philosophy's relations to women (thus, a different philosophy): and the question she*

*poses of possible places for speech, places other than those
prescribed by the Outside/Inside alternative, is an operational
question for feminism raised by every page of her book. (Morris,
1981/82:75)*

Le Doeuff's project of opening up philosophy to its own histo-
ricity, its contingencies, its historical and socio-cultural positioning,
is not unrelated to Foucault's analysis of the power and desire
operative in knowledges (especially in 'The Discourse on
Language', in Foucault, 1972), where Foucault asks not what
discourses *say* but what they *do*, not as bodies of truth but as
institutionally produced and supervised practices. Like Derrida,
Le Doeuff is also interested in what texts say, and in particular
how they articulate their positions. Yet unlike either Foucault or
Derrida, she is unwilling to emphasise either a text's interior (its
discursive means) or its exterior (its place as a practice and an
event) at the expense of the other. Like Irigaray, she is committed
to revealing the elisions, repressions and disavowals of femininity
within philosophical and other discourses; and like Kristeva, she is
concerned with the literary devices, sites of multiple meaning and
ambiguity within texts; yet unlike either, her project is not limited
to the discursive realm but is also directed to the relations between
discourses and social practices. Unlike Irigaray, she is not interested
in constructing or speaking in a feminine voice; nor, like Kristeva,
does she advocate the transgressive impetus of experimental and
avant-garde forms of writing as part of a struggle for women's
liberation. These French theorists may well mark out the intellectual space within which Le Doeuff works, but they do not cover
the same issues nor share similar methods or general goals.

A more interrogative project than Irigaray's or Kristeva's, Le
Doeuff's aims at a rigorous deconstruction of philosophy which
may open it up to its own lacks and inadequacies, not as a source
of weakness but as a site for its growth and development. She
confronts philosophy with its own techniques of evasion and thus
with its own concrete limits and spcificity. In doing so she forces
the discipline to accept its partial access to the real, the true and
the good such that the discipline may be able to accept from, and
give more to, other disciplines, other knowledges, so that some sort
of exchange relation becomes possible. This is an eminently feminist gesture insofar as only such a notion of philosophy will
enable it to accept whatever contributions feminism may offer
without pre-empting what either may find useful in the other. An

open-ended philosophy heralds a future in which the contributions of men and women may change the discipline, reorient its fundamental questions, inflect its paths of historical development, changing the way that the discipline is practised as well as the subjects who constitute the intellectual community producing and affected by philosophy.

Conclusion

ETWEEN them, Kristeva, Irigaray and Le Doeuff raise the possibility of a sexual subversion of received or malestream notions of subjectivity, representation, knowledge and power. Each challenges the assumed neutrality and universality of logo-centric and phallocentric principles, conceptual schemas and methodologies in acknowledging the cultural and epistemological debt the production of knowledges owes to women, femininity and maternity. Each makes explicit the silencing, submersion and containment of one half of humanity effected in the most 'rational', 'civilised' and 'noble' of cultural activities, the violence and coercion veiled beneath the most glorified and pure of 'human endeavours' — the creation of knowledges.

This recognition of the latent brutality of knowledges does not induce a lament or nostalgia for a more perfect and representative knowledge, a knowledge capable of completion through the con-tributions of women. Instead of aspiring to complete those projects men alone are incapable of perfecting for themselves, these three feminists question the goals and desires of knowledge production with the aim of destabilising them and making possible other kinds of writing and knowing. Their writings play a dual role: de(con)structive, insofar as they dismantle and destabilise the perceived unities of texts, knowledges and disciplines; and con-structive insofar as they create new alignments between terms, new modes of organisation within and between texts, and new networks of interlocking concepts. The subversion of existing knowledges, textual conventions and doctrinal adherences relies, in each case, on an assertion of the unrecognised or repressed contributions of femininity, whether, as in Kristeva's case, this is identified with a series of feminine sexual drives and energies; or, as in Irigaray's case, with the specificities of women's desires and perspectives; or, as in Le Doeuff's case, with the images and

230

metaphors of femininity. Destabilising existing forms of writing and knowing is a precondition for the positive assertion of femininity. Without the fissuring of existing intellectual categories and textual norms, there is simply no conceptual space available for women's positive self-representations. Kristeva, Irigaray and Le Doeuff have each undertaken the more or less preliminary task of clearing a conceptual terrain of the sexist, patriarchal and imperialist territorialisations, and of mapping sites which may now be appropriate for feminine or feminist occupation. This seems less a form of colonisation than the search for a place in which to live, to inhabit, to cultivate, to produce in ways undreamed of before. This occupation is not a proprietorial seizure but more a stake in and commitment to the kinds of intellectual struggle and productivity feminists today recognise is necessary in the transvaluation of existing knowledges.

Kristeva's subversion consists in her challenge to the presumed unity, transparency and cohesion of texts. Texts are the consequences of the violent repression of psychical pleasures and energies and their subsumption under the principles of law, order and authority. The veneer of singular meaning, transparent expression and realist representations conceals a series of repressions, forms of renunciation and sacrifice which cannot themselves be represented. She makes explicit the unspeakable cost of representation, which requires the child's abandonment of the immediacy of its pleasures and experiences, together with the loss of the most privileged and powerful of all its love objects. For her the maternal body is the unspoken underside of all discourse. Articulating and representing this abyss in representation, and indicating textual fragments in which this body is able even minimally or indirectly to be spoken, Kristeva's subversion involves breaching the limits of intelligibility, transgressing the borders between desire and language. She asserts the play of sexual differentiation running within and between all texts, and overflowing their intentions, which always leaves ineradicable, traceable residues in texts which make these texts amenable to different readings and to the play of sexual pleasures they contain.

Irigaray's subversion takes knowledges, particularly meta-knowledges of the kind to which philosophy and psychoanalysis aspire, knowledge about knowledges, as its critical object. The mirror of philosophical speculation, the reflection of male sexuality in phallocentric discourses, and the isomorphism between these discourses and male subjectivity needs to be shattered, fragmented and traversed; the space subtending representation which remains invisible to/in specular reflection, the space of the mirror-surface itself, must be seen as the precondition of the self-reflecting image. If philosophy and psychoanalysis represent the pinnacle of male reflection (man's rendering of others, the world and the cosmos in his own image), Irigaray's strategy is to focus on that opaque surface which makes reflection possible: women's bodies are the space and matter whose containment or 'blackout' make male self-projection possible. Until the flat mirror surface is curved back on itself, until it becomes the speculum, it is unable to represent women's modes of self-reflection. Such self-representations, Irigaray suggests, cannot deny their materiality and corporeality as representations: this is why the speculum renders itself, as well as its object, visible. The hierarchical privilege granted to the mirror which mirrors everything but itself is a visual correlate of the space of metalanguage and metaknowledge: these are discourses and knowledges which take up to the right to reflect on everything but themselves. Irigaray's strategy consists in disentangling the human (and the divine) from the masculine in order to make women's self-representations (of the human and the divine) possible. This is not simply the placing of female and male viewpoints side by side but the transformation of the 'universal', neutral human. Her subversion involves calling the masculine by its name, refusing it the status of the universal. It involves the proliferating of the positions *in medio* between binary oppositions — a pluralisation and ultimately a diversification of what had been previously governed by a singular universal. Irigaray affirms the play of sexual difference and exchange undermining the homeomorphism of male mirror reflection.

Le Doeuff's subversion is directed towards the institutional historical and (con)textual position of philosophy. Philosophy as a discipline is possible only because *it* relies on unacknowledged relations with previous texts, philosophical, literary and 'popular', from which it borrows images, metaphors and textual devices. Its history is not the consequence of the gradual accumulation of rational principles and rigorously tested postulates but is the result of the discipline's investment in networks of power–knowledge. Non-philosophical considerations, including those involved in the teaching, learning and assessment of philosophy, as well as the discipline's role in providing support, justification or testimony for other social practices (including politics, religion and science), impinge on the way the discipline is practised and conceives of itself. Philosophy's carefully drawn boundaries, which mark its exclusions and provide it with a self-chosen identity, are not the results of rational reflection but desire and fantasy. Le Doeuff makes it clear that the discipline functions as it does only by hiding, covering over and disavowing its reliance on alterity — the alterity of other disciplines and discourses, the alterity of social practices, and the alterity of other subjects/knowers. The 'masculinity' of philosophy is the result not only of the limited access it has granted to women but also of the 'feminine', non-philosophical other it constructs as 'external' but which is in fact its internal condition. Philosophy's boundaries, its very identity, depend on its being able to exclude or explain away the image, the figure of speech, the turn of phrase which it can neither accept nor expel. Le Doeuff affirms the position of images, models and metaphors of femininity in masculinist philosophies, seeing them as points of tension and contradiction, points which can illuminate what is at stake in various philosophical positions.

Each subverts the perceived unities of the self-contained text, the self-reflecting representational system and the self-defined knowledge. Each asserts that underlying and overflowing this perilous unity is a play of differences — sexual differences — which cannot be accepted without major upheavals in the forms knowledge and writing have taken. Each advocates an open-ended, ambiguous, proliferative upheaval, one which challenges the fixity and closure of discourses and knowledges. Such an upheaval throws into question the goals of truth, knowledge, objectivity, self-evidence and mastery presumed by malestream knowledges. These norms are seen as forms of intellectual violence which efface their own processes of production and ensure that other possibilities, other ways of knowing, remain undeveloped.

If the three French feminists examined in this book have a common denominator, it is the identification of prevailing intellectual norms and categories of knowledge as masculine; and the demonstration of the tenuous hold such knowledges have on their disavowed feminine preconditions and foundations. The affirmation of sexual difference, located either psychically, corporeally or textually, is the major strategy each deploys to challenge phallocentrism. It is the hinge which problematises phallocentrism and which enables alternatives, feminine or feminist texts, to be developed. It would, however, be misleading to assume that these French feminists share more than this. The privileged objects of their investigations, the methods they rely on, their goals, are diverse, and at times incompatible (most pertinently, concerning the affirmation or deconstruction of female sexual identity). They differ as much from each other as they do from the malestream.

It may seem strange in the context of Anglo-Saxon feminisms that these French feminists have little to say about women's day-to-day lives and experiences. Each seems more concerned with femininity as metaphor and concept than the empirical reality of women's lives in patriarchy. By this, I do not want to suggest that their work has no relevance to women in their everyday struggles. Simply, that their work is not *on* or *about* women. If anything, they are 'about' male-dominated knowledges. This does not, by that token, mean that they are either not feminist or that they are elitist. Rather, it implies that feminist struggles are multidirectional, occurring in many different practices, including the practice of the production of meanings, discourses and knowledges. In challenging male-dominated knowledges, at the same time they question the ways in which women's everyday lives are made meaningful, explained and justified conceptually. In all three cases they undertake a struggle within representation, involving a political contestation of the privileged positions of enunciation. This struggle for the right to write, read and know differently is not merely a minor or secondary task within feminist politics. Clearly it cannot replace the other forms of struggle in which feminists are engaged. Without a critical feminist awareness of the ways patriarchal knowledges inform everyday language and life, and without alternative frameworks of knowledge and representation, women will remain tied to a series of concepts and values which oppress them. Kristeva, Irigaray and Le Doeuff do not proclaim a new female language, nor new non-patriarchal knowledges: instead they rupture the apparent self-evidence of prevailing models in order to make new modes of knowing and writing possible. They celebrate the possibility of different forms of desire, pleasure and representation.

If woman has always functioned 'within' the discourse of man ... it is time for her to dislocate this 'within', to explode it, turn it around, and seize it; to make it hers, containing it, taking it into her own mouth, biting that tongue with her very own teeth to invent for herself a language to get inside of. (Cixous, 1980b:257)

Notes

Chapter 1

1   This can be seen as Hegel's reply to Descartes' solipsism. In place of the *cogito*, the self-conscious or self-knowing subject presumed by Descartes as the origin, source and guarantee of knowledge, Hegel substitutes a self-consciousness which could have no existence as such without the other. Hegel introduces into the *plenitude* or givenness of the *cogito* the notion of a *negativity* or *alterity* as its necessary condition.

2   Compare: ... *it does the man of the Fight no good to kill his adversary. He must leave him life and consciousness, and destroy only his autonomy. He must overcome the adversary only insofar as the adversary is opposed to him and acts against him. In other words, he must enslave him. (Kojève, 1969:15)*

3   Significantly, Sartre was not the first existentialist to acknowledge the constraints and limits placed on freedom by oppression. In *The Second Sex* de Beauvoir had already accepted the relevance of patriarchal oppression in limiting women's capacities for freedom and transcendence — a proposition Sartre could not adopt himself, or even recognise in de Beauvoir's work, for many years. See Chapter 6 for further discussion of de Beauvoir's relation to Sartre.

4   His self-criticisms had already been published before 1979, when he murdered his wife — a well-known feminist. He never came to trial but was hospitalised. His name is consequently rarely mentioned today, and always in hushed tones.

5   This was a period of unorganised, 'spontaneous' upheaval, when students, teachers, workers, radicals, and even professionals of all kinds took to the streets. It was spurred by student riots in West Germany, whose most well-known writer was Daniel Cohn-Bendit. The ostensive object of protest was the educational system, but criticism soon spread to all institutional structures and forms of authority, including what were previously considered radical — particularly the PCF. A national students strike, and full-scale street-fighting strikes through industry and in offices created a major crisis of culture and politics, whose character has marked French thought ever since. See Conley, 1984:2–4; Hirsch, 1981:139–54; and Guattari, 1984:208–17.

235

6   His doctoral dissertation was submitted in 1932; his annual seminars began in 1952; and his major text, *Écrits*, was published in France in 1966.

7   When Lacan was censured by the International Psychoanalytic Association (IPA) in 1964, he was 'banned' (in his words, 1977b:3) from teaching. Althusser, however, offered him space at the École Normale Supériere in 1966, where his seminars continued until the Department of Psychoanalysis was moved to Vincennes (see Turkle, 1976; and Schneiderman, 1983).

8   *... we know that what begins at the level of the subject is never without consequence on condition that we know what the term* subject *means.*

   Descartes did not know, except that it involved the subject of a certainty and the rejection of all previous knowledge — but we know since Freud, that the subject of the unconscious manifests itself, that it thinks before it attains certainty. (Lacan, 1977b:37)

9   Lacan remains highly critical of the communicational model of language, which posits a sender or transmitter, a receiver, and a message that passes from the first to the second. He denounces his first English translator's, Anthony Wilden, preoccupation with general systems theory and communication theory in his book *System and Structure, Essays in Communication and Exchange.*

10 Compare: *What we have been able to observe is the privileged way in which a person expresses himself as the ego: it is precisely this —* Verneinung, *or denial.*

   We have learned to be quite sure that when someone says 'It is not so' it is because it is so; that when he says 'I do not mean' he does mean ... we are ... convinced that our researches justify the epigram of the philosopher who said that speech was given to man to hide his thoughts; our view is that the essential function of the ego is very nearly a systematic refusal to recognise reality that the French analysts refer to in talking about psychoses. (Lacan, 1953:11–12)

11 Lacan refers to the work of Emile Benveniste, especially *Problems in General Linguistics* (1961), to explain his structuralist interlocking of language and subjectivity as mutually defining categories. See especially Chapters 19 and 20.

12 Lacan derives his understanding from Saussure, for whom the term refers to the material rather than the conceptual component of the sign. For Saussure, because the verbal sign is paradigmatic of all signs, the signifier is the 'sound-image'; in the case of the graphic text, it consists in pen markings on paper.

13 See Foucault's 'Nietzsche, Genealogy, History' in D. Bouchard (ed.) 1977 *Language, Counter-Memory, Practice.*

14 Derrida remains elusive about his relation to Marx. He concedes that Marx's critique of idealism shares a common ground with his own project; and he also suggests that his analysis/deconstruction of Marx is 'still to come'. He claims that his project and marxism's are different, whose differences should not be too readily effaced:

   Reading is transformational. I believe that this would be confirmed by certain of Althusser's propositions. But this transformation cannot be executed however one wishes. It requires protocols of reading. Why not say it bluntly: I have not yet found any that satisfy me. (Derrida, 1981:63)

For further details on his relation to marxism, see M. Ryan (1984) *Marxism and Deconstruction*, especially Chapter 2.

15 'The hymen is therefore not the truth of unveiling. There is not *alethia* (truth as unveiling), only a blink of the hymen' (Derrida, 1981a:293).

16 Spivak articulates the more explicitly masculinised approach in Derrida's more recent texts, where it is no longer woman, but *man* who is the object of a deconstructive disentanglement:

the product of the feminisation of philosophy has changed within Derrida's own work. It didn't go in the direction of 'devenir femme'... the direction of Derrida's later work is to see that anthropos is defined as 'man' as a sign that has no history. So Derrida then begins to worry about the history of the sign 'woman'. (Spivak, 1984/5:186)

Chapter 2

1 This terminology is Emile Benveniste's. He brings together a Lacanian/ Freudian notion of the split subject, and a Saussurian conception of language, differentiating the subject of *énonciation* (utterance act) from the subject of the *énoncé* (statement). The subject that speaks, in other words, must be differentiated from the subject spoken about. Even in apparently autobiographical statements, the 'I' who speaks is not the same as the 'I' about which it speaks. One subject (of the *énonciation*) is the subject of the production of discourses and the other is the subject of the statement, the 'I' internal to a discourse. Benveniste's analysis of pronouns provides a fascinating and highly fertile understanding of the functioning of the 'I', which he points out is necessarily bound up with units of discourse, and not with the naming of an object (the self). See his *Problems in General Linguistics* (1961).

2 My aim is to present Kristeva's (and the other feminists') position as sympathetically as possible, if only to be able to assess it fairly and rigorously. It is only if one understands the terms of a theoretical system from inside its framework that criticisms are most powerful and effective. External critiques tend to leave the system being criticised intact and to pose alternatives to it from the outside. In the case of Kristeva's work, I will avoid, where possible, any overly detailed discussion of her technical linguistic, literary and phonematic researches, which are of more interest to the specialist, in order to concentrate on the more interdisciplinary, and thus more accessible feminist components of her work. Clearly, however, it is not possible to sidestep her technical contributions altogether.

3 Freud notes these procedures of representation as early as *The Project for a Scientific Psychology* (1895), and uses them as explanations of symptom and dream formation in his subsequent work.

4 Lacan derives considerable support from the work of Roger Caillois, particularly in his remarkable paper 'Mimickry and Legendary Psychaesthenia' (1984). There Caillois argues that the instinct does not use

camouflage or mimicry for survival or adaptive purposes—its *visual* camouflage gives it no protection against most predators, who use the sense of smell rather than vision in hunting prey. Rather, the animal's or insect's ability to blend in with its environment is an instance of a broader, and more profound phenomenon Caillois describes as a *captivation by and derealisation of space*. Lacan sees in Caillois' work the outlines of the child's merger with and captivation by a virtual or specular image and space, the space of mirror reflections, which duplicate (and reverse) the space of a perspectival real. As Caillois notes and Lacan affirms, this captivation by space is a feature of certain psychoses, where the subject cannot locate itself as a being *in* space, but is absorbed by its space and is thus unlocated, unbounded.

5   In *La traversée des signes* Paris: Editions du Seuill, 1975.
6   For Freud and Lacan, castration can only take hold of the child when he/she attributes it to the mother, the child's primordial love object. She becomes the living illustration of the dismembering power of the symbolic father. More importantly, castration is the correlate and repressed condition of the phallic, for only by relegating women to the category of castrated object can man take up the phallic position.
7   Compare: *the conditions are gathered together, not to sweep away the unity entirely (for that would be equivalent to the dissolution of sociality itself) but to subject it to analysis ... unity would no longer be a block but a condition. (Kristeva, 1976:66–7)*
8   Compare: *The debate [surrounding the events of 1968] was a debate about political culture of modernism. It was a debate about the vision of a non-technocratic yet non-humanistic culture that would celebrate our 'decentered' relation to language in sublime laughter and 'transgression' about an avant-garde culture ... presenting itself as the rupture, the threshold, the limits of our age; and about a non-populist or elitist culture which was nevertheless committed to the left. (John Rajchman, 1986:10–11)*
9   There is clearly a broad range of feminist conceptions of *écriture feminine*: some understand by this term a quasi-biological concept of writings by *women*, by biological females; others take it to mean writings by *feminists*, that is, by women with particular orientations. Both these positions classify texts on the basis of the sex or politics *of the author*. Other feminists, by contrast, understand that it refers to writing, produced by women or even some men, which challenge the prevailing norms of patriarchal culture; and others again will presume it to mean those writings containing certain positive attributes not directly related to the sex of the author. Many of Kristeva's objections seem valid and appropriate. My disagreement with her is about her refusal to specify which feminist positions, given that there is a broad variety, she rejects and which ones she accepts.

Chapter 3

1   At any given time it is plausible to claim that the majority of women within a given population do not menstruate: pre-pubertal girls, pregnant

and menopausal women, athletes, anorexics, women with health problems, etc. could in fact comprise a slight majority of women!

2 *By symbolising the abject, through a masterful delivery of the jouissance
produced uttering it, Dostoyevsky delivered himself of that ruthless
maternal burden.*

    *But it is with Proust that we find the most immediately erotic, sexual
and desiring mainspring of abjection; and it is with Joyce that we shall
discover the maternal body in its most un-signifiable, un-symbolizable
aspect, shores up, in the individual, the fantasy of the loss in which he is
engulfed or becomes inebriated, for want of the ability to name the
object of desire. (1982:20)*

3 *the simple-minded anti-semitism that besets the tumultuous pages of the
pamphlets, are no accident; they thwart the disintegration of identity
that is co-extensive with a scription that effects the most archaic
distinctions, that bridges the gaps insuring life and meaning. (1982:136)*

4 *Dostoyevsky has X-rayed sexual, moral and religious abjection, dis-
playing it as collapse of paternal laws ... And by symbolizing the abject,
through a masterful delivery of the jouissance produced by uttering it,
Dostoyevsky delivered himself of that ruthless maternal burden.
(1982:20)*

5 *'if we suppose her to be* master *of a process that is prior to the socio-
symbolic-linguistic contract of the group, then we acknowledge the risk
of losing identity at the same time as we ward it off' (1980:238).*

6 *By giving birth, the woman enters into contact with her own mother; she
becomes, she is her own mother: they are the same continuity differentiating itself. She thus actualises the homosexual facet of motherhood,
through which a woman is simultaneously closer to her instinctual
memory, more open to her psychosis, and consequently, more negatory
of the social, symbolic bond.* (1980:239)

7 *'It is precisely the child that, for a* mother *(as opposed to a* genetrix*),
constitutes an* access *(an* excess*) towards the Other' (1980:279).*

8 She does not, of course, ignore the Judaic contributions to the symbolic
order either. My point here is simply that, in the context of a discussion
of the maternal function, her remarks are largely irrelevant. Indeed, she
claims that Judaism represents the paternity of the symbolic: 'Judaism
thus makes the paternal function the support, along with the subject, of
symbolism and sociality, while at the same time, through its emphasis,
sociality ...' (1976:66).

9 One of the five figures Kristeva discusses in *Tales of Love*—Narcissus,
Don Juan, Romeo and Juliet—which, together with the Virgin Mary,
comprise our culture's privileged representations of love: the self-
contained narcissistic love; a masculine 'love' craving confirmation of his
phallic status; the amorous couple, whose love is impossible, forbidden,
marked by death; and maternal love, selfless love of the Other.

10 Freud notes, in a footnote to this passage, that the pre-oedipal child is
not yet familiar with the differences between the sexes, and thus presumes a sexually indifferent object of primary identifications. 'Perhaps it
would be safer to say "with the parents"; for before the child has arrived

at a definite knowledge of the differences between the sexes, the lack of a penis, it does not distinguish between its father and its mother' (Freud, 1923:31n).

11 With the exception of Marianite discourses, which, in any case, code maternity through the father (God) and the son (Christ).

Chapter 4

1 Her earliest writings reflect these two interests, in particular, her analysis of the different language patterns in the speech of male and female schizophrenics demonstrates her concern for a psychological and linguistic analysis that is nonetheless free from Lacan's equation of psychical and signifying elements. See *Les langages des déments* and *Parler n'est jamais neutre* (1985).

2 This, for example, warrants their inclusion in Marks and Courtivron's collection, *New French Feminisms* (1981).

3 Irigaray claims that she has self-consciously attempted to write different kinds of texts, depending on the texts she is analysing. Her projected tetralogy 'on' the four elements, *Amante Marine*, is written using the element of water as metaphor for Nietzsche's writings; air is the element for Heidegger's texts; a projected volume on Marx would explore his writing from the point of view of a metaphorics of fire, and a fourth book on the dividing up/sharing (*partage*) of the earth is also projected. She makes it clear that each is written in a different style: 'It rapidly became obvious to me that the same type of writing couldn't be used for Nietzsche as for Heidegger' (1981).

4 In my opinion, Jane Gallop is the only one out of many commentators who succeeds in using Irigaray's own techniques and strategies to analyse Irigaray's texts. See *Feminism and Psychoanalysis: The Daughter's Seduction* (1982). Unfortunately, my own writing skills do not match Gallop's witty erudition. Thus instead of attempting to develop a 'poetic', Irigarayan reading of Irigaray, one which stays faithful to her ideals, I am content to analyse her position 'straight', using whatever phallocentric or patriarchal devices I need without, hopefully, unfairly attributing them to Irigaray. More 'dutiful' (in Gallop's terms) than Gallop's reading — although Gallop's text gives the impression that, if she accuses Irigaray of maintaining an oedipal relation to Freud and Lacan, she herself must also be guilty of *both* the same oedipal relation *and* an added dimension of *sibling rivalry* — my reading aims to provide as clear an introduction to Irigaray's works as is possible in a limited space and a foreign language. On the relation between Gallop and Irigaray, see Anna Munster's 'Playing with a Different Sex ...' in E. A. Grosz, T. Threadgold et al. (1987) (eds) *Futur*Fall: Excursions into Post-Modernity*.

5 Irigaray articulates her ambivalence regarding Freud in a number of papers, and most particularly in *This Sex Which Is Not One* (1985b). For example,

It is not a matter of naively accusing Freud, as if he were a 'bastard'. Freud's discourse represents the symptom of a particular social and

cultural economy, which has been maintained in the West since the time of the Greeks.

What we have to question is the system of representation, the discursive system at work in this socio-cultural functioning. And, in this respect, what Freud demonstrates is quite useful ... He describes rigorously the consequence of our socio-cultural system ... In some sense, this is not false. (1977:63–4)

6   In the history of philosophy, truth is most commonly understood as a form of reference or correspondence. A proposition can be regarded as true if its 'picture' of the world corresponds to the way the world really is. The true proposition is a mirror reflection of reality. Irigaray's traversal of the mirror in *This Sex Which Is Not One*, especially her use of Lewis Carroll's *Through the Looking-Glass*, is aimed not only at challenging the Lacanian notion of mirror identifications, but also the prevailing, originally Platonic understanding of truth.

7   Probably the most common objection raised against her position is the charge of essentialism. Sayers, for example, charges her with biological essentialism (1982:131); Moi argues that she defines 'woman' in essentialist terms based on women's sexual organs (1985:143); Jones criticises Irigaray for concentrating only on the female body, considered (by Jones) only in physiological terms (1981:224–5); Plaza accuses her of seeking an essence in the pure experiences submerged under patriarchal accretions (1978:8); and Rose argues that she posits an essence based on women's natural or maternal origins (1986:136). My argument is that these claims are based on a profound misreading of Irigaray's claims. They substantialise or ontologise what, for Irigaray, is a discursive or deconstructive strategy.

8   Many of her critics claim that she essentialises both women's and men's natures, using the latter to explain the existence of patriarchy. This is why Plaza, for example, accuses her of psychologising women's oppression:

When Luce Irigaray proposes that 'Western logic' has discredited the Difference to satisfy man's narcissism, she makes a reductionist and hence false interpretation ... [S]he psychologises her investigation: she proposes the existence of a 'man' with an eternal psyche and hostile to everything which escapes him ... she confers on man an original power, an initial wish for domination ... (1978:14)

9   For example, 'To found a field of study on this belief in the inevitability of natural sex differences can only compound patriarchal logic and not subvert it ...' (Plaza, 1978:8). Or, in a similar vein,

the material conditions of her analysis are spectacularly absent from her work. But without specific material analysis, a feminist account of power cannot transcend the simplistic and defeatist vision of male power pitted against female helplessness that underpins Irigaray's theoretical investigations. (Moi, 1985:147)

10   This claim — a strikingly materialist position, at least insofar as language is regarded as material — demonstrates Moi's misunderstanding of

Irigaray. It is surprising that, in a text like Moi's, which purports to be antihumanist, materialist and (marxist?) feminist, and is specifically concerned with how texts function, she refuses to see Irigaray's discursive strategies as material. Her confusion may spring from a mistaken identification of Irigaray's project with the general elimination of women's oppression. (Clearly, if this is her project, to concentrate only on the discursive is a limitation.) As I understand it, her project is more specific and regionalised, located at the level of her own practices as a writer, teacher and theorist—the dismantling of a representational and epistemic economy and the introduction of other forms of representation more amenable to women's specificity (see Moi, 1985:147).

11 For more on the inscriptions of power on bodies, see M. Gatens, 1983.
12 NB The two exceptions of whom I am aware are Carolyn Burke and Margaret Whitford. Whitford confirms my suspicion that Irigaray's work is either not read, misread or misleadingly read:

Now the idea that Irigaray is proclaiming a biologically given essential femininity in which biology in some unclear fashion simply 'constitutes' femininity seems to me quite simply a misreading of Irigaray (based on the only English translation available in 1982). (Whitford, 1986:7)

13 *The mouth, that's also lips! That's exactly what's special about women, that they have lips up here and down there! Perhaps they [men] have silenced her mouth throughout history because she also has lips down there! Man doesn't have a set of lips, woman does ... (Irigaray, 1983d:195)*

14 For example, Jones suggests that Irigaray's objective is to reveal an innate or natural femininity:

can the body be a source of self-knowledge? Does female sexuality exist prior to or in spite of social existence? Do women in fact experience their bodies purely or essentially, outside the damaging acculturation so sharply analysed by women in France and elsewhere? The answer is no ... (Jones, 1981:253)

15 This may explain the extraordinary incidence of so-called 'eating disorders'—the modern form of hysteria. Anorexia and bulimia seem most interestingly interpreted in terms of a mourning or nostalgia for the lost (maternal) object, and either an attempt to devour or consume it (bulimia) or to harden oneself against its loss (in anorexia).
16 See Lacan's and Benveniste's structural use of Saussure in explaining the construction of subjectivity. See particularly Lacan's 'The Agency of the Letter in the Unconscious' in 1977a; and Chapters 19 and 20 in Benveniste's *Problems in General Linguistics* (1961).

Chapter 5
1 Among the texts to be examined in this chapter are *Amante Marine, L'Oubli d'air, Passions elémentaires, Le Corps-à-corps avec la mère, L'Ethique de la différence sexuelle, Parler n'est jamais neutre* and *Sexe et parentés.*

2   Levinas' writings on the question of ethics include *Otherwise than Being or Beyond Existence, Ethics and Infinity, Totality and Infinity: An Essay on Exteriority, Existence and Existents, Collected Philosophical Papers, Being and Totality*; as well, there is a recent collection of papers on and by Levinas edited by Richard A. Cohen, *Face-to-Face with Levinas*; and his main English translator, Alphonso Lingis, discusses his work in some detail in *Libido*.

3   In this sense Levinas is closer to Spinoza than to Kant: ethics is not the domain of rules and imperatives but that of living life in recognition of its rich plurality.

4   For further detail, see my paper 'The People of the Book' *Art and Text* 26, Nov. 1987.

5   Sartre's statements in *Being and Nothingness*.

6   See Toril Moi's critical review of Girard, 'The Missing Mother: The Oedipal Rivalries of René Girard' in *Diacritics* 12, 2, 1982.

7   See, for example, R. Bell's (1985) analysis of the rampant anorexia which seemed to dominate the lives of literally hundreds of holy saints in *Holy Anorexia*.

8   See also 'To Love the Torah More than God', *Judaism* 28, 1979.

9   As Susan Handelman claims, the Torah is itself a book of rather strange dimension, being both primary and secondary text, text and commentary in one:

> *In the standard edition of the Talmud, a brief part of the Mishnah is set in the center of the page, followed by the Gemara's discussion and commentary. The commentary of Rashi is printed on the one side, and that of the tosafists [the commentaries on Rashi's commentary, made by his sons and grandsons] on the other. Bordering these columns are additional notes, cross-references, glosses, emendations, and comments by later authorities ... The central pattern of the text surrounded by commentary was followed in other works of rabbinic thought. (Handelman, 1982:47)*

10 This point is particularly pertinently developed in Carolyn Burke's (1987) excellent paper 'Romancing the Philosophers'; see especially footnote 21.

Chapter 6

1   In, for example, *The Order of Things, The Archaeology of Knowledge* and, in a different way, in *Madness and Civilization* and *Discipline and Punish*.

2   In 'La Face honteuse de la philosophie', and 'La Rêverie dans "Utopia"' in *L'Imaginaire* (1980), and in the paper 'Utopias: Scholarly' (1982).

3   It is rumoured that, because Descartes was in the habit of sleeping late, when he acted as a philosophy tutor for Queen Christina in Sweden he was forced to rise before sunrise, and, in the damp chill of the morning air, caught a cold from which he eventually died.

4   Kant's claims are variants of a frequently echoed theme throughout the history of philosophy:

Laborious learning or painful pandering, even if a woman should succeed in it, she would destroy the merits that are proper to her sex and because of their rarity, they can make her the object of cold admiration; but all the same, they will weaken the charms with which she exercises her great power over the other sex. (Kant, quoted in Mahawald, 1978:78)

Bibliography

THIS section is divided into three parts. In the first are listed the texts of Kristeva, Irigaray and Le Doeuff; in the second are secondary texts and related materials on each of these writers; and in the third are miscellaneous texts broadly relevant to the concerns of these three French feminists.

Julia Kristeva

(1972a) 'The Semiotic Activity' *Screen* 14, 1
(1972b) 'Phonetics, Phonology and Impulsional Basis' *Diacritics*, fall
(1972c) 'Four Types of Signifying Practice' *Semiotext(e)* 1
(1975) 'The Subject in Signifying Practice' *Semiotext(e)* 3
(1976a) 'China, Women and the Symbolic' *Sub-Stance* 13
(1976b) 'Signifying Practice and Mode of Production' *Edinburgh Review* 1
(1977a) 'L'Héréthique de l'amour' *Tel Quel* 74
(1977b) 'Modern Theater Does Not Take (a) Place' *Sub-Stance* 18/19
(1977c) *About Chinese Women* London: Marion Boyars
(1978) 'The U.S. Now: A Conversation' *October* 6
(1980) *Desire in Language* Leon S. Roudiez (transl.) Oxford: Basil Blackwell's
(1981a) 'The Maternal Body' *m/f* 5/6
(1981b) 'Interview' ibid.
(1981c) 'Women's Time' *Signs* 7, 1
(1982a) *Powers of Horror: An Essay on Abjection* Leon S. Roudiez (transl.) New York: Columbia University Press
(1982b) 'Psychoanalysis and the Polis' *Critical Inquiry* 9, 1
(1982c) 'Ne dis rien: A propos de l'interdict de la représentation' *Tel Quel* 91
(1983) 'The Father, Love and Banishment' in E. Kurzweil and W. Phillips (eds) *Literature and Psychoanalysis* New York: Columbia University Press
(1984a) *The Revolution in Poetic Language* Maragaret Waller (transl.) New York: Columbia University Press
(1984b) 'My Memory's Hyperbole' in D. C. Stanton (ed.) *The Female Autograph* New York: Library Forum
(1984c) 'Julia Kristeva in Conversation with Rosalind Coward' *ICA Documents*, special issue on *Desire*
(1984d) 'Histoires d'amour' ibid.
(1984e) 'Two Interviews with Kristeva' (with E. H. Baruch) *Partisan Review* 51, 1

245

(1985) 'The Speaking Subject' in M. Blonsky (ed.) *On Signs* Baltimore: Johns Hopkins University Press
(1986) 'An Interview with Julia Kristeva' (with I. Lipkowitz and A. Loselle) *Critical Texts* 3, 3
(1987) *Tales of Love* Leon S. Roudiez (transl.) New York: Columbia University Press
Moi, T. (ed.) (1986) *The Kristeva Reader* Oxford: Basil Blackwell

Luce Irigaray
(1973) *Les Langages des déments* Paris: Mouton
(1974) *Speculum: de l'autre femme* Paris: Les Editions de Minuit
(1975a) 'La Femme, son sexe et le langage' *La Nouvelle Critique* 82, mars
(1977) 'Women's exile' *Ideology and Consciousness* 1
(1978) 'That Sex Which Is Not One' in P. Foss and M. Morris (eds) *Language, Sexuality and Subversion* Sydney: Feral
(1979a) 'Établir un généalogie de femmes' *Maintenant* 12, 28 mai
(1979b) 'Mères et filles vues par Luce Irigaray' *Libération* 21 mai
(1980) *Amante Marine: de Friedrich Nietzsche* Paris: Les Editions de Minuit
(1981a) *Le Corps-à-corps avec la mère* Montréal: Les Editions de la pleine lune
(1981b) 'And One Doesn't Stir Without the Other' *Signs* 7, 1
(1982) *Passions elémentaires* Paris: Les Editions de Minuit
(1983a) *La Croyance même* Paris: Editions Galilee
(1983b) *L'Oubli de l'air: Chez Martin Heidegger* Paris: Les Editions de Minuit
(1983c) 'Veiled Lips' *Mississippi Review* 11, 3
(1983d) 'For Centuries We've Been Living in the Mother–Son Relation ...' *Hecate* 9, 1/2
(1984) *L'Ethique de la différence sexuelle* Paris: Les Editions de Minuit
(1985a) *Speculum of the Other Woman* Gillian Gill (transl.) Ithaca: Cornell University Press
(1985b) *This Sex Which Is Not One* Catherine Porter with Carolyn Burke (transl.) Ithaca: Cornell University Press
(1985c) *Parler n'est jamais neutre* Paris: Les Editions de Minuit
(1985d) 'Any Theory of the "Subject" Has Always Been Appropriated by the Masculine' *Trivia* winter
(1985e) 'Is the Subject of Science Sexed?' *Cultural Critique* 1
(1986a) *Divine Women* Stephen Muecke (transl.) Sydney: Local Consumption Occasional Papers, 8
(1986b) 'Women, the Sacred and Money' *Paragraph* 8
(1986c) 'The Fecundity of the Caress' in R. A. Cohen (ed.) *Face-to-Face with Levinas* New York: State University of New York Press
(1987a) *Sexes et parentés* Paris: Les Editions de Minuit
(1987b) 'L'ordre sexuel du discours' *Langages* 85, mars

Michèle Le Doeuff
(1977) 'Women and Philosophy' *Radical Philosophy* 17

Bibliography

(1979) 'Operative Philosophy: Simone de Beauvoir and Existentialism' *I. and C.* 6
(1980a) *Recherches sur l'imaginaire philosophique* Paris: Payot
(1980b) 'La philosophie renseignée' in C. Delaceaupagne et R. Maggiosi (eds) *Philosopher* Paris: Fayerd
(1981/2) 'Pierre Roussel's chiasmas' *I and C* 9
(1982a) 'Utopias: Scholarly' *Social Research* 49, 2
(1982b) 'Special-femmes, un grumeau sur la langue' *Alidades* automne–hiver
(1982c) 'Quelle modernité philosophique' *La revue d'en face* 12
(1984) 'L'unique sujet parlant' *Éspirit* mai–juin
(1986) *Vénus et Adonis suivi de genèse d'une catastrophe* Paris: Alidades

Secondary texts and commentaries

On Kristeva

Caws, M. A. (1973) '*Tel Quel*: text and revolution' *Diacritics* spring
Conley, V. (1975) 'Kristeva's China' *Diacritics* winter
Creech, J. (1977) 'Kristeva's Bataille: Reading as Triumph' *Diacritics* summer
Gross, E. (1982) 'Women and Writing: The Work of Julia Kristeva in Perspective' *Refactory Girl Writes* 23, October
———— (1986) 'Philosophy, Subjectivity and the Body: Kristeva and Irigaray' in C. Pateman and E. Gross (eds) *Feminist Challenges: Social and Political Theory* Sydney: Allen & Unwin
Grosz, E. A. (1987) 'Language and the Limits of the Body: Kristeva and Abjection' in E. A. Grosz, T. Threadgold et al. (eds) *Futur*Fall: Excursions into Post-Modernity* Sydney: Pathfinder Press and the Power Institute
Jones, R. A. (1981a) 'Writing the Body: Toward an Understanding of *Écriture Feminine*' *Feminist Studies* 7, 1
———— (1981b) 'Assimilation with a Difference' *Yale French Studies* 62
Jardine, A. (1980) 'Theories of the Feminine: Kristeva' *enclitic* 4, 2
———— (1981a) 'Pre-texts for the Transatlantic Feminist' *Yale French Studies* 62
———— (1981b) 'Introduction to "Women's Time"' *Signs* 7, 1
———— (1985) *Gynesis: Configurations of Woman and Modernity* Ithaca: Cornell University Press
———— (1986) 'Opaque Texts and Transparent Contexts: The Political Difference of Julia Kristeva' in N. K. Miller (ed.) *The Poetics of Gender* New York: Columbia University Press
Johnson, B. (1978) 'The Critical Difference' *Diacritics* summer
Lewis, P. E. (1974) 'Revolutionary Semiotics' *Diacritics* fall
Moi, T. (1985) *Sexual/Textual Politics: Feminist Literary Theory* London: Methuen
Pajaczkowska, C. (1981) 'Introduction to Kristeva' *m/f* 5/6
———— (1985) 'On Love and Language' *Free Associations* 2V
Wenzel, H. (1981) 'The Text as Body/Politics' *Feminist Studies* 7, 2
White, H. (1976) 'Exposition and Critique of Kristeva' *CCS Occasional Paper* London

On Irigaray

Adlam, D. and Venn, C. (1977) 'Introduction to Irigaray' *Ideology and Consciousness* 1

Atack, M. (1986) 'The Other: Feminist' *Paragraph* 8

Berg, E. (1982) 'The Third Woman' *Diacritics* 12

Burke, C. (1978) 'Report from Paris' *Signs* 3, 4

—————— (1980) 'Introduction to "When Our Lips Speak Together"' *Signs* autumn

—————— (1981) 'Luce Irigaray Through the Looking Glass' *Feminist Studies* 7, 2

—————— (1987) 'Romancing the Philosophers: Luce Irigaray' *The Minnesota Review* 29

Felman, S. (1975) 'The Critical Phallacy' *Diacritics* winter

Foss, P. (1978) 'On the Text Which Is Not One' in P. Foss and M. Morris (eds) *Language, Sexuality and Subversion* Sydney: Feral

Gallop, J. (1981) 'Phallus/Penis: Same Difference' in J. Todd, Homes and Meier (eds) *Men by Women* New York

—————— (1982) *Feminism and Psychoanalysis: The Daughter's Seduction* London: MacMillan

—————— (1983) '*Quand nos lèvres s'écrivent*: Irigaray's Body Politic' *Romantic Review* 74, 1

—————— (1986) 'French Theory and the Seduction of the Feminine' *Paragraph* 8

Gearhart, S. (1985) 'The Scene of Psychoanalysis: The Unanswered Questions of Dora' in C. Bernheimer and C. Kahane (eds) *In Dora's Case: Freud-Hysteria-Feminism* London: MacMillan

Gross, E. (1976) 'Lacan, the Symbolic, the Imaginary and the Real' *Working Papers in Sex, Science and Culture*, 1, 2

—————— (1986a) 'Philosophy, Subjectivity and the Body: Kristeva and Irigaray' in Pateman and Gross (eds) *Feminist Challenges*

—————— (1986b) 'Review of *Speculum* and *This Sex*' *Australian Feminist Studies* 2

—————— (1986c) *Irigaray and the Divine* Sydney: Local Consumption Occasional Papers, 9

—————— (1987) 'Notes Towards a Corporeal Feminism' *Australian Feminist Studies* 5

—————— (1988) 'The Hetero and the Homo: The Sexual Ethics of Luce Irigaray' *Gay Information* 17–18

Jones, R. A. (1981) 'Writing the Body: Toward an Understanding of *Écriture Feminine*' *Feminist Studies* 7, 1

Lyon, E. (1979) 'Discourse and Difference' *Camera Obscura* 3/4

Munster, A. (1987) 'Playing with a Different Sex: Between the Covers of Irigaray and Gallop' in Grosz, Threadgold et al. (eds) *Futur*Fall*

Plaza, M. (1978) '"Phallomorphic Power" and the Psychology of "Woman"' *Ideology and Consciousness* 4

Sayers, J. (1986) *Sexual Contradictions: Psychology, Psychoanalysis and Feminism* London: Tavistock

Wenzel, V. H. (1981a) 'The Text as Body/Politics' *Feminist Studies* 7, 2

Bibliography

_____ (1981b) 'Introduction to "And One Doesn't Stir Without the Other"' *Signs* 7, 1

Whitford, M. (1986a) 'Luce Irigaray and the Female Imaginary: Speaking as a Woman' *Radical Philosophy* 43

_____ (1986b) 'Luce Irigaray: The Problem of Feminist Theory' *Paragraph* 8

On Le Doeuff

Deutscher, M. (1984) Michèle Le Doeuff and the Imaginary of Philosophy (unpublished manuscript)

Emerton, K. (1987) Women and Philosophy: An Introduction to the Work of Michèle Le Doeuff (unpublished manuscript)

Gatens, M. (1986) 'Feminism, Philosophy and Riddles Without Answers' in Pateman and Gross (eds) *Feminist Challenges*

Lloyd, G. (1983) 'Masters, Slaves and Others' *Radical Philosophy* 34

MacKenzie, C. (1986) 'Simone de Beauvoir: Philosophy and/or the Female Body' in Pateman and Gross (eds) *Feminist Challenges*

Morris, M. (1981/2) 'Operative Reasoning: Michèle Le Doeuff, Philosophy and Feminism' *I. and C.* 9

Miscellaneous

Adams, P. (1978) 'Representation and sexuality' *m/f* 1

Adams, P. and Minson, J. (1978) 'The "Subject" of Feminism' *m/f* 2

Andermatt, V. (1977) 'Hélène Cixous and the Uncovery of Feminine Language' *Women and Literature* 7, 1

Bachelard G. (1969) *The Poetics of Space*, Boston: Beacon Press

Bartkowski, F. (1980) 'Feminism and Deconstruction: "A Union Forever Deferred"' *enclitic* 4, 2

de Beauvoir, S. (1972) *The Second Sex*, H.M. Parshley (transl.) London: Penguin

Brown, B. and Adams, P. (1979) 'The Feminine Body and Feminist Politics' *m/f* 3

Benveniste, E. (1961) *Problems in General Linguistics* Bloomington: Indiana University Press

Braidotti, R., Weinstock, J. et al. (1980) 'Round and Round the Looking Glass ...' *Hecate* 6, 2

Caillois, R. (1984) 'Mimickry and Legendary Psychaesthenia' J. Shepley (transl.) *October* 31

Cohen, R.A. (ed.) (1980) *Textes pour Emmanuel Levinas* Paris: J.M. Place

_____ (1986) *Face-to-Face with Levinas* New York: State University of New York Press

Cousins, M. (1978) 'The Logic of Deconstruction' *Oxford Literary Review* 3, 2

Cixous, H. (1976) 'Interview' *Sub-Stance* 13

_____ (1980a) 'Sorties' in E. Marks and I. de Courtivron (eds) *New French Feminisms* Amherst: University of Massachusetts Press

_____ (1980b) 'The laugh of the Medusa' in ibid.

249

———— (1981) 'Castration or decapitation?' *Signs* 7, 1
———— (1982) 'Introduction to Lewis Carroll's *Through the Looking-Glass* and *The Hunting of the Snark*' *New Literary History* 13
Cixous, H. and Clément, C. (1985) *The Newly Born Woman* B. Wing (transl.) Minneapolis: University of Minnesota Press
Clément, C. (1983) *The Lives and Legends of Jacques Lacan* A. Goldhammer (transl.) New York: Columbia University Press
———— (1987) *The Weary Sons of Freud* N. Ball (transl.) London: Verso
Conley, V. (1977) 'Missexual Misstery' *Diacritics* summer
———— (1984) *Hélène Cixous: Writing the Feminine* Lincoln and London: University of Nebraska Press
———— (ed.) (1985) 'On Feminine Writing' special issue of *Boundary 2*
Derrida, J. (1973) *Speech and Phenomena and Other Essays on Husserl's Theory of Signs* Alan Bass (transl.) Evanston: Northwestern University Press
———— (1974) *Glas* Paris: Editions Galilee
———— (1976) *Of Grammatology* G. C. Spivak (transl.) Baltimore: Johns Hopkins University Press
———— (1979) *Spurs: Nietzsche's Styles* B. Harlow (transl.) Chicago: University of Chicago Press
———— (1981a) *Dissemination* B. Johnson (transl.) London: The Athlone Press
———— (1981b) *Positions* Alan Bass (transl.) London: The Athlone Press
———— (1982a) *Margins of Philosophy* Alan Bass (transl.) Chicago: University of Chicago Press
———— (1982b) 'Choreographies' *Diacritics* Summer
———— (1985) *The Ear of the Other: Otobiography, Transference, Translation* A. Ronell (transl.) New York: Schocken Books
———— (1986) *Memoires for Paul de Man* C. Lindsay, J. Culler and E. Cadava (transl.) New York: Columbia University Press
———— (1987a) *The Post Card: From Socrates to Freud and Beyond* Alan Bass (transl.) Chicago: University of Chicago Press
———— (1987b) *The Truth in Painting* G. Bennington and I. McLeod (transl.) Chicago: University of Chicago Press
Descartes, R. (1970) *The Philosophical work of Descartes*, E. S. Haldane and G. R. T. Ross (transls) London: Cambridge University Press
Descombes, V. (1980) *Modern French Philosophy* Cambridge: Cambridge University Press
Douglas, M. (1966) *Purity and Danger: An Analysis of the Concept of Pollution and Taboo* London: Routledge & Kegan Paul
Duchin, C. (1986) *Feminism in France: From May 1968 to Mitterand* London: Routledge & Kegan Paul
Duren, B. (1981) 'Cixous' Exorbitant Texts' *Sub-Stance* 32
Eisenstein, H. and Jardine, A. (eds) (1980) *The Future of Difference* Boston: G. K. Hall and Barnard Women's College
Fedkiw, P. (1982) 'Marguerite Duras: The Feminine Field of Hysteria' *enclitic* 4, 2
Felman, S. (1975) 'The Critical Phallacy' *Diacritics* winter
———— (1977) 'To Open the Question' *Yale French Studies* 55/56

———— (1981) 'Rereading Femininity' *Yale French Studies* 62
———— (1985) *Writing and Madness (Literature/Philosophy/Psychoanalysis)* Ithaca: Cornell University Press
Feuerbach, L. (1957) *The Essence of Christianity* G. Eliot (transl.) New York: Harper & Row
Féral, J. (1978) 'Antigone or the Irony of the Tribe' *Diacritics* fall
Foss, P. and Morris, M. (eds) (1978) *Language, Sexuality and Subversion* Sydney: Feral
Foucault, M. (1972) *The Archaeology of Knowledge* New York: Harper Torchbooks
———— (1977) 'Nietzsche, Genealogy, History', *Langiage-Counter-Memory-Practice*, D. Bouchard (ed.), Ithaca: Cornell University Press
Freud, S. (1900) *The Interpretation of Dreams* standard edn of *The Complete Psychological Works* J. Strachey (transl.) London: the Hogarth Press
———— (1913) *Totem and Taboo* standard edn, vol. 13
———— (1914a) 'On Narcissism: An Introduction' standard edn, vol. 14
———— (1914b) 'The Unconscious' ibid.
———— (1925) 'A Note upon a Mystic Writing Pad' standard edn, vol. 19
———— (1930) *Civilisation and its Discontents* standard edn, vol. 21
———— (1977) *On Sexuality* vol. 7, London: Penguin
Fynsk, C. (1978) 'A Decelebration of Philosophy' *Diacritics* spring
Gallop, J. (1981) *Intersections: A Reading of Sade with Bataille, Blanchot and Klossowski* Lincoln: University of Nebraska Press
———— (1986) *Reading Lacan* Ithaca: Cornell University Press
Gasché, R. (1979) 'Deconstruction as Criticism' *Glyph* 6
Gatens, M. (1983) 'A Critique of the Sex–Gender Distinction' in J. Allen and P. Patton (eds) *Interventions After Marx* Sydney: Intervention
———— (1986) 'Feminism, Philosophy and Riddles Without Answers' in Pateman and Gross (eds) *Feminist Challenges*
Girard, R. (1977) *Violence and the Sacred* P. Gregory (transl.) Baltimore: Johns Hopkins University Press
Gross, E. (1976) 'Lacan, the Symbolic, the Imaginary and the Real' *Working Papers in Sex, Science and Culture* 2
Grosz, E. (1987) 'The People of the Book' *Art and Text* 26
Guattari, F. (1984) *Molecular Revolution: Psychiatry and Politics* R. Sheed (transl.) London: Penguin
Handelman, S. (1982) *The Slayers of Moses: The Emergence of Rabbinic Interpretation in Modern Literary Theory* New York: State University of New York Press
———— (1983) 'Jacques Derrida and the Heretical Hermeneutic' in M. Krupnick (ed.) *Displacement. Derrida and After* Madison: University of Wisconsin Press
Hartman, G. (1978) *Psychoanalysis and the Question of the Text* Baltimore: Johns Hopkins University Press
Hawkes, T. (1977) *Structuralism and Semiotics* London: Methuen
Heath, S. (1978) 'Difference' *Screen* 19, 3
———— (1982) *The Sexual Fix* London: MacMillan
Hegel, G. W. F. (1967) *The Phenomenology of Mind* A. V. Miller (transl.) Oxford: Clarendon Press

Hirsch, A. (1981) *The French New Left: An Intellectual History From Sartre to Gorz* London: South End Press

Hyppolite, J. (1969) *Studies on Marx and Hegel* London: Heinemann

———— (1974) *Genesis and Structure in Hegel's Phenomenology of Spirit* Evanston: Northwestern University Press

Jardine, A. (1981) *Gynesis: Configurations of Woman and Modernity* Ithaca: Cornell University Press

Jay, N. (1981) 'Gender and dichotomy' *Feminist Studies* 7, 1

Jacobus, M. (1986) *Reading Woman: Essays in Feminist Criticism* New York: Columbia University Press

Johnson, B. (1980) *The Critical Difference* Baltimore: Johns Hopkins University Press

Kant, I. (1973) *The Critique of Pure Reason* N. Kemp Smith (transl.) London: MacMillan

Kirk, G. S., Raven, J. E. and Schofield, M. (1983) *The Presocratic Philosophers: A Critical History with a Selection of Texts* Cambridge: University of Cambridge Press

Kofman, S. (1980a) 'The Narcissistic Woman: Freud and Girard' *Diacritics* fall

———— (1980b) 'Ex: The Woman's Enigma' *enclitic* 4, 2

———— (1981) 'No Longer Full-fledged Autobiogriffe' *Sub-Stance* 29

———— (1986) *The Enigma of Woman: Woman in Freud's Writings* Urbana: University of Illinois Press

Kojève, A. (1969) *Introduction to the Reading of Hegel* J. Nichols (transl.) New York: Basic Books

Kuhn, A. (1981) 'Introduction to Cixous' "Castration or decapitation"' *Signs* 7, 1

Krupnick, M. (ed.) (1983) *Displacement: Derrida and After* Madison: University of Wisconsin

Lacan, J. (1977a) *Écrits: A Selection* A. Sheridan (transl.) London: Tavistock

———— (1977b) *The Four Fundamental Concepts of Psychoanalysis* A. Sheridan (transl.) London: the Hogarth Press

Levinas, E. (1968) *Quatre lectures Talmudique* Paris: Les Editions de Minuit

———— (1979a) 'To Love the Torah more than God' *Judaism* 28

———— (1979b) *Existence and Existents* A. Lingis (transl.) The Hague: Martinus Nijhoff

———— (1979c) *Totality and Infinity: An Essay on Exteriority* A. Lingis (transl.) The Hague: Martinus Nijhoff

———— (1981) *Otherwise than Being or Beyond Existence* A. Lingis (transl.) The Hague: Martinus Nijhoff

———— (1985) *Ethics and Infinity: Conversations with Phillipe Nemo* R. A. Cohen (transl.) Pittsburgh: Dusquesne University Press

———— (1986) 'Dialogue with Emmanuel Levinas' in R. A. Cohen (ed.) *Face-to-Face with Levinas* New York: State University of New York Press

———— (1987) *Collected Philosophical Papers* A. Lingis (transl.) The Hague: Martinus Nijhoff

Lingis, A. (1982) *Excesses: Eros and Culture* New York: State University of New York Press

Bibliography

_____ (1985) *Libido: Six Existential Thinkers* New York: State University of New York Press
Lloyd, G. (1984) *The Man of Reason: 'Male' and 'Female' in Western Philosophy* London: Methuen
Lyotard, J.–F. (1977) 'Jewish Oedipus' *Genre* 10
Mahawald, M. (ed.) (1978) *Philosophy of Woman: Classical to Current Concepts* Indianapolis: Hackett
Mitchell, J. (1974) *Psychoanalysis and Feminism* London: Allen Lane
Mitchell, J. and Rose, J. (eds) (1982) *Feminine Sexuality: Jacques Lacan and the École Freudienne* London: MacMillan
MacCabe, C. (ed.) (1981) *The Talking Cure: Essays in Psychoanalysis and Language* London: MacMillan
Montefiore, A. (1983) *Philosophy in France Today* Cambridge: Cambridge University Press
Moi, T. (1982) 'The Missing Mother: The Oedipal Rivalries of René Girard' *Diacritics* summer
Morris, M. (1981–82) 'Import Rhetoric: "Semiotics in/and Australia"' *The Foreign Bodies Papers* series 1, Sydney: Local Consumption Publications
Nietzsche, F. (1969) *Ecce Homo* W. Kaufman (transl.) New York: Vintage Press
_____ (1974) *The Gay Science* W. Kaufman (transl.) New York: Vintage Press
Norris, C. (1982) *Deconstruction: Theory and Practice* London: Methuen
_____ (1987) *Derrida* London: Fontana
Ragland-Sullivan, E. (1986) *Jacques Lacan and the Philosophy of Psycho-Analysis* Urbana and Chicago: University of Illinois Press
Rajchman, J. (1986) *Michel Foucault. The Freedom of Philosophy* New York: Columbia University Press
Rose, J. (1986) *Sexuality in the Field of Vision* London: Verso
J. J. Rousseau (1972) *Emile*, B. Foxley (transl.), London: Everyman's Library
_____ (1975) *The Social Contract*, M. Cranston (transl.), London: Penguin
Roustang, F. (1982) *Dire Mastery: Discipleship from Freud to Lacan* Baltimore: Johns Hopkins University Press
Sartre, J.–P. (1968) *The Search for a Method* H. E. Barnes (transl.) New York: Vintage Books
_____ (1976) *Critique of Dialectical Reason* A. Sheridan-Smith (transl.) London: New Left Books
_____ (1977) *Being and Nothingness* London: Methuen
F. de Saussure (1974) *Course in General Linguistics* New York: Fontana/Collins
Schor, N. (1985) *Breaking the Chain: Women, Theory and French Realist Fiction* New York: Columbia University Press
Schneiderman, S. (1983) *Jacques Lacan: The Death of an Intellectual Hero* Cambridge: Cambridge University Press
Smith, J. H. and Kerrigan, W. (eds) (1984) *Taking Chances: Derrida, Psychoanalysis and Literature* Baltimore: Johns Hopkins University Press
Spender, D. (1980) *Man Made Language* London: Routledge & Kegan Paul
Spivak, G. C. (1981) 'French Feminism in an International Frame' *Yale French Studies* 62

——— (1983) 'Displacement and the Discourse of Woman' in Krupnick (ed.) *Displacement*

——— (1984/85) 'Women, Intellectuals and Power: An Interview' *Thesis XI* 9

——— (1987) *In Other Worlds: Essays in Cultural Politics* London: Methuen

Suleiman, S. R. (1986) (ed.) *The Female Body in Western Culture: Contemporary Perspectives* Cambridge, Mass.: Harvard University Press

Turkle, S. (1976) *Psychoanalytic Politics: Freud's French Revolution* New York: Basic Books

Warner, M. (1976) *Alone of All Her Sex: The Myth and Cult of the Virgin Mary* New York: Knopf

Weedon, C. (1987) *Feminist Practice and Poststructuralist Theory* Oxford: Basil Blackwell's

Wright, E. (1984) *Psychoanalytic Criticism: Theory in Practice* London: Methuen

Index